CITY LIGHTS ANTHOLOGY

CITY LIGHTS BOOKS

Edited by Lawrence Ferlinghetti

Production: Nancy J. Phillips

© *1974 City Lights Books*
All Rights Reserved for the Authors

Library of Congress Catalog Card Number: 74-75061

ISBN: 0-87286-076-0

Cover: "Thelonious Monk." by Victor Brauner

"Greece" by Philippe Weisbecker is from ART OF THE TIMES, by permission of the Publisher, Darien House, Inc.

CITY LIGHTS BOOKS are published at the City Lights Bookstore. Editorial & Publishing offices: 1562 Grant Avenue, San Francisco, California 94133.

CONTENTS

CITY LIGHTS ANTHOLOGY

The contributors to this international collection of new writing come from half a dozen countries and as many movements, some much opposed to each other. Many of the North Americans are, or have recently been, in the San Francisco Bay Area (that literary estuary containing both fresh and salt water).

The cover drawing of Thelonious Monk is by Victor Brauner, the Roumanian-born Paris surrealist painter and sculptor.

Allen Ginsberg was co-winner of the National Book Award for Poetry in 1974 for his City Lights Book, *The Fall of America.*

Andrei Voznesensky visited this country last in 1971 when he was presented by City Lights in a mass reading at Project Artaud in San Francisco.

Richard Baker-roshi of the San Francisco Zen Center will write an introduction to the book by Huey P. Newton and Ericka Huggins, *Insights & Poems*, to be published by City Lights.

Roland Topor's drawings are from his City Lights book, *Panic*, and from *Dessins* (Editions Albin Michel, © 1968).

Judson Crews has lived and written poetry for a long time near Taos, New Mexico, but this year is at the University of Zambia, Africa.

Herbert Marcuse, professor emeritus at the University of California, San Diego, is author of *Eros & Civilization*, *Essay on Liberation*, *One-Dimensional Man* and other seminal works.

Diane di Prima, author of *Revolutionary Letters*, will soon publish her new book, *Loba.*

Gail Chiarrello's books of poetry, *The Mark* and *The Bhangra Dance*, are published by Oyez in Berkeley.

Kathleen Teague is included in the Dremen Press *Anthology of Women Poets* and now lives in Eureka, California.

Barbara Guest, long associated with the New York School of Poets and painters, has a book in print entitled *Blue Stairs* (Corinth Press, N.Y.)

Bobbie Louise Hawkins in Bolinas, California, has been making a large leap from painting to writing, now working on Texas stories.

Linda King is a sculptor and writer, as well as a cohort of Charles Bukowski in Los Angeles. She has a book of poems, *Sweet and Dirty.*

Jack Micheline's short story is from his unpublished book, *Skinny Dynamite.*

Jerry Kamstra is author of *Weed: Adventures of a Dope Smuggler* (Harper & Row). His autobiographical novel, *The Frisco Kid* (which should be retitled *Tropic of Frisco*) will be put into print by Harper & Row in 1975.

Charles Bukowski generally does not write 'fiction'—he writes his own life, as did Henry Miller and Jack Kerouac. A movie is being made from his *Erections, Ejaculations, Exhibitions & General Tales of Ordinary Madness* (City Lights, 1972)

Michael Rumaker in Nyack, N.Y., has been published by the Grove Press (*Gringos & Other Stories*) and by Scribner's (*The Butterfly*).

Gary Snyder's latest books are published by New Directions, including *Earth House Hold*. He was seen recently in the woods above the Yuba River near Nevada City, California, carrying a huge load of Manzanita on his back, shouting as he crashed through the underbrush, "Picture of Old Man Carrying Firewood!" and looking like an ancient Japanese painting of same.

Robert Creeley is a master of the very private poem—an intensely introspective voice which nevertheless manages to communicate deeply with a large audience. He is now published by Scribner's.

Jack Kerouac's poems herein are from a large manuscript of *Pomes All Sizes* which City Lights hopes to print whenever his heirs will allow it.

Dennis Fritzinger has been published by the Arif Press in Berkeley. He is a Chess Master and teaches chess at San Francisco State University.

Tom Cuson has directed poetry series at the Coffee Gallery and the Intersection in San Francisco. His poems have appeared among other places in "Gallery" and in Panjandrum Press anthologies.

Thomas Head is past editor of "Amphora" and his *3 pinball pomes* 1971) and *Dark Water* (1972) were published by Thorp Springs Press, Berkeley.

Richard Brautigan has lately followed his fish from the West Coast to Montana, having gone a long way from the first trout stream he bought by the foot at the Cleveland Wrecking Company. It's rumored he's using smaller and smaller hooks, which may account for the shorter and shorter poems he brings back. His net is very fine.

Kaye McDonough was associate editor of *185 Anthology* (1973). The drawing of Bob Kaufman facing her poem is from a series of poets' portraits by Peter Leblanc which will be the center of an exhibition at the M. H. De Young Museum in San Francisco late in 1974.

Ed Bullins left the West Coast in the 1960's and became the leading playwright-in-residence at the New Lafayette Theatre in Harlem. He's famous for such plays as "The Electronic Nigger" and "Charlie's Old Man," and his Black Ritual Mystical Drama is a new direction for him.

Michael McClure's latest book of poems is *September Blackberries*, published recently by New Directions.

Charles Upton's *Panic Grass* sprang up as a City Lights book in 1968, followed by *Time Raid* from Donald M. Allen's Four Seasons Foundation.

Reinhard Lettau is a dissident German writer, now a professor at University of California, San Diego. His Kafkaesque *Obstacles* was brought out by Pantheon in 1965.

Harold Norse's *Hotel Nirvana; Selected Poems* was published this year by City Lights in its Pocket Poets Series, and "Greece Answers" is from it.

The selection of modern Greek poets herein is from a book of *Voices Out of Junta Greece* to be published by City Lights. The translators are at present in Greece, gathering the texts.

Reza Baraheni was at last report still in an Iranian jail, originally arrested on unspecified charges in 1973. At the end of that year he had been in solitary confinement for 102 days and was not allowed to read or write.

(Political repression in Iran is well-documented by the Committee for Artistic & Intellectual Freedom on Iran (Address: 156 Fifth Avenue, Room 703, New York, N.Y. 10010)

Vicente Huidobro (1893-1948), born in Santiago, Chile, published *Canciones de la Noche* (1912), *La Grita del Silencio* (1913), *Espejo de Agua* (1916). In the same year in France, with Pierre Reverdy and Guillaume Apollinaire he helped found the revue "Nord/Sud." In Madrid in 1918 he published *Poemas Articos* and *Ecuatorial. Altazor* came out in 1931. Nicanor Parra recently wrote: "Huidobro, in Chile and in South America in general, is still considered the foremost exponent of the avant-garde . . . . I admire in him not only the poet but also the free spirit he represents. No one is further from the authoritarian mafias in fashion. He is one of the few not hypnotized by Stalinism." William Witherup and Sergio Echeverria have been doing pioneering work in new translations of Latin American poets including Parra, Antonio Machado, Enrique Lihn, and Huidobro.

Isabelle Eberhardt's story herein is from a book of her selected writings now being translated for City Lights Books by Paul Bowles in Tangiers, Morocco.

Jean Genet's book on Giacometti from which our selection is taken was first published in French by Marc Barbezat in 1958 and remains unpublished in America. Its translator, Daniel Peri Lucid is at the University of Massachusetts.

Bertrand Mathieu, whose unique American translation of Rimbaud's *A Season in Hell* appears here, is on leave from the University of New Haven and writes from Greece: "Rimbaud's *Hell* is an enigmatic poem but not an entirely hermetic one. There's some merit to thinking of it as a psycho-drama. The stage is the poet's brain. The dual characters adopt a variety of shifting shapes: angel/demon, bride/bridegroom, happiness/misery, good/evil. But *yin* and *yang* are one."

The portraits of Rimbaud by Jim Dine are from a series of six etchings done progressively on the same plate. (They may be seen together in the January 1974 issue of "Arts.")

The Surrealist Movement in the U.S. has edited its own section in this anthology, many of the contributors being active in the publication, "ARSENAL: Surrealist Subversion."

TOPOR

ALLEN GINSBERG

ENCOUNTERS WITH EZRA POUND

JOURNAL NOTES

22 Sept. 1967

Drive up to Rapallo from Bogliasco on super bridge across green-castled canyons, bright day and blue water between railroad and hedged cypress—

Pound rose from garden chair as we rounded path from the road surveying downhill large red house gardened. We sat, drank wine under a tree, I opened Indian harmonium and sang Harekrishna. In the house he spoke, at Olga Rudge's prompting,

"She asks, do you want to wash your hands?"

So then no more speech, except "too much" of the white plate of pasta almost eaten, and chicken/ham broiled, in a plate, he drank white wine— "Too much." O. Rudge lady peeled the grapes, or washed them in crystal bowl. "Too much," but set on a plate he reached out aged pink fingers, thumbnail white frayed.

O.R.: She felt too bad to go to Montreal, woke that night ill, cancelled airplane, sent telegram Montreal, E.P. had said " I won't go without you." Tornado in Milan, planes late anyway, might've missed London connection—

The *Book of Changes* in Italian. Pound had a copy, and the coins were loose in a tiny alabaster bowl Olga Rudge showed.

"If this atmosphere (Blue Rapallo and Torquello Bay to Portofino under mountain verdure on promontory below daylit distance) is fine enough for Ezra Pound then these young men, who come to see Pound territory, should try to look at it . . . take time . . ."

"Zoagli" of *Cantos* is town other side of mountain south of Rapallo.

Stared in tiny pupiled eye, he blinked twice, our eyes shifted aside, I meditated.

Later sang, "*Prajnaparamita Sutra*, eyes open on him, eyes turned away, he shifted back to gaze direct.

After lunch we drove to Portofino—he silent in car—ivory handled cane at side—sat on the quai, he drank iced tea. Long time quiet. Ancient paranoid silent—

"Did you ever try hashish all these years?" I was curious. He looked at me, blinked eyes, shook thin white-bearded cheeks, no, twice—

"Swinburne the only miss . . . he'd a been the one to turn you on," I murmured to myself half aloud.

10/3/67. I went to bed last nite, thinking to consult dream worlds as I have neglected to record dreams for a year or two now.

10/7/67. Dream

In large hotel Europe, wandering down twilit corridor having seen Pound —thin beard and stark face upswept hair from *Observer* photo—I am ruminating over his silence, walking along polished marble Italian floor—thinking also to tell friend Ettore to send Pound photos taken at Portofino us sitting together silent at Café waterfront table—Tell Olga Rudge I want to publish photos, money given to poets, or to C.O.P. [Committee on Poetry, Inc]—or I'll tell her myself and ask if it's alright—ruminating in the dream about newspaper publicity—I go out on balcony and sit alone in obscurity after sunset on deckchair—*His silence unhappy*—I begin to sob and then many sobs come and tears wet my closed eyes—I open eyes and see maid with dry mop cleaning the balcony, and another lady in deck chair watching my cry, I am pleased that someone heard me cry, wonder if she understands why—I get up to leave—wake in front room Milan crash of trolleys on tracks 5 P.M. afternoon, my eyelids wet.

10/21/67. Arrived Venice—settled in Pension near Salute, consulting map on wall, turned saw Olga Rudge and then Pound emerging from dining room. We sat for coffee. Mrs. Rudge explained I wouldn't have had trouble finding their house, "oftentimes Venetians will walk half a mile to show you a tiny alley."

Pound spoke up, "Forty years since I've seen anybody do that . . ."

"Do what, Ezra?" she asked.

"Take the trouble to walk you along to show you the way." He said no more that hour; I arranged to come to lunch next day.

10/22/67. Going to Pound's house—how old?—"How old are you, old man?" I said, several wines and a stick of pot midway between meal.

"82 in several days," he said. That's all he said—all day, with the Italian-Ivanchich speaking of the Afric desert simultaneous—"82"—and I smoked at front of fire, smoked and spoke, and no one reproved me in Venice—perfect balanced, the consciousness—played him *Eleanor Rigby, and Yellow Submarine,* and *Dylan's Sad Eyed Lady of Lowland* and *Gates of Eden* and *Where are you tonite, Sweet Marie?* and Donovan's *Sunshine Superman.* I gave Pound Beatles, Dylan, Donovan—the experts suave and velvet for Futurity—I walked silent out Vio where meets the Grand Canale—I gave Beatles, gave Dylan, gave Donovan—to listen? Forever—tomorrow give Ali Akbar Khan.

[added later]—(This note written blind drunk Sun. nite 1 a.m. returning from Harry's Bar.)

What follows is sober recapitulation days later of what happened Oct. 22.

All afternoon, lunch and wine and upstairs conversation with Ivanchich visiting and Pound silent. I lit a stick of grass at lunch and smoked it, saying nothing about it.

Later high, as I played him music; he had come upstairs swiftly when I asked him to listen, and folded self in chair, silent hands crossed on lap, picking at skin, absorbed—occasionally with a slight smile—at *Eleanor Rigby*. "No one was saved" and *Sweet Marie* "six white horses/that you promised me/were finally delivered/down to the Penitentiary." I repeated the words aloud, in fragments—for him to hear clearly. So he sat. "Is this all too much electric noise?" He smiled and sat still. "I just want you to hear this *other*"—and I continued playing, *Gates of Eden,* and even *Yellow Submarine*. Sat there all along, I drunk, he impassive, earnest, attentive, asmile.

Also that day I chanted Mantras to Krishna, and Tara, and Sarva Dakini, fragment of Allah, and *Om a ra ba tsa na de de de de to* Manjusri, describing His book and flaming Sword of Intelligence—Olga hearing Majusri downstairs came up to top floor where we were (Ivanchich and Pound) and said "It sounded lovely down there" so sat and listened—I was drunk.

A finality "that binds things together." Depression all last week—read papers and *Time*—read *Cantos,* feel better.

10/28/67. Supper at Cici, Olga and Pound at table, "You like the Beatles records? . . . or too much noise?"

Silence.

"You mean those discs?" he said.

"Yes."

Silence.

"No! No!" to the waiter offering zucchini also with sliced mutton.

"Oh yes, take some zucchini, it is good for you—" Olga.

"You liked the Noh, heard first time at the Sanctus Spiriti Church?" Olga asked. He stared thinking, then shook head No, slowly, added "Palladio's theater—"

10/28/67. Lunch w/Olga Rudge, Pound, Michael Reck, Peter Russell. 1:30 P.M. Pension Cici 22 Salute Oct. 28, 1967—

Pound ate, fish, mostly silent during meal, others conversed, he responded occasionally with head nods—re a performance of Monteverdi (?) at S. Friari—

I had one question (being told he responds to specific textual questions from the turn of century—memorabilia)—

That I had found the "place of Carpaccio's skulls"—but where's the place where

"in the font to the right as you enter
     are all the gold domes of San Marco"—?

He looked up and in even, tho high voice, said "Yes, when the font was filled—now they've changed it—used to be like that—"

For yesterday I'd looked in that same holywater basin, a stone bowl, but "for some sanitation reason" as Olga R. added a few minutes later, they'd placed a copper round-rim lip on inside of bowl, for water—and no longer filled the center of the bowl, just the metal canal around the rim.

"I walked half a mile yesterday," I added, "looking for the spot in Dei Grecii, in San Georgio—finally looked in San Marco."

"It used to be like that—the center was filled with water, and the reflection had the domes," he explained, Perhaps less extensively.

"And the 'casa que fue de Don Carlos'—the house that used to be Don Carlos'?"

"That is on the way to San Vio."

"But I've been there—is that near the English church?"

"That's on the corner where San Vio meets the Canal."

"But Salviati's is down the street here at the end—the sign."

"Salviati was in another place in that time," said Pound.

"Oh—but *who* was Don Carlos."

"The *Pretender*."—he answered.

"So the house is on the corner of San Vio & Canal?"

He nodded, yes.

I continued—explaining that there were a great many specific perceptions —descriptions—of exact language composed—throughout *Cantos*—"tin flash in the sun dazzle" and "Soapsmooth stone posts"—and added I'd gone to San Vio looking for the soapsmooth stone posts—Were they on the bridge to the private door off the square? or the posts at the end of the quai at the canal-edge, or the plinth at the center of the square? Which was it, because they were all rough—changed perhaps—replaced. "Was it a specific stone post you had in mind, or just all the stone posts?"

"No, general—" he said, or nodding negatively, not a specific one.

A few moments silence while I looked thru my notebook for a phrase. "I've been trying to find language equivalent for that light on water— yesterday I arrived at this—

'Leaped on Vaporetto,
    sun yellow in white haze, Salute's
silver light, crooked-mirrored on the glassy surface' "

and repeated to him, while he looked me in eye—fine blue pupil—'light, crooked-mirrored on the glassy surface,' and smiled at him. "You approve of that?"

"That's good," he smiled back—hands steady on the table, with almost invisible tremor, white hair straight back above high-slanted forehead—his skin wrinkled at wrists and back of hand, dry, slight white flakes of dead skin, fingernails whitened by picking or rubbing, membrane-white roughness scraped on surface of thumb-nail—clean skin of face and brow, with slight flaking of age (not dandruff) but dryness of skin surface under the thin white straight hair above his brow.

Had been talking with Reck about Buddhism, meditation, mantras, last nite at supper and today earlier—and continued the conversation into Pound's ear, leaning toward him talking quietly—Reck's child, Mickey, playing with 14 postcards distracted him, Russell conversing with Olga Rudge at other side of Pound, she at end of table.

Reck asked, "You ever meet Kitasono Katsue?

Pound, "No." Reck described meeting with Katsue, whom he found clerkish.

Sometime at table—conversing w/Reck, who on basis of previous nite's conversation (Reck'd noted there were Taoist elements in Confucian tradition at origin) was encouraging open discussion of Oriental heresies, asked about Indian gods—in relation to Greek—I had mentioned Vedic Hymns, asking Pound if he'd ever heard Vedic chanting—

"No"—shook his head, he hadn't—I continued, referring to UNESCO new volumes of Hymns to Surya (Apollo), Rudra (Thunder God)—also mentioned Ganesh Chant (White Yajur Veda).

So explained to him—"You remember I was telling you about hearing Blake's voice—?"

He hesitated and then pursed his mouth, nodded up and down slightly, looking away.

"But I didn't tell it coherently."—so described to him the occasion— "a series of moments of altered modes of consciousness over a period of weeks, etc."—ending "no way of presenting that except thru things external perceived in that state" and so continued explaining how his attention to specific perceptions, & WcW's "No ideas but in things" had been great help to me in finding language and balancing my mind—and to many young poets—and asked "am I making sense to you?"

"Yes," he replied finally, and then mumbled "but my own work does not make sense." [or "but I haven't made sense."]

I had asked him before if he would like to come to give a reading in the U.S., or Buffalo or S.F. say, he replied, "Too late—"

"Too late for what—for us or for your voice?" I laughed, and continued, explaining my and our (Creeley, etc.) debt to his language perceptions— speaking specifically of the sequence of phanopoeic images—"soapsmooth stone posts"—even his irritations and angers characteristic, humors, dramatic, as manifest in procession as time mosaic.

"Bunting told me," said Pound, "that there was too little presentation and too much reference"—referring to things, not presenting them.

I replied that in the last year [Basil] Bunting had told me to look at Pound because *I* had too many words, and shewed Pound as model for economy in *presentation* of sensory phenomena, via words. I went on to describe recent history of Bunting—I'd before asked him if he'd seen *"Brigflatts* and he had nodded, swifly, affirmative. So Pound's work, I concluded to him, had been, in "Praxis of perception, ground I could walk on."

"A mess," he said.

"What, you or the *Cantos* or me?"

"My writing—stupidity and ignorance all the way through." he said, "Stupidity and ignorance."

Reck had been adding "encouragement" in general terms, and here said, "But the great lesson has been in prosody, your ear, which everyone has learned from . . ." and described also effect of Pound on Hemingway and Hemingway on Bengali writers—Babel—or Japanese—"Did you," Reck concluded "teach Hemingway?"—as a question to which Pound was silent —doubtful? I opened my mouth to continue the communion—

"Direct presentation"—"Yes," said Reck, "No adjectives"—

Turning to Pound, Reck continued, "your poetry's shockingly direct."

"It's all doubletalk—" Pound re *Cantos* answered.

Reck—"But you have a marvelous ear, one can't praise that too much —great ear—It's hard for you to write a bad line."

Pound—"It's hard for me to write anything."

Reck—"You're reading has been so extensive, and led people to many areas."

Pound—"Not enough . . . I didn't read enough poetry."

Reck—"What you did read you made good use of." . . .

"For the ear—[William Carlos] Williams told me," I continued, "in 1961—we were talking about prosody, I'd asked him to explain your prosody to me in general, something toward approximation of quantitative any- way Williams said, 'Pound has a mystical ear—did he ever tell you that?'

"No," said Pound, "he never said that to me"—smiling almost shyly and pleased—eyes averted, but smiling, almost curious and childlike.

"Well I'm reporting it to you now to you 7 years later—the judgement of the tender-eyed Doctor that you had a 'mystical ear'—not gaseous mysti- cal he meant—but a natural ear for changes of rhythm and tone."

I continued explaining the concrete value of his perceptions manifested in phrasing, as reference points for my own sensory perceptions—I added that as humor—HUMOR—the ancient *humours*—his irritations, against Buddhists, Taoists and Jews—fitted into place, despite his intentions, as part of the drama, the theater, the presentation, record of flux of mind-con- sciousness. "The Paradise is in the desire, not in the imperfection of accom- plishment—it was the intention of Desire we all respond to—Bhakti—the Paradise is in the magnanimity of the *desire* to manifest coherent perceptions in language."

"The intention was bad—that's the trouble—anything I've done has been an accident—any good has been spoiled by my intentions—the pre- occupation with irrelevant and stupid things—" Pound said this quietly, rusty voiced like old child, looked directly in my eye while pronouncing "intention."

"Ah well, what I'm trying to tell you—what I came here for all this time—was to give you my blessing then, because despite your disillusion— unless you *want* to be a messiah—then you'd have to be a Buddhist to be the perfect Messiah" (he smiled)—"But I'm a Buddhist Jew—perceptions have been strengthened by the series of practical exact language models which are scattered thruout the *Cantos* like stepping stones—ground for *me* to occupy, walk on—so that despite your intentions, the practical effect has been to clarify my perceptions—and, anyway, now, do you accept my blessing?"

He hesitated, opening his mouth, like an old turtle.

"I do," he said—"but my worst mistake was the stupid suburban prejudice of antisemitism, all along, that spoiled everything—" This is almost exact.

"Well no, because anyone with any sense can see it as a humour, in that sense part of the drama—you manifest the process of thoughts—make a model of the consciousness and antisemitism is your fuck-up like not liking Buddhists but it's part of the model as it proceeds—and the great accomplishment was to make a working model of yr. mind—I mean nobody cares if it's Ezra Pound's mind—it is a *mind*, like all our minds, and that's never been done before—so you made a working model all along, with all the dramatic imperfections, fuck-ups—anyone with sense can always see the crazy part and see the perfect clear lucid perception-language-ground—"

He had nodded a little when I said "Nobody cares if it's Ezra Pound's mind"—and I added, and "so, fine, it's Ezra Pound's mind a fine mind but the important thing, *a model of mind process*—Gertrude Stein also made one, usable—yours however as I've experimented in transcription the nearest to a natural model—a model *from* Nature—as Cezanne had worked *from* Nature, to reconstitute the optical field perceptions . . ."

It may have been at this point that he said as recorded above, that his worst mistake had been "the stupid suburban prejudice antisemitism"—

and I responded, "Ah, that's lovely to hear you say that . . ." and later "as it says in *I Ching*, 'No Harm.'"

Sometime in this conversation he'd concluded, "I found out after seventy years I was not a lunatic but a moron."

And I paraphrased "Beginning of Wisdom, Prospero," and was continuing—Reck turning aside from his child asked me to repeat what Pound'd said, which I did and turned eyes to Pound, remembered I'd quoted epilogue verses *Tempest* last Sunday, so repeated them again to Pound, saying "You remember?

'Now all my charms are overthrown
& what strength I have's my own
Which is most faint'—I drew that out—'Tis true,
Unless I pardoned be by you . . .
Prayers of yours my sails must fill . . .'
and continued—"Can't remember exact language . . . 'Prayer/which pierces so that it assaults

Mercy
itself
and frees all faults.'

So throwing staff and books "deeper than ever did plummet sound"

He looked at me in my eye kind smiling, I looked at him and then (must've been at this point) asked if he'd accept my blessing—more conversation—the sequence at this hour later inexactly rememberable—We rose, he got coat cane and Olga gave him grey wool small-brim'd hate, walked all of us out on San Gregorio by small canal lined with iron rail—started walking, still talking up street to his alley—T.V. cameramen waiting, a black cable snaked from his door to powerline across alley—and at door we all stood, he outside still while Olga went in—So took him by shoulders looked in his eye and asked "and I also came here for your blessing, and now may I have it sir?"

"Yes," he nodded, "for whatever it's worth—"

"And more, and more," I said, "I'd like you to give me yr. blessing to take to Sheri Martinelli"—for I'd described her late history Big Sur, eyes seeing Zodiac everywhere hair bound up like Marianne Moore—which gossip perhaps he hadn't even heard—"To at least say hello to her, I'll tell her, so I can tell her," and stood looking in his eyes. "Please . . . because it's worth a lot of *happiness* to her, now . . ." and so he looked at me impassive for a moment and then without speaking, smiling slightly, also, slight redness of cheeks awrinkle, nodded up and down, affirm, looking me in eye, clear no mistake, ok.

Then he stood, silent, Peter Russell said adieux, I waited, talked to Olga while, "It's horrible, so many come and ask him if he's still writing—" she had said at table; there were now enough *Cantos* for new volumes, scattered and as yet uncollated or edited whatever—"to ask him if he's writing—of course it's different with someone like yourself, to discuss as fellow"—fellow professional or something. "Well it makes him self conscious"—"Yes self conscious," she agreed to that language exact—"But if you wait," she had said "and have patience, he needs to talk—he thinks all his work so bad—whereas when he reads it into tape, you can tell he reads with enthusiasm, some parts—other parts, of course he dislikes but that's natural, after years to be self-critical, anyone would . . ." She spoke very sensibly, explaining how she viewed the apparent perplexity as it was made more difficult by outside uncomprehension of the nature of his present alertness and character.

Then he turned to me—I had kissed him on right cheek—held my hand, and said "I should have been able to do better . . ."

"It was perfect," I replied—"I haven't properly yet sung Harekrishna to you either . . . I'll be around a few days more anyway maybe . . . see you . . ." He stood then at his door, hesitating to enter—waved down the alley, I walked away with Reck and Russell, who suggested I try to transcribe details of the conversation while it is still fresh to ear.

His remarks several days ago "82 in several days" exact to this Monday Oct. 30. his birthday.

10/29/67.—12 P.M.—Out on Salute boat-station waiting for Vaporetto, Peggy G. with two tiny dogs and Paolo art friend, met gossiping, I related some of conversation with Pound day before—she thought his wartime activities "unforgivable" . . . also asked me if I'd written poem called *Howl* and another poem *Gasoline?* Olga Rudge and Ezra Pound appeared on the floating platform—9 P.M. dark—she said they were going to Carmini Church for Vivaldi concert, 5 year celebration of priest, a lady friend singing that night—social appearance—I asked "May I come" and as she said, certainly, we went on vaporetto—

Sitting on bench behind them, addressed her and Pound's ear, told story of Julius Orlovsky, as Manichean who wouldn't speak for 14 years because he believed all the evil in the universe issued from his body and mouth. "Are you a Manichean, Ezra?" she laughed. No answer. Walked long time, slightly lost in alleys past open flagstone campo S. Margherita to church (I'd visited it earlier today on walk starting from Zatteria, when I'd met Pound in afternoon sunlight, blinking, waiting on Fondamenta [quai-waterside, facing Juidecca] with Olga for film crew trailing them—standing then in bright clear light long sun yellow rays bathing the buildingsides—I wanted to stay get in the picture, but said I was taking walk, so continued on my way and left them in group with TV director, a large serious artistic looking Italian—I walked several hundred feet on and stepped out on a swaying wooden jetty, sat crosslegged, and watched from distance, as their group slowly ambled back to San Gregorio.)

Evening now, we three went into S. Maria Del Carmelo—wrote note there, sitting behind Pound—

> Carmini, organ, apse brilliant yellow
> gilt angels, violincello,
>   Byzance cross hung silhouette,
> Flowers on altar, Pillars wrapped in red velvet—
> old man sat before me,
> brown canvas shoes, one heel raised alert,
>   hat and cane in hand
> Smooth woodslab resting
>   under a fold in his coatback—
> white cheek beard dyed red by
> velvet light,
> black not entirely faded from
> back of his skull,
> fringed with grey hair,
>   candle gleam through white web.

Some very delicate Vivaldi violin beginning soft and rising — Olga, Pound following, walked forward along pillared candle-lit left aisle to look closer to her singing friend, they stood there listening to the end. Then without waiting for next pieces of concert to finish, headed home thru alleys, walking—silent awhile, then I began again—as I'd been to look, today, at "lacquer in sunlight . . . russet brown . . . lions out of benevolence," to the left of San Marco (Olga on vaporetto had pointed out House of Don Carlos—other side of San Vio Campo, on corner—Questioned where Salviati's had been, Pound didn't answer)—he didn't respond either, to reference to the lions; anyway it wasn't a question.

I began: "I've been thinking about problem you raised yesterday, the *Cantos* a mess—If they made a static crystaline ideological structure, it would be unresolvable, now. But as it is an open-ended work, that is, epic, "including history," of movement of yr. mind and record of focused perceptions, existing in *time*, and changing in time, anything you write now will refer back to the beginnings and alter all that went before—like turning a

Venetian blind. Same thing as in Lombardo's Sirens—. Beginning back in time with serpent tails, going thru transformation thru Breast *Pisan Cantos* poignancy—ending in present time sculpting clear human eyes. In short, what I'm saying is, — Einstinian changing universe is recorded, not static crystal shit model—so *anything* you do now is OK and will be proper appropriate, as means of altering preceding thought-flow by hindsight—Am I making sense?" This addressed to problem of finishing *Cantos*.

Replied, "It's all tags and patches."

I explained lots more, in answer, ending "I've read *Cantos* thru this month and in each canto there's always some condensed perception concrete image round which the other tags, ideologies, irritations and projections and references revolve, so whole work has solid vertebrae." Then continued, "Is your problem one of physical depression that keeps you from recording and registering these final perceptions—whatever you are *now?*"

"The depression's more mental than physical," Pound answered.

Later in conversation I said the *Cantos* were solid—good as Dickens' *Bleak House* I started reading, that was full of exaggerations—said I'd read *The Pit* lately, Frank Norris, had he read it ever?

"No."

So I described the roar of wheat trading on the floor of the Stock Exchange. We got to house, after more on *Cantos*, he not replying, but when he entered his house he said immediately,

"It's too hot in here."

Olga built a fire. I sat down, and next described effect of his poetry on younger poets—Do you know the enormous influence you've had? I asked—

"I'd be surprised if there was any," he said dubiously, looked down, but interested—I recited a few short poems of Creeley, talked briefly of Olson, Wieners—asked him if he knew Creeley's work at all, he nodded up and down, thin beard affirmative. "But do you understand the influence your writing had been as a model for whole generation of younger poets—that is my age half yours now 41 and say Creeley?"

"It would be ingenious work to see any influence," sd. he.

Explained the influence WCW, Zuke (Zukofsky), Bunting, etc. Said that at first, myself of Paterson, I'd found WCW more usable—

"*Williams* was in touch with human feelings . . ." he said, nodding his head slightly in disgust at himself. I explained it was the practical matter of listening to "I'll kick yuh eye." And I went on explaining the models we had — that Williams didn't have Fire Excitement — Crane had — did Pound know Crane's "Bridge?"

"No." I was surprised, so recited several verses of *Atlantis* comparing it to Shelley *West Wind*, and Pound's own anger-inspiration rhythm Canto 46 "Heliandros! Kai Heleptolis! Kai Helarxe!" Asked if he'd tape recorded that, he nodded no.

Olga serving ovaltine, brought me copy of Canto 110, "Has Mr. Ginsberg seen this?" I said I'd return it, she asked him to sign it for me—he hesitated long time, and said.

"Oh, he doesn't *want* it."

"Well, yes sure, I do," I pointed my finger, "if you want to check yr. perceptions. I absolutely do."

So he signed, "Alan Ginzberg—dall'autore—Oct. 29, 1967 Ezra Pound."

At home, I also at one point asked him if he was at all familiar with my poetry, he shook his head negative. I said, Well, oddly, it might even please you. This led on to discussion of his influence on younger poets.

10/30/67—3:30 P.M.—Met Pound by Teodoro's statue, cafe there, with Ivanchich and girlfriend—Ivanchich had invited me to lunch at Malamocco's, Pound's birthday today—conversation about Huxley, re. electronic spying, I repeated notion that best anti-police state strategy was total exposure of all secrets, rather than electronic monopoly-control of classified information—i.e. unclassify everybody's private life, Johnson's as well as mine— thence conversation re. intrusion of machinery universe—Olga asked Pound for old quotation, which he repeated complete after her fragmentary reference, "As for living, our servants can do that for us."

As habitual, he hesitated over choice of foods, refused vegetables—I gave him 1½ stringbeans from my side dish, which he picked up with fork and ate—toasted him and drank wine, he at first didn't respond, then swiftly took his glass and drank.

I talked a great deal about modern use of drugs as distinct from '20s opiate romanticism (as I saw it)—turned finally and asked him again— "Does all this make nonsense to you now—'immortality pills' and all?"

"You know a great deal about the subject," he replied.

Ivanchich identified Olga's reference to the can of opium Pound brought —Was it Hemingway's story or Williams'—to friend (Forrest Read?) Ivanchich saying it was in *Movable Feast*. Pound commented:

"Hemingway had the correct version."

Olga asked me if I knew Michaux,— then asked Pound if he remembered Michaux—Pound shook head No, she said, "Oh, you must remember, he came to lunch with us in Paris two years ago" . . . she had described him as very charming.

I had also asked, earlier, if Pound had not ever *met* Hart Crane, he shook head No.

Walked back slowly along Riva Schiavoni, on top of white bridge (Ponte de Pieta across from Sighs Bridge by Ducal Palace) Pound in brown wool hat, St. Georgio Maggiore dome and tower above his head silhouetted in brilliant yellow-blue afternoon light, few people and many grey pigeons crowded on stone ground—we waited by vaporetto for Olga to check at pastry shop—on the way, passing Todero's column I repeated,

"Shd/I shift to the other side,
    or wait 24 hours,"

and asked what does that mean, shift to the other side of the column, or cross over to Salute?

"Fantasia." he replied.

"What?"

"Just fantasy."

"I thought meant, shift sleeping to other side of the column of Teodoro, or, maybe, change in life—or just writing *poetry*."

He was silent.

Olga returning, we sat waiting for vaporetto, asked if Reck'd left copy of *Hsi-yu hu* by Yeh-Lu Ch'u-Ts' Ai, (Tr. Igor de Rachewiltz, Monumenta Serica, Vol. XXI, 1962). Said Pound's "Immortality Pills" phraseology was from notes in that monograph—also reference to Incense Cults—all Canto 99.

At door this evening, returning from an errand, Mrs. Rudge invited me to return later to sing to Pound on his birthday nite. Came by at 10 attired in silken London-Indic shirt, woven gold, and Buddhist Trikaya emblem round neck—he was silent, by fire (he'd come downstairs)—so chanted Prajnaparamita Hrydya Sutra in Jap and English, then Hare Krishna, and after some birthday cake and a little more champagne, Buddhist 3 Vows. Buddham Saranam Gochamee, Dhamam Saranam Gochamee, Sangham Saranam Gochamee. Then in silence still, to illustrate effect of his composition on mine, read — with indifferent voice alas — few pages of "Middle Section of Long Poem on These States." oops! Silence. Eek! Put that down fast after asking, do you see the relationship in method of composition? Silence. So picked up harmonium and chanted 50 verses of Gopala Gopala Devaka Nandina Gopala—high and sweet, and low solemn. Then explained "Gopala means Krishna cowboy" and said goodnite and "Happy Birthday Krishna," he smiled at that. Leaving from door I demanded, "Well, say *Goodnight!*" He nodded amiably, said "Goodnight." So I left.

11/6/67—2.30 A.M. Sun. Nite—

Nov. 2, saw Pound on Zatteria, walking at 1 P.M. in sunlight along the stones—Onnisanti Day—asked him "How are you today? Alive!"

He answered, "Worse. And alive."

Several days later met at lunch, he was silent, curious reddish cast to cheeks, observed the elderly waitress carefully bone his fried trout—silent, then swiftly picked up fork, cut a piece and ate. But didn't finish his plate, refused cake and coffee. New clean lavender shirt with wide collar, and monocolored yellow tie. Always hangs his hat outside Pension dining room, and his scarf, on brass hook, and carries ivory-handled cane inside to table. Said, "Goodbye, Mr. Pound," and he turned, hesitated, looked at me, smiling slightly, but dumb, shook my extended hand.

Yesterday came down in mid-afternoon to dining room back of Pension kitchen, acompanying Otto Endrenyi—Hungarian-Bolognesi exrefugee friend of Olga—who'd heard me sing in room an hour earlier—(high with Israeli architect I'd met in flooded San Marco Plaza and we'd walked and smoked his last brown stick of Kif, along street from Academia to Zatteria, then up to my room I sang awhile Hare Krishna)—So Otto invited me to coffee

—found Pound sitting there alone, Olga at telephone in front office preparing trip to Padua to escape rain floods of early November.

I sat across from Pound at another table, asked him if there was old or classical music to St. Francis *Canticle to Creatures*—repeated question, he answered. "There is no contemporary music." So, high on Pot still, I improvised in Hebraic-Indian modes the complete canticle, with drone harmony on Peter Orlovsky's brown school harmonium, chanting thru "Frate Morte."

An hour later saw him and Olga Rudge outside hotel, and followed after them with Otto, they to take vaporetto to R.R. to Padua, we to promenade in San Marco at red clouded sunset hour—Pound walked energetically, white raincoat flowing behind him, walked with speedy strength, slowed to climb small bridge-steps to Salute's platform and stepped up firmly, then with youthful balance stepped from the tipsy floating platform onto boatbus and walked ahead into cabin, sat down; vaporetto pulled away from shore, moving upstream.

Morning— . . . empty life, revolving on the surface of a mirror, myriads passing by —

Woke, and realizing late date, only another month and half before reading tour, and fatal time in USA, and I gotta get back soon see Peter, and finish texts once for all, collect books, cash in verbal chips, dropout—all last nite at Luigi Nonno's house talk of Cuba and Revolution and Guevara photos on wall and avant garde collections with machinery, lights, Guevara images fair faced and smiling thru boyish beard—Time passing.

ANDREI VOZNESENSKY

EXEGI MONUMENTUM

(after Horace)

excerpt from "Rezanov"

I've created a monument to myself, marvelous, eternal . . .
Our distorted
fleeting reason clutches at pyramids, statues, memorial places . . .
Vanity!
Ten thousand years more or less, and further—nothing!

I am the last poet of civilization,
not of ours—Roman—but of civilization in general.
In an epoch of spiritual crisis and cipherization
culture is the most shameful of things.
It's shameful to recognize an untruth and not call it that,
or having branded it shameful not to uproot it;
shameful to call funerals "weddings,"
still more shameful to pose at funerals.
For these words my contemporaries will strangle me
but the future afro-euro-ameri-asiat
will tear my pedestal out by its roots
and a hole will gape in the planet.

Then they'll get down to proving that my words were absurd.
Make up better songs, dances, write a few books.
And I'll be happy that I was justly strung up.
That will be another kind of monument!

Translated from the Russian by Maureen Sager

HUEY P. NEWTON

from
INSIGHTS & POEMS

HIMSELF

If one does not realize himself
how can one give himself
If one does not realize himself
how can one receive himself
And if one realizes
how can he give or receive

I DIMINISH MYSELF

If I define myself as my thumb
I deny myself my fingers
If I define myself as my fingers
I deny myself my hand
If I define myself as my hand
I deny myself my arm
If I define myself as my arm
I deny myself my body
If I define myself as my body
I deny myself my universe
I diminish myself

EGO

one day i suddenly realized i had forgotten:
name
age
sex
address
race
I had found myself

REVOLUTIONARY SUICIDE

By having no family
I inherited the family of humanity.
By having no possessions
I have possessed all.
By rejecting the love of one
I received the love of all.
By surrendering my life to the revolution
I found eternal life.
Revolutionary suicide

THE UNKNOWN

I heard God call
I got my gun and waited
When he appeared I realized
and I took the gun from my head.

ERICKA HUGGINS

from

INSIGHTS & POEMS

AFTER LOOKING AT A PICTURE OF AN INDIANSISTERWOMAN

Red woman
mother of this country,
on whose bones (and those of your daughters/sons)
this country's soil was fertilized,
did you see them bring my people here?
Did you cry?
did you see them bring others of all colors
                  all poor
                        to this corrupt, confused,
mis used land? — mother earth, red beauty — do you see us
all now — struggling — inside this country, once yours,
America the beast?
do you see us all trying to go back to our home?
        to the real life/natural life?
            freedom?
do you see us trying to love? are we on the right path?
do we see the right signs in the clouds, the air, the animals,
the people . . . do you hear the winds of change?

                motorcycles
                    horns
                    trucks
                    car exhausts
              a television voice
                    memories
                    songs
                    dreams
                    a smile
              a comrade's voice
                    a silver ring
                    a gold one
                    a wooden box
             an oval stone
                    a gravesite near the water
                    jail
                    keys
                    locks
                    bars

a wilted, wrinkled flower
    letters
    laughter
    wishes
    tears
a night of silent sounds
    children
    brothers
    sisters
    friends
a thousand lonely fuschias

JUDSON CREWS

DOLORES HERRERA

I

Dolores Herrera, a dark eyed Chicana
Dolores Herrera, with a child's spirit, yet a woman
Dolores Herrera, who may prove to be
       the most important American of the 1970's
       the personality of the decade
Dolores Herrera, with a child's spirit but
       with the fierce intensity
       of banked fire

Dolores Herrera, whose I.D. card is a blur
       whose birthplace is a blank
       whose ancestry is not quite certain
Dolores Herrera, who harbored a Brown Beret
       wanted for questioning by the police
       who may be a wet-back
       who may have smoked pot
Dolores Herrera, who has known brutality
       and deprivation
       and stark terror
Dolores Herrera, whose food stamps
       the country could no longer afford

Dolores Herrera, stripped naked in a bare cell
       under a blazing light
Fucked by the brazen beak of the bald eagle
Aborted in a barren field watched over by crows
       and by coyotes
       aborted among cadavers

Dolores Herrera, who treasured solitude
       who liked to walk in the quiet twilight
       among the small hills and the brooding stones
       who liked to think of quiet water and deep places
       who thought upon the years ground to pieces in
       an abrasive crazy existence
       who thought upon the long droughts
       the barren soil, the gutted arroyos
Dolores Herrera, who never knew before that her
       meagre needs could bankrupt the country
       who had never realized before
       that the solvency of the state was so shakey
       who had never come to grips with the fact
       that the government was built on sand

II

Dolores Herrera
     you were caught off base
Dolores Herrera
     you have been fucked

Fucked by the little men in the gratuitous pay
     of the senile giants
Fucked by the fart-knockers and the turd-tumblers
Fucked by the route-man and
     the chicken-shit junior executive
     in the Department of Accounts-now-closed
Dolores Herrera, your credit has been over-extended
     cough it up, today and not tomorrow
     every penny of it
     one hundred and nineteen dollars and seventy-six cents
     plus eighty-six dollars and forty-seven cents carrying charges
     and seven dollars and fifty-nine cents
     at eleven and one-half percent
     plus seventeen dollars and twenty-eight cents indemnity
Dolores Herrera, your past, present, and future accounts
     are now due, and past due, and are all now in arrears
Cough it up, Dolores Herrera
     by three twenty-seven in the afternoon, Dolores Herrera
     or your ass can rot
     in the county jail, Dolores Herrera
     forever

Dolores Herrera, you are fucked

Fucked by the Cristo Rey and the balance of power
You were fucked on the steps of the temple
     of Justice
     while the lady with the scales
     and the sword
     was impassive as ever
     in her white Anglo-Saxon splendor
You were aborted on the courthouse lawn
     at the foot of the proud statue of
     the Defender of the People
You were fucked by the court clerk
     who said you put two X's in the wrong box
     who said you must be cross-eyed
     as he ogled your tits through correctional lenses
Fucked in the rectum by the Attorney General's Office
     who says Equal Protection is outside
     of his jurisdiction
     and is no concern of his Department
Fucked by the Senator who turned the other way

        knowing this is no proper issue
        to get mixed up in
        with an election year at hand and Party problems
        a constant worry

Dolores Herrera, you are fucked

Dolores Herrera, you jailbird
        and you cheat
Don't you know your troubles could bankrupt the State?
Dolores Herrera, don't you know
        you are an embarrassment to the Establishment?
        don't you know your story must be kept quiet?
        don't you know the Attorney General doesn't want
        to hear about you?
        don't you know that officialdom wishes that you
        had never been born?
Dolores Herrera, why don't you get lost
        you leper, and you bum

Dolores Herrera

You could slice off your nipples
        you could de-pigment your skin
        you could pluck out your eyelashes
        you could tape up your slit
        you could shave yourself clean
You could play the topless-bottomless circuit
        for a season
You could earn your own keep
        just for a change

You are fucked, Dolores Herrera
        you are fucked

Now that they have perfected castration of the mind
        with bloodless surgery
Now that the newscasters know how
        their bread is buttered
Now that the nightingale is asphyxiated
        with a feedback of his own melody

Fucked by the beast nurtured in the vaunted chambers
        of the highest council
Fucked by the beast sanctified at the sacred altar
Fucked by the beast belching ash and steam
        vaporing the sky, cankering the lung
Fucked in the Chapel of the Singing Sorrow

Aborted in the center of the open arena
        at the Inter-Tribal Ceremonial
        at the State Fair
        at the Fiesta in September
Dolores Herrera

The Office of Departments and Ombudsmen fucked you
        with a runaround and a rubber stamp because
        you had not been fucked yet
        by the Ombudsman of the Division
        of Community Ombudsmen
The Department of Risks and Reprisals said you
        didn't stand a chance
        but fucked you through a fumigation dip
        and a delousing chamber
        just in case

You are fucked, Dolores Herrera

Fucked because you have seen your brothers
        gutted with methadone, fucked
        because you have seen their minds
        blanked out with stellazine
Fucked by a thirty-inch night-stick drumming
        the left kidney and then the right
        crushing above the buttocks
        to the small of the spine
Fucked by a cannister of tear gas with
        an emetic additive
Fucked by a poisoned bayonet in the hands of a rookie
        a brave Guardsman shitting in his pants
        for fear of his life at the sight of
        your clenched fist held high over your head
        as a symbol because of what you have seen
        and because of what you know
As a symbol of the certain calendar
        of the clock approaching the hour

The sea is gutted, the sea is a grave
        the mountains are corroded with isotopes
        malign blunder pollutes the throats of children
        avaricious cowardice grinds it into
        the marrow of their bones

III

Dolores, the children are weeping
   the mothers are weeping
Your sisters are sobbing, Dolores, at the sight of
   garlands of their lover's bowels
   and their brother's entrails

Weep, Dolores Herrera, with the weeping
   weep for the new ghosts
   weep for the land-mined jungles
   weep for the depth-charged sea
   weep for God's mercy and his crown

Dolores, you are not alone
   Did you know there are hands reaching out?
Dolores Herrera, there are infants wrenched
   from their mother's breasts, her tears bleeding
   down her mute cheeks
   there are the aged-decrepit cast out from
   their last uneasy haven, with their broken prayers
   wondering that all their journeys
   have ended like this
Dolores Herrera, you are not alone, and because
   you are not alone
   you are frightening the Establishment
   did you ever know that they
   were so very fearful?
Did you ever know before that they could be
   frightened as easily as that?

Weep, Dolores, with the starry-eyed
   poets of the spirit
   for those fallen by their own hands
   for those castrated and hanged
   those bludgeoned to their knees
Weep in quiet mercy
   but weep as well in anger
You will yet weep in joy. Joy because
   the clock has been turned round
   joy because the calendar has been renewed
   renewed with brighter dates
   renewed with commemorations of mercy
Weep joyous tears for those fighters fighting worthy
   with weapons naked as their hands
   with words naked as their hearts
   fighting above the convulsed streets
   fighting the fog that blankets the fighting

IV

Oh snot-asses who have fucked her
        you have fucked her mind with maggots
        but her heart is clean
You have fucked her with forty-five linear feet
        of paper work, in quadruplicate
        on the IBM machine, with no-carbon-required

You fuckers
You have fucked her with a double handful
        of punched cards in three colors
        filed in every branch office where
        she might have gotten born but didn't
You fucked her with a green card
        that turned yellow when she waded ashore
        out of the scum-fucked river
You fucking murderers

She has seen the spume of your farts
        bloated with fat
She has seen your navels gorged
        with the milk of infants
She has seen your ass-holes sucking up
        the blood of her brothers
She has seen your altars covered with entrails
        your bank-vaults covered with entrails
        your court benches covered with entrails
She has seen this tripe torn from
        the bowels of her brothers
        ground to an essence of unction
        to grease your machinery of war
        your machinery of industry
        and of law and order
        to make its wheels seem to glisten
        to make its pistons appear to maintain
        a show of motion and power

But they are frightened of you, Dolores Herrera
        they are hurrying in secret meetings
        to make new rules to keep you silent
        did you ever know before that a voice
        could be quieted so easily?
        did you ever know before that hands could be
        shackled as easily as that?
They would like to put you out of the way
        forever

Dolores Herrera
      they want to tape your lips tight
Dolores Herrera
      they want to shackle your hands
Dolores Herrera
      they want to be shed of you for good
      the Attorney General wishes he had never never
      heard your name
      they wish you had never been born

Why don't you drop dead, Dolores Herrera?
How can the Department of Slights and Oversights
      meet its budget with you
      there on top of everything else?
How can they complete their paper work
      and get it out on time?
How can the politicos keep going with the likes of you
      fooling around here and getting in their way?
But don't think you are alone, Dolores Herrera
      you are not *you alone*
      you are the red, the brown, the black, all
      rolled into one
You are the puking brat and the crippled crone
      in one neat package
      yet you are you, Dolores Herrera
      dark eyed and soft voiced
      intense
      liked banked fire
The personality of the decade
      not because you are a woman
      nor because you are an ethnic
      but because you know that change is
      a special calendar, because you know
      that change is the only clock of this eon

V

Dolores Herrera, they are frightened of you
      they are afraid of what you know
      they are afraid of what you dream
      they wish you had never been born
      they want to get you out of sight
      to shut you up for good
They are falling over themselves in their frenzy
      their fear brings a nausea rising in their throats
      their fear is making their teeth chatter in the dark

They are afraid of you, Dolores Herrera, because
        they know they have wronged you
They are afraid of you, Dolores Herrera, because
        you are not you alone

They are as if tossed in a gathering gale
         will the East wind let them last?
         will the torrent whip over them?
         will their vomit choke their lungs?
They are afraid of you, because of
        your child's spirit, because of
        your fierce intensity
        like banked fire
They are afraid of you, Dolores Herrera, because
        you are many, because
          there are many hands reaching out
          to join your hands
They are afraid
        and their nausea rises in their throats
They are afraid, Dolores Herrera, because
        they know the time has come
        it is now

Gallup, New Mexico, July, 1973

HERBERT MARCUSE

MARXISM & FEMINISM

(Lecture delivered by Herbert Marcuse on March 7, 1974 under the auspices of the Center for Research on Women at Stanford University.)

This text was written and re-written after intensive, rigorous and often heated discussions with women. In these discussions I gained insight into largely neglected problems of socialism and into the radical potential of the Women's Movement as a subversive force. With grateful appreciation, this text is dedicated to:

Catherine Asmann
Carol Becker
Anne-Marie Feenberg

Ruth George
Antonia Kaus
Susan Orlofsky

I shall take the liberty of beginning and ending with some rather personal remarks. For the beginning I just want to say that this is the only invitation to lecture which I have accepted during the entire academic year. The reason is a very simple one. I believe the Women's Liberation Movement today is perhaps the most important and potentially the most radical political movement that we have, even if the consciousness of this fact has not yet penetrated the Movement as a whole.

Now, two preliminary remarks on the situation of the Women's Liberation Movement as I see it. The Movement originates and operates within patriarchal civilization; it follows that it must be initially discussed in terms of the actual status of women in the male dominated civilization.

Secondly, the Movement operates within a class society—here is the first problem: women are not a class in the Marxian sense. The male-female relationship cuts across class lines but the immediate needs and potentialities of women are definitely class-conditioned to a high degree. Nevertheless there are good reasons why "woman" should be discussed as a general category versus "man." Namely the long historical process in which the social, mental and even physiological characteristics of women developed as different from and contrasting with those of men.

Here, a word on the question whether the "feminine" or "female" characteristics are socially conditioned or in any sense "natural," biological. My answer is: over and above the obviously physiological differences between male and female, the feminine characteristics are socially conditioned. However, the long process of thousands of years of social conditioning means that they may become "second nature" which is not changed automatically by the establishment of new social institutions. There can be discrimination against women even under socialism.

In patriarchal civilization, women have been subjected to a specific kind of repression, and their mental and physical development has been channeled in a specific direction. On these grounds a separate Women's Liberation Movement is not only justified, but it is necessary. But the very goals of this Movement require changes of such enormity in the material as well as intellectual culture, that they can be attained only by a change in the entire social system. By virtue of its own dynamic, the Movement is linked with the political struggle for revolution, freedom for men *and* women. Because beneath and beyond the male-female dichotomy is the human being, common to male and female: the human being whose liberation, whose realization is still at stake.

The Movement operates on two levels: first, the struggle for full economic, social and cultural equality. Question: is such economic, social and cultural equality attainable within the capitalist framework? I will come back to this question, but I want to submit a preliminary hypothesis: there are no economic reasons why such equality should not be attainable within the capitalist framework, although a largely modified capitalism. But the potentialities, the goals of the Women's Liberation Movement, go far beyond it, namely into regions which never can be attained within a capitalist framework, nor within the framework of any class society. Their realization would call for a second stage, where the Movement would transcend the framework within which it now operates. At this stage "beyond equality," liberation implies the construction of a society governed by a different Reality Principle, a society where the established dichotomy between masculine and feminine is overcome in the social and individual relationships between human beings.

Thus, in the Movement itself is contained the image, not only of new social institutions, but also of a change in consciousness, of a change in the instinctual needs of men and women, freed from the requirements of domination and exploitation. And this is the Movement's most radical, subversive potential. It means not only a commitment to socialism (full equality of women has always been a basic socialist demand), but commitment to a specific form of socialism which has been called "feminist socialism." I will return to this concept later.

What is at stake in this transcendence is the negation of the exploiting and repressive values of patriarchal civilization. What is at stake is the negation of the values enforced and reproduced in society by male domination. And such radical subversion of values can never be the mere by-product of new social institutions. It must have its roots in the men and women who build the new institutions.

What is the meaning of this subversion of values in the transition to socialism? And secondly, is this transition, in any sense, the liberation and ascent of *specifically feminine* characteristics on a social scale?

To start with the first question, here are the governing values in capitalist society: profitable productivity, assertiveness, efficiency, competitiveness; in other words, the Performance Principle, the rule of functional rationality discriminating against emotions, a dual morality, the "work ethic," which means for the vast majority of the population condemnation to alienated and inhuman labor, and the will to power, the display of strength, virility.

Now, according to Freud, this value hierarchy is expressive of a mental structure in which primary aggressive energy tends to reduce and to weaken the life instincts, that is, erotic energy. According to Freud, the destructive tendency in society will gain momentum as civilization necessitates intensified repression in order to maintain domination in the face of the ever more realistic possibilities of liberation, and intensified repression in turn leads to the activation of surplus aggressiveness, and its channeling into socially useful aggression. This total mobilization of aggressiveness is only too familiar to us today: militarization, brutalization of the forces of law and order, fusion of sexuality and violence, direct attack on the life instincts in their drive to save the environment, attack on the legislation against pollution and so on.

These tendencies are rooted in the infrastructure of advanced capitalism itself. The aggravating economic crisis, the limits of imperialism, the reproduction of the established society through waste and destruction, make themselves increasingly felt and necessitate more intensified and extended controls in order to keep the population in line, controls and manipulation which go down into the depth of the mental structure, into the realm of the instincts themselves. Now, to the degree to which the totalization of aggressiveness and repression today permeates the entire society, the image of socialism is modified at an essential point. Socialism, as a *qualitatively* different society, must embody the *antithesis*, the definite negation of the aggressive and repressive needs and values of capitalism as a form of male-dominated culture.

The objective conditions for such an antithesis and subversion of values are maturing, and they make possible the ascent, at least as a transitory phase in the reconstruction of society, of characteristics which, in the long history of patriarchal civilization, have been attributed to the female rather than the male. Formulated as the antithesis of the dominating masculine qualities, such feminine qualities would be receptivity, sensitivity, non-violence, tenderness and so on. These characteristics appear indeed as opposite of domination and exploitation. On the primary psychological level, they would pertain to the domain of Eros, they would express the energy of the life instincts, against the death instinct and destructive energy. And the question here arises: why do these life-protecting characteristics appear as specifically *feminine* characteristics? Why did the very same characteristics not also shape the dominant masculine qualities? This process has a history of thousands of years, during which the defence of the established society and of its hierarchy originally depended on physical strength, and thereby reduced the role of the female who was periodically disabled by bearing and then caring for children. Male domination, once established on these grounds, spread from the originally military sphere to other social and political institutions. The woman came to be regarded as inferior, as weaker, mainly as support for, or as adjunct to man, as sexual object, as tool of reproduction. And only as worker had she a form of equality, a repressive equality, with man. Her body and her mind were reified, became objects. And just as her intellectual development was blocked, so was her erotic development. Sexuality was objectified as a means to an end, procreation or prostitution.

A first countertrend became effective at the very beginning of the modern period, in the 12th and 13th centuries, and, highly significantly, in direct context with the great and radical heretic movements with the Cathars and the Albigensians. In these centuries, the autonomy of love, the autonomy of the woman was proclaimed, contrasting and counteracting male aggressiveness and brutality. Romantic Love: I am perfectly well aware of the fact that the term has become entirely pejorative, especially within the Movement. Still, I take it a little more seriously, and I take it in the historical context in which these developments should be taken. This was the first great subversion of the established hierarchy of values: the first great protest against the feudal hierarchy and the loyalties established in the feudal hierarchy, with its specifically pernicious repression of the woman.

To be sure, this protest, this antithesis was largely ideological, and confined to the nobility. However, it was not entirely ideological. The prevailing social norms were subverted in the famous Courts of Love, established by Elinor d'Aquitaine, where the judgment was practically always in favor of the lovers and against the husband, the right of love superseding the right of the feudal lord. And it was a woman who reportedly defended the last stronghold of the Albigensians against the murderous armies of the northern barons.

These progressive movements were cruelly suppressed. The weak beginnings of feminism, anyway on a weak class basis, were destroyed. But nevertheless, the role of the woman gradually changed in the development of industrial society. Under the impact of technical progress, social reproduction depends increasingly less on physical strength and prowess, either in war or in the material process of production, or in commerce. The result was the enlarged exploitation of women as instruments of labor. The weakening of the social basis of male dominance did not do away with the perpetuation of male dominance by the new ruling class. The increasing participation of women in the industrial work process, which undermined the material grounds of the male hierarchy, also enlarged the human base of exploitation and the surplus exploitation of the woman as housewife, mother, servant, in addition to her work in the process of production.

However, advanced capitalism gradually created the material conditions for translating the ideology of feminine characteristics into reality, the objective conditions for turning the weakness that was attached to them into strength, turning the sexual object into a subject, and making feminism a political force in the struggle against capitalism, against the Performance Principle. It is with the view of these prospects that Angela Davis speaks of the revolutionary function of the female as antithesis to the Performance Principle, in a paper written in the Palo Alto Jail, "Women and Capitalism," December, 1971.

The emerging conditions of such a development are mainly:
—the alleviation of heavy physical labor,
—the reduction of labor time,
—the production of pleasant and cheap clothing,
—the liberalization of sexual morality,
—birth control,
—general education . . .

These factors indicate the social basis for the antithesis to the Performance Principle, the emancipation of female and feminine energy, physical
and intellectual, in the established society. But at the same time, this
emancipation is arrested, manipulated, and exploited by this society. For
capitalism cannot possibly allow the ascent of the libidinal qualities which
would endanger the repressive work ethic of the Performance Principle and
the constant reproduction of this work ethic by human individuals themselves. Thus, at this stage, these liberating tendencies, in manipulated form,
are made part of the reproduction of the established system. They become
exchange values, selling the system, and sold by the system. The exchange
society comes to completion with the commercialization of sex: the female
body not only a commodity, but also a vital factor in the realization of
surplus value. And the working woman continues, in ever larger numbers, to
suffer the double exploitation as worker and housewife. In this form, the
reification of the woman persists in a particularly effective manner. How can
this reification be dissolved? How can the emancipation of the woman
become a decisive force in the construction of socialism as a qualitatively
different society?

Let's go back to the first stage in the development of this Movement, and
assume the achievement of complete equality. As equals in the economy and
politics of capitalism, women must share with men the competitive, aggressive characteristics required to keep a job and to get ahead in the job. Thus,
the Performance Principle, and the alienation implied in it would be sustained and reproduced by a larger number of individuals. In order to achieve
equality, which is the absolute prerequisite of liberation, the Movement must
be aggressive. But equality is not yet freedom. Only as equal economic and
political subject can the woman claim a leading role in the radical reconstruction of society. But beyond equality, liberation subverts the established
hierarchy of needs—a subversion of values and norms which would make for
the emergence of a society governed by a new Reality Principle. And this, in
my view, is the radical potential of *feminist socialism.*

Feminist socialism: I spoke of a necessary modification of the notion of
socialism, because I believe that in Marxian socialism there are remnants,
elements of the continuation of the Performance Principle and its values. I
see these elements, for example, in the emphasis on the ever more effective
development of the productive forces, the ever more productive exploitation
of nature, the separation of the "realm of freedom" from the work world.

The potentialities of socialism today transcend this image. Socialism, as a
qualitatively different way of life, would not only use the productive forces
for the reduction of alienated labor and labor time, but also for making life
an end in itself, for the development of the senses and the intellect for
pacification of aggressiveness, the enjoyment of being, for the emancipation
of the senses and of the intellect from the rationality of domination: creative
receptivity versus repressive productivity.

In this context, the liberation of the woman would indeed appear "as the
antithesis to the Performance Principle," would indeed appear as the revolutionary function of the female in the reconstruction of society. Far from
fostering submissiveness and weakness, in this reconstruction, the feminine

characteristics would activate aggressive energy against domination and exploitation. They would operate as needs and eventual goals in the socialist organization of production, in the social division of labor, in the setting of priorities once scarcity has been conquered. And thus, entering the reconstruction of society as a whole, the feminine characteristics would cease to be specifically feminine, to the degree to which they would be universalized in socialist culture, material and intellectual. Primary aggressiveness would persist, as it would in any form of society, but it may well lose the specifically masculine quality of domination and exploitation. Technical progress, the chief vehicle of productive aggressiveness, would be freed from its capitalist features and channelled into the destruction of the ugly destructiveness of capitalism.

I think there are good reasons for calling this image of socialist society feminist socialism: the woman would have achieved full economic, political, and cultural equality in the all-round development of her faculties, and over and above this equality, social as well as personal relationships would be permeated with the receptive sensitivity which, under male domination, was largely concentrated in the woman: the masculine-feminine antithesis would then have been transformed into a synthesis—the legendary idea of *androgynism.*

I will say a few words about this extreme of (if you wish) Romantic or speculative thought, which I think is neither so extreme nor so speculative.

No other rational meaning can possibly be attributed to the idea of androgynism than the fusion, in the individual, of the mental and somatic characteristics, which in patriarchal civilization were unequally developed in men and women, a fusion in which feminine characteristics, in cancellation of male dominance, would prevail over their repression. But, no degree of androgynous fusion could ever abolish the natural differences between male and female as individuals. All joy, and all sorrow are rooted in these differences, in this relation to the other, of whom you want to become part, and whom you want to become part of yourself, and who never can and never will become such a part of yourself. Feminist socialism would thus continue to be riddled with conflicts arising from this condition, the ineradicable conflicts of needs and values, but the androgynous character of society might gradually diminish the violence and humiliation in the resolution of these conflicts.

To conclude:

The Woman's Movement has gained political significance because of recent changes in the capitalist mode of production itself which provided the movement with a material base. I recall the main features:

1) the increasing number of women employed in the production process,
2) the increasingly technical form of production, gradually diminishing the use of heavy physical labor power,
3) the spread of an *aesthetic* commodity form: systematic commercial appeal to sensuousness, luxuries; the diversion of purchasing power to pleasurable things and services.

4) the disintegration of the patriarchal family through "socialization" of the children from outside (mass media, peer groups, etc.)

5) the ever more wasteful and destructive productivity of the Performance Principle.

Feminism is a revolt against decaying capitalism, against the historical obsolescence of the capitalist mode of production. This is the precarious link between the utopia and reality: the social ground for the movement as a potentially radical and revolutionary force is there, this is the hard core of the dream. But capitalism is still capable of keeping it a dream, of suppressing the transcending forces which strive for the subversion of the inhuman values of our civilization.

The struggle is still a political one, for abolition of these conditions, and in this struggle, the feminist movement plays an ever more vital part. Its mental and physiological forces assert themselves in political education and action, and in the relationship between the individuals, at work and at leisure. I stressed that liberation cannot be expected as a by-product of new institutions, that it must emerge in the individuals themselves. The Liberation of women begins at home, before it can enter society at large.

And here is my concluding personal statement. You may if you wish interpret it as a statement of surrender, or a statement of commitment. I believe that we men have to pay for the sins of a patriarchal civilization and its tyranny of power: women must become free to determine their own life, not as wife, not as mother, not as mistress, not as girl friend, but as an individual human being. This will be a struggle permeated with bitter conflicts, torment and suffering (mental and physical). Only the most familiar example today, which occurs again and again, where a man and a woman have jobs or can get jobs at places distant from each other, and the question naturally arises: who follows whom?

An even more serious example, the conflicting erotic relationships, which inevitably will arise in the process of liberation. These erotic conflicts cannot be resolved in a facile, playful way, nor by being tough, nor by establishing exchange relationships. That you should leave to the exchange society where it belongs. Feminist socialism will have to develop its own morality, which will be more, and other, than the mere cancellation of bourgeois morality. Women's Liberation will be a painful process, but I believe it will be a necessary, a vital stage in the transition to a better society for men and women.

La Jolla, California
March, 1974

HERBERT MARCUSE ──────── MARXISM AND FEMINISM

Explanation of terms:

REALITY PRINCIPLE
   —the sum total of the norms and values which govern behavior in an
   established society, embodied in its institutions, relationships, etc.
PERFORMANCE PRINCIPLE
   —A Reality Principle based on efficiency and prowess in the fulfillment of competitive economic and acquisitive functions.
EROS, as distinguished from SEXUALITY
   —sexuality: a partial drive, libidinal energy confined and concentrated in
   the erotogenic zones of the body, mainly: genital sexuality.
   —Eros: libidinal energy, in the struggle with aggressive energy, striving
   for the intensification, gratification, and unification of life and of the life
   environment: the Life Instincts versus the Death Instinct (Freud).
REIFICATION, VERDINGLICHUNG
   —the appearance of human beings, and relationships between human
   beings, as objects, things, and as relationships between objects, things.

TOPOR

DIANE di PRIMA

from LOBA

"Her power is to open what is shut
Shut what is open"

Her power is to fall like razors
on the fine wind of yr spirit.
Still water
            in the current,
                        unmoving air
that the wind blows thru;
hers is the fire that clings, but does not
consume, dark fire that does not
light the night.

Torches in her labyrinth
                        throw shadows
on ice-cut walls. Flickering stalagtites
cut out of garnet.
                        Her bower
lurks in the unseen muddy places
of yr soul, she waits you under the steps
of yr tenement.

                        She gleams
in the wildwood where you have not dared
to walk. Wild yew & blackberries
tight, dried meat
of skinny winter deer, these
she holds out, like a key.
                        Her door
cannot be found, it is close-shut, it crumbles
it wafts in wind. Her power is to raise
the pale green grass of spring, the pale wildflower
carpets which fly starward like primroses w/dogs
asleep on them. Her power is in spittle
& in the lentil,
                        it rises like smoke
from the reopened furrow. She terraces the hills
w/her glance, her white breast gleams
in mossy caves you remember where the smoke
curled on the greenwood fires

she is the wind you never leave behind
black cat you killed in empty lot, she is
smell of the summer weeds, the one who lurks
in open childhood closets, she coughs
in the next room, hoots, nests in your hair
she is incubus
                        face at the window
                                        she is
harpy on your fire-escape, marble figurine
carved in the mantelpiece.
                                She is cornucopia
that wails in the night, deathgrip
you cannot cut away, black limpid eyes
of mad girl singing carols behind mesh, she is
the hiss in your goodbyes.
Black grain in green jade, sound
from the silent koto, she is
tapestry burned
                        in your brain, the fiery cloak
of feathers carries you
                                off hills
when you run flaming
                        down
                                        to the black sea

she is the scrub oak, juniper
on the mesa, she is joshua tree
in your desert, she grows
in cracks in the pavement
she tastes of sage, tastes bitter
as chapparal

she is born in tangled woodlands of kelp
she walks those slippery hills beneath
the waves; she rises again & again
from coral cities
floats glistening to shore on
turquoise seas

She lay
on the straw mat
in the warm room
thinking about love, all the
afternoon, at least
.remembering, not thinking
at all. There was no wind.
child voices in the street.
Sleep on her eyes, she lay
slightly absurd, headband askew
daydreaming, a silly smile
on her lips, her legs
akimbo.

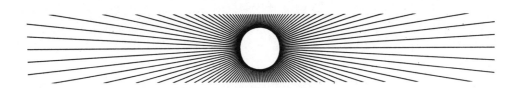

GAIL CHIARRELLO

I CARRIED WITH ME POEMS...

I carried with me poems, poems which spewed out of everything;
  I saw poems hanging from the clotheslines, hanging from the
    streetlamps:
  I saw poems glowing in the bushes, pushing out of the earth
    as tulips do;
I felt poems breathe in the dark March night like ghosts which
  squared and wheeled through the air;
I felt poems brushing the tops of chimneys, brushing by in the
  dark; I felt poems being born in the city, Venuses breaking
  through a shattered sea of mirrors;
  I felt all the poets of the city straining,
    isolated poets, knowing none of the others, straining;
I felt that some gazed into the March night, looking, and finding;
and others were running down the steep streets, seeking, and
  seeking to embrace;
and others stood in empty bookstores turning over pages of fellow
  poets whom they loved but didn't know;
and some pondered over coffee growing cold, in harshly lit cafe-
  terias,
    and gazed at the reflections of the eaters in the wall-to-wall
    mirrors;
some dwelt on what it was to grow old;
some dwelled on love;
some had gone out of time;
some, going out of time, looked back into time, and started;

I felt all of these lives and existences, all with poems at
  their center;
I knew none of these poets;
but I felt these intimations augured well, for me, and for poetry;
and my steps grew big, giant steps, I bounded down Parker Street,
a tall, taciturn, fast-walking poets' accomplice.

I SHALL GO CRAZY WITH DELIGHT

I shall go crazy with delight;
with the long, liquid silences
of vessels, rocked all night
on the mortal bosom of the Milky Way:

can I use English language to describe
all that is beautiful in a man's visage:
dark side of the moon; crow's wing; brooding;

a relentless, ten-stringed instrument;
sorrow's storm, covering me;
forgotten like some Latin manuscript
when the whole Zodiac wheels forth
erupting
in volcanic longing—

November storm brewing;
all the waters of the world
coldly boiling
poured forth by the ruthless power of Scorpio:

Blow, winter rains,
for you are much less unkind
than someone who is always on my mind
with his curling lip, and his one
raised eyebrow.

—November 5, 1973

LAST DAY OF THE OLD YEAR 1973 POEM

For Julie, "because there are so many of us."

It's raining on the long grass across Parker Street,
and the rain comes drizzling down on Oakland,
on the flat Bay near Solomon Grundy's;
the rain; the rain; on the Warren Expressway;
raining on Jewel Lake; raining on Anza;
and it rains on the bright girls, with their curly hair
   and bandannas;
and it rains on the smart girls from Cornell, or Barnard;
and it's raining on all those kind girls, those very
   eager, intense girls,
with their PH.D.'s and their Phi Beta Kappas;
their Army fatigue jackets, and their interest in Israel;
all those young, and somewhat older, girls
with their enduring interest in capuchino, and Freud;
and it's raining on the girls in green sweaters
who study karate; have one child; on Welfare;
who sing Lotte Lenya and Piaf
in an old Buick at midnight with four friends;
and it's raining on those fresh-looking, warm girls
   who read Baudelaire,
   and take the initiative;
and it's raining in New York, and raining in Paris,
and they keep on laughing, and reading, and hugging,
and they keep on cooking, and dancing, and crying,
and it's raining in Oakland, and it's raining in Berkeley,
and these girls are plunging into the future
   on the crest of a wave.
and it's raining in London,
and the wave is carrying them forward,
and there's no one behind them
but the green grass on Parker Street,
and no one before them but the rain out of heaven,
and even now, no one, and nothing, but their wonderful rain-dance
   of courage and caring,
all these bright girls of Oakland, and
these bright girls of Berkeley.

—December 31, 1973

BARBARA GUEST

SOUR ORANGES

Chinese girl chorus singing Ave Maria
with Gilbert and Sullivan graciousness
do you suppose the West will succeed in its Christianization
of the East — Ho Ho

   —like the pollination of oranges for sweetness

But these are sour oranges although they ripened
in the backyard of sunny California

   —they are sour oranges not bitter Corfu lemons

Although Lawrence Durrell is lecturing three blocks away
in Southern California and that represents a kind of pollination

   —these are sour oranges

Although I have been given attar of roses from Bulgaria
in a wooden vial (to be used when empty for further purposes)
and this can be considered a form of pollination

   —these are uncolonized oranges
    and they are sour

Although Mrs Jones English Chutney is on my shelf
here in New York City and this might be thought to be
a purchase of colonization

   —these are sour oranges

Although I possess French, German, Greek, Jugoslav
poetry anthologies
and for many poets these are good pollinizers

   —these oranges are sour

Because I refuse to put ash at their roots
or spray their leaves with toxic agents
or pick them while they are green
to glow artificially in the market

These oranges are growing more and more into Alexander Pope
oranges dwarfed and bitter
yet capable of seductive landscape plans
where the problems are not of pollination
but symmetry and the irony of an unnatural order

Suddenly there spreads a career for these sour oranges
on the map a new garden for the inedible
a prince searches for them among Prokofieff trellises
and a few assassinations take place
of those who have reported these quiet oranges
to have sullen personalities

Several republics have sewn
this orange emblem onto their flag as ministries fall
a sour orange season is contemplated
by agronomists to prevent
inflation amid the orange enthusiasts

Like the delicate cranes that demolish our passages
or the cats who prowl our terraces, the carrion birds
who destroy our deaths

      —the sour infertile oranges

are prepared in the underground by a fellowship of voyagers
for whom day and night are indiscriminate
and the eunuch who dwells in each of them
shall rule his kingdom as the Sultan of Turkey
was out manoeuvered by his castrates and crippled wives

BOBBIE LOUISE HAWKINS

MOUTH TASTES

Mouth tastes a bitter taste
face grows dark
It is the other bitter side
The exile we live our lives in

How can we bear it

All of us
who know more than we know
and move in that correctness
beyond ourselves

Walking
the ground passed
falls away
Footprints
fade in rhythms
we have no eye to watch

There was never a way
back
never ever
a way back
every time
all along
no way back

The ways have faded all away
and we're left
here in this far region

Distant strangers
among
the most ordinary
turns of mind

And where the shape of loss is clear
there is a seepage there
of fear that fills the shape

As on the beach footprints fill
with water

at our backs the
history
a lengthening
graph of small lakes
shaped
each one
like a foot
to fit a foot
and fades

Courage grows so weary
How can we bear it

The sky's above
The eyes below
The endless view
in mind

Distance and going
our familiar place
We name this journey
"Home"

We keep ourselves
in mind
and moving

THERE WHERE...

There where the word grows dark

persevering
despite
bright knowledge

The flower unfolding
holding
its center
intact
but turns it all turns
toward day's light
that in the night was
no bloom at all
a pale ghost
latent and pale

There is no day and no night
for the word
all its bright knowledge
held latent
a pale shimmer
all its leaves are open
all the time

Only at its very center
as if an eye blinked once
there is the shock
of strange life
strange distance
there where the word goes dark

KATHLEEN TEAGUE

THE GREATEST SHOW

The mouth awakes
inside the ring

the red bulbs bloom
a rim of steamy hair

The Etruscan faces
a Vesuvian light

yields,

bringing down a veil
the black-gartered eyes

wanting.

A Nubian sings
in the garden at night

a ship on the Nile

between the banks
the high priestess

her grand thighs
of calcified sand

The boat heaves;
the throat gives way,
aye . . .

A small body floats
between the lips, slips

outside, into light

O flowers!

The mouth, a nest,
goes back to sleep

sewn back
    inside
the dream.

LINDA KING

TOO SOON LIGHT

for T. R.

he finally
asked me to dance
and the tingling
started like it
always did
me against him
feeling, knowing
his eyes firing me
like a winter furnace

in his old green chevy
on the dump road
we kissed like animals
hungry for food
long kisses
trying to fill
the desire

too young and afraid
to make love
morning light
scared us home
separating our
dizzy, dangerous ache
suspending it
untouched still

WHEN LOVE FALLS DOWN

when love falls down
on you in the night
and you feel it on you
in you, around you
through you
it breathes down on you
hot and heavy and thick
and you know it is love
you know it's love
know it's love
there is no doubt
and there can never
again be any doubt
that is not a lie
love lays in on you
and is part of you
like finger or skin
and it feels good
it feels so good

when love is on
you like that
you want everybody
to have it
some way
some how
some time
everything and everybody
feeling love and loving
feeling like you do
in your throat and your arms
your breath and blood
simmering love
he loves me
he loves me
I love him

TAXI DANCER

7:15
turn on the tub water
plug in the ten minute hot rollers
bathe, towel, lotion, roll hair
make up, blush, mascara
erase dark shadows under the eyes
blue shadow over the eyes
into panti-hose
a short dress
with plenty of cleavage showing
platform shoes
out with the rollers
tease, tangle, spray
key, money, certs
a thrift store fur
and twelve minutes to Danceland
in the door by 8:00
where the men
pay fifteen cents a minute
to dance with the lovely lady of their choice
a chiropractor, a factory worker, a machinist
a five foot white-haired gentleman
who is not a gentleman
a Japanese business man separated from a cold wife
salesmen, a truck driver
a nut with a pass from the mental hospital
a priest
a prophet
blacks looking for a stable addition
blacks beautiful, dressed, dancing professionals
the ugly
the fat
the lonely
the lustful, the alone
the one in love with a beautiful Korean girl
horny and broke Mexican boys
who dance only when they call 'ten free minutes'
watching the clock closely
all for $9.00 an hour
breast, legs, lips and looks
the illusion of love
hung up on a dance floor
the music plays fast
the bodies dance slow

twisting, grinding
with only an occasional waster
spinning apart way from his blond
they like the blonds
the shortest skirts
the braless
the brazen
the beautiful
and especially those who will meet after hours
watched and overseen by Albert
with a face stamped
with lust and greed
greed, adding up extra minutes
shorting on tickets
lust, pinching bottoms
asking each new girl to his bed
the girls try the job
half-believing the ad saying $200.00+ a week
getting fingerprinted for permits
settling for $72.00 or $80.00
maybe a hundred with good nights
bought by the minute
realizing quick tips
come with extra service
on the dance floor
dancing, fighting hands
smiling and warm
hardly whores
hardly ladies
but curious
and like myself 3/4 unemployable
with only a marriage
as a work record
not quite a poetess
not quite a sculptress
not quite a playwright or novelist
not quite an actress
not desperate enough for marriage
not rich enough to lounge
not immoral enough to sell
work it is
over stimulating, underpaid
and the *Times* has a large
'want ad' section
the one for dance hostesses
runs daily

JACK MICHELINE

PINK, RED AND BLUE

Malugee was born in back of a grove on the shady side of Memphis. He was born screaming in the dark night. The night he was born the stars raced across the Zodiac. The big dipper and Orion did a dance in the higher heavens and the moon was full and the frogs slid slowly into the swamps and the whippoorwills and the crickets sang their songs in the night air. On his second day Malugee laughed as the sun broke through the morning dawn. His eyes were clear and bright and blue like the streams of mountains and the music of the Creole washwomen filtered through his skin and through his heart and up to his straight red hair. The bells tolled in the churches and old darks sang the blues and drank from old rickety porches. His mother sold her body for quarters and half dollars and sometimes she would get two dollars for a quick trick, putting the money in an old silk stocking underneath her mattress. When the workers from the saw mill got paid each week. Malugee's father had died in prison from a dose of highly developed syphilis which he had gotten very young in the back streets of New Orleans. Malugee heard music all the time, even when he shined shoes outside the churches in the streets on Sunday, hearing the clear music of the violin, and the clear streams of water surrounding the brow of his flowing red hair. Malugee had smooth silky skin. Malugee heard music of the bluejays and the swamps. Pink fucked guys with one arm and one leg, gave love to the blind eye and one lip. Pink sucked guys with small cock and big cock and enormous cock. Malugee's mother, Pink, with her orange ass giggling and laughing in the moonlight, even the poor Chinaman Louis with one ball came to the grey shack with the red light. The Lumberjacks came and the bushboys came and the skinny long haired hippies came. Pink had big round tits, her left tit scarred from the sadists of her youth. It wasn't the money she got paid that made her spread her legs east of Memphis. South of Tucumcari, North of Tallahassee, West of Fresno and Eugene and Mendocino. Pink took cock to her cunt, took mouth and teeth to her nipple, took change and greenbacks with Washington and Lincoln's face on it. Tookem all that came with their pain, every sore ass loser with a droopy eye. Every braggart who never had a sister. Every son of a priest who thought sex was evil. A moment to forget the pain was inside, that loneliness was a void like an empty canyon, that there were no heroes not even in the movie shows or the newspapers that were printed daily. Malugee's mother was a good piece of ass and they whispered in school Pink had a big pussy and anyone could fuck her for a dollar bill or for a half a dollar. Shame had no color or pain, no religion, and the ones that went to church had no monopoly on virtue. Malugee hated and was ashamed of his mother and could not feel sorrow for her, nor could he understand what was real and no one knew each other or had time to find out. Malugee tried not to hide his head from the deep sorrow that the truth was economic like rent or bananas or beer in the icebox. Malugee's head hung limp and he could not see the tops of trees, nor the sky, nor the shooting stars that crossed the horizon. At fourteen Malugee ran away from home. He did not know what he wanted to be and could not love his mother nor accept her, and he wanted to love and holler and scream and shout and dance all at the same time. But he was tied up in knots inside and it was hard to open up. He did not know what he wanted to be. He ran away and went to Biloxi, Shreveport, New Orleans, Houston, El Paso, Santa Fe, working as a drifter, a busboy, a dishwasher, a geek at a carnival. Two weeks at a car wash, three weeks as a waiter at an Italian restaurant. He was not black or white or green or blue. Malugee was the Albino with creamy skin and straight red hair who drank wine and slept in the parks or under the trees in the high grass. Malugee sought out his fantasies in movies and skid row bars, in public libraries he sought books in which he could identify his life, to find someone else who had already lived similar experiences. Each individual person had a want in them that was strong, a desire to love and touch someone without fear or hate or reprisal or retaliation.

He could not ask his mother Pink to love him. He could go to church and cry that the world was rotten. For the sky was not there. Nor were the trees there and some shaggy dog was not there, and the open road of the heart was not there. He walked in the concrete of cities with an alcoholic woman with a pimply face and a large stomach and a big ass wanting to share his flop and touch his wild red hair and put his cock in between her legs to forget the loneliness of the road that was in all of us. Malugee raced past the multitudes of the concrete cities, his head bowed, people pushing and shoving to work and weeping and crying and dying and laughing and boozing and shouting and worrying the mass of pain and compromise called man. The thighs of young girls gleaming through the eye of sunlight.

Malugee began to take pills, red birds and blue birds and dexies and bennies and speed. Malugee wildly racing through the streets and into the counties east of San Francisco Bay.

One morning Malugee stole some blond's horse in Forest Knolls and galloped across the highway into the woods heading North to the sea at Bolinas. Fourteen miles and two hundred yards high above the cowfields and the pine trees and the creeks and the shallow eyes of the lost. Half out of his mind, his eyes blazing from the pills and the heat of the sun. He galloped on, his mind racing half across a nation. Full of automobiles and highways and supermarkets and drug stores, past the fearful who lost courage, past the hospitals where the wounded and the sick lay, past the fir trees and the lonely sassafras. Past his mother's eyes across the Memphis swamp. Past the race track of dreamers at Santa Anita and Yonkers, Laurel and Aqueduct, Saratoga, Green Mountain, Belmont and Hollywood Park. Past the gambling midnight of dreamers in the prisons of the unlucky and damned and the lost queens laughing in the cell blocks. Malugee urged the horse on out into the sea, into the choppy water and infinite void and the death that comes when life diminishes into stone and dry beds of creeks and the lost memories of what was. For there was no one and nobody to hit back. No one to scream to but the empty wilderness what man is and what was and what will be. Malugee's body floated out to the sea. The white horse dead to the gnatting flies unto the shore of sand and wind and sea and earth and rain.

Pink's ass rose in the wind. Arnie the lumberjack was coming. Four weeks in the redwoods without a woman. Pink grabbed his long, thick, skinny dick and sucked Arnie off. The night rose from the sky. Malugee was dead. Arnie pulled up his pants and went to the bar to drink and laugh. It was a good night he released some of his pent up passion. Pink took on three more, the dogs barked in the woods. Pink combed her long red hair. Soon the night would be over and dawn would come and she would get some sleep. A star crossed the heavens. The creek was silent. The moss waited for the frost. Pink took a swallow of rock and rye. The night soon would be over, soon the dawn would come, like the new day. Like the buds of new flowers and the trees on the hillsides. Pink scratched her ass. It was a busy night. She finished with her last customer and she yawned putting her night's earnings from her silk stocking into a tin box inside an opening in the fireplace. Pink fell exhausted on her bed. Her son was no longer on the earth. His pink body floated in the blue waters of the ocean. The dawn slowly lit the early morning sky. The birds sang.

JERRY KAMSTRA

THE FRISCO KID

From Chapter 20

Walter is trying to con d'Artagnan Pig into driving us to Big Sur for the weekend. "I want to ride in the Caja Flash," Walter says. "We'll have a ball! I want to soak my body in those tubs all weekend."

"It'd be good to get away from the Beach for awhile," I say.

"C'mon, d'Artagnan, crank up the Caja Flash, I'll buy the gas."

"Perhaps a medicinal soak in a rural spa would be beneficial," d'Artagnan Pig says, huffing up his belt.

Two hours later we're tooling down Highway 1 in the Caja Flash. We're all sitting in the front seat, d'Artagnan Pig behind the wheel, me in the middle, Walter next to the window. The back seat is full of wine bottles and bennies and a little weed to keep us going when our bones get weary. The Caja Flash speeds through Westlake and Pacifica and drops like a light down Devil's Slide, flashing toward Half Moon Bay. I feel happy, really crazy all of a sudden, the soft Central Coast rhythm quickening my blood. "Whaaa-hooo!" Walter cries, cracking the cap on a jug and handing it to me.

I feel insane. The joy of Big Sur lies ahead of us, a magic juxtaposition of mountains and sea that sets up an energy cycle no one can explain. The Caja Flash's engine hums and brussel sprout plants ripple by while d'Artagnan Pig and Walter burp and laugh, point and stare and cry aloud at each knot of hitchhikers passed, slowing down for some, stopping, backing up for the girls, picking them up and cramming them onto laps and back seats, stopping further down the road for more, a crazy hipster wagon making it down the coast along the fast rugged no nonsense craggy western edge of America; alive, alight, away and gone like a light toward Davenport, Santa Cruz, Aptos and Freedom, through little California coastal towns with no names, just wide spots in the road where strangers stop their cars and get out to stare into the gloom, holding onto hats as the Caja Flash's windstream rushes by.

Walter and I share the jug while d'Artagnan drives. I look out the window. I always get the same feeling on the road, how many times now, always and forever the journey down the road becoming like a dream, a strange feeling sweeping over me, the way the road turns and dips along the sea's edge, the musky smell of the brussel sprout plants, the Japanese farmers who always make such a success of their farms, at the dunegrass blowing across the bluffs above the sea, the plowed fields, manicured carefully as backyards, stretching away for miles and miles toward the sea . . . .

Walter yips and shakes the jug while d'Artagnan laughs and whips the Caja Flash around the bends. I fall deeper into my coastal dream, reverent and afraid at the same time, knowing this is both the way toward and the way away from where I want to go. Inside the car there is a warmth that soaks into my blood, yet outside there is a road and a roadedge that seems mine, like a heartstring tied through all the places I've ever been and will ever go . . . . perhaps I should explain:

I have never understood my feeling for America. Something in the roads, the way the land smells at night, an overwhelming sadness about my friends, these in this book and others, a genuine feeling of loss, a mysterious lessening as one grows old . . . all part, perhaps, of a realization that something in our heart is sick, something in our backbone not quite right, a loneliness all out of proportion to its pain, a devastation that seems somehow so overwhelming as to be inexplicable, a passionlessness that exudes the smell of prisons, emptiness and decay like a light over the land that showers the soil with dread . . . .

I love America and yet am so alone in it, so cut off from everything, so panicked by the strangeness, aloofness, costliness of its life. On the road all this assuaged. Perhaps it's the movement, maybe the stillness, but somehow the highway leads me to a fullness, a completeness that is unattainable on any streetcorner, in any room. It's the link between places that makes these places livable, that gives them content, that sends us down them with such hope, such expectancy, such emotional wish-fulfillment that we imagine on the long dark silent stretches of beribboned concrete that the next town will really be the America we were taught to believe in . . . .

from Chapter 13

JoJay rolled five joints in preparation for a visit to his cousin, Walk In Many Suns. Walk In Many Suns is a plumber who lives in YumYum Estates. He has invited Walter and JoJay and his brothers and me to participate in the Bonanza Ceremony.

"YumYum Estates," Walter said. "What's that?"

"I think it's some kind of pueblo," JoJay said. He licked joint number five and placed it in his medicine bag. "Walk In Many Suns said that lots of Indians live there. It's in Oakland."

"YumYum," Walter said. Maybe Walk In Many Suns knows something we don't know."

We drove across the Bay Bridge in Walter's jeep. JoJay lit a joint and passed it around, Jose, Joselito, Trinidad Archelito and I sat in the back of the jeep behind Walter and JoJay. Between tokes on the joint, JoJay blew on his holy hollow left wingbone of an eagle whistle. His brothers pounded on their goatskin drums while Walter rattled his turquoise jewelry and beat on the dashboard with one hand.

"I feel like I'm taking a journey into a giant gumdrop," Walter said.

"Don't feel bad," JoJay said. "Walk In Many Suns said the Bonanza Ceremony is worth the trip."

JoJay was dressed in full Indian regalia in honor of the Bonanza Ceremony. I had on an ancient buckskin jacket JoJay had given me the day before. I was standing in JoJay's teepee admiring the coat when he told me to try it on. I tried it on. The coat was handmade, sewn with beautiful beads and porcupine quill scrollwork, with fringes around the edges. On each breast were small blue and yellow feathers, woven in between the beads and porcupine quills. The coat was beautiful. "It's yours," JoJay said. "For a white man with an Indian's soul." I sat up in the back of the jeep in my new ancient buckskin jacket, proud to be a white man with an Indian's soul.

"This Bonanza Ceremony is a big thing," JoJay said. "Walk In Many Suns said it's the high point of the week. It's some kind of city Indian celebration."

"As long as Walk In Many Suns serves some of that wild rice and pickled moosenose soup you told me about," Walter said. "I'll celebrate anything for some of that."

"Don't worry," JoJay said. "Walk In Many Suns said the Bonanza Ceremony wouldn't be the Bonanza Ceremony without the wild rice and pickled moosenose soup."

We sailed across the Bay Bridge. JoJay's feathered headdress flapped and furled in the jeep's windstream. Passing drivers gawked and rapidly cleared a path for Walter's jeep. JoJay shrieked on his holy whistle and Walter sailed through the tollbooth.

"Uh . . . Walter . . . . I think you're supposed to stop and pay a quarter at the tollbooth," I said.

JoJay screeched louder on his whistle and Walter pounded his open hand on the dashboard in time with the music and drums. The jeep was really swinging. I looked behind us and saw the black and white patrol car coming with red light flashing.

I tapped JoJay on the shoulder and nodded towards the patrol car. "Maybe we better swallow those joints, JoJay," I said.

By the time the Highway Patrol caught up with us, all the joints were swallowed except half of one which was lodged somewhere near JoJay's esophagus. It's hard swallowing four marijuana cigarettes on the spur of the moment. It's something that can be done with a bit of reflection, but on the spur of the moment it's very difficult. To be democratic, each of us should have swallowed three-fourths of a marijuana cigarette but JoJay was holding so he swallowed three-and-a-half joints and was busy working on the last half of the fourth joint. The rest of us watched solemnly as JoJay's jaws worked overtime. The Highway Patrol stopped his car behind us and walked around to the driver's side of the jeep. It seemed to me that JoJay's jaws were working in slow motion, but that was because JoJay was choking on the dry marijuana and was slowly asphyxiating in front of our eyes. It tends to make you slightly paranoid seeing an Indian in full ceremonial regalia slowly asphyxiating in front of your eyes while a Highway Patrolman is walking up behind you. It's hard to describe the exact feeling. It's like reaching for the husk of a dead sparrow and picking up a fifteen pound bird.

The Highway Patrolman was very polite. He told Walter it was customary to stop at the bridge tollbooth and pay twenty-five cents.

"It's been the custom for a long time," he said. "People have been doing it for years."

While the Highway Patrolman was talking to Walter, JoJay was slowly turning blue. He was wheezing carefully somewhere down in his lower tract. It's disconcerting to see a redman turning blue right in front of your eyes.

"What's wrong with that purple Indian?" the Highway Patrolman said. "He took some Indian medicine to prepare for the Bonanza Ceremony and he's slowly asphyxiating," Walter said. "That's why I didn't stop at the tollbooth, we have to find some water."

"Why didn't you say so?" the Highway Patrolman said. "I'll get my thermos."

The Highway Patrolman ran back to his car and returned with a thermos of coffee. By this time JoJay was turning a colorful shade of mauve. JoJay took the thermos from the Highway Patrolman and drank some of the coffee. It might have been his last act. Instead, the coffee washed down the last half of the fourth joint and saved JoJay's Life.

"That's why I always respect the law," JoJay said later. "You never know when the law's going to wash down half a marijuana cigarette."

*

JoJay thanked the Highway Patrolman for saving his life and Walter backed up to the tollbooth and paid a quarter and then we continued on. YumYum Estates is in the hills of Oakland but it is not a pueblo. YumYum Estates is a housing tract surrounded by Boca Raton Estates, Dawn Vision Estates and Sherwood Forest Estates.

"I wish I'd brought my longbow," JoJay said, as we entered the development. "You never know who you're going to meet in Sherwood Forest."

Walter circled identical streets for half an hour before finding Walk In Many Sun's house. When we drove up in front of his house, Walk In Many Suns was standing in the driveway, wearing a pair of one-hundred-pocketed Can't Bust-'em bib overalls and no undershirt. He looked like a Cherokee plumber. He raised his hand in the traditional "hou" sign as Walter stopped the jeep.

"Hou, cousin!" JoJay answered.

As we were getting out of the jeep, Neck Like A Swan, Walk In Many Sun's wife, and her five children came out of the house. Neck Like A Swan was shaped like a soft ball-bearing. She was wearing a beaded buckskin dress and her five children hid behind her. There was not enough buckskin dress to hide five children, however, so some of them spilled out.

"These friends are not tradingpost whites," JoJay said. "They are not cowshit whitemen."

Walk In Many Suns made the hand-upraised sign. "Welcome to my house," he said.

Inside the house were many Indians. Walk In Many Suns introduced us and from each Indian we received the traditional handshake and sign. Jose and Joselito and Trinidad Archelito brought in their drums from the jeep and set them up in the powwow room. The powwow room was the den. Neck Like A Swan brought us beer and we sat down on the floor. The floor was covered with thick sheepskin rugs and colorful handwoven blankets. When I asked about them, Neck Line A Swan blushed and said yes, she wove them.

At the far end of the powwow room was a giant television set, sitting in the place of honor. Against the walls were hundreds of old bottles, bones, rusty locks and pieces of metal and artifacts Walk In Many Suns had dug up while working as a plumber. Walk In Many Suns was an amateur archeologist.

"I am glad you could come to our Bonanza Ceremony," Walk In Many Suns said. "It starts in half an hour."

"I never knew Indians had a Bonanza Ceremony," Walter said. "I have never heard of a Bonanza Ceremony in Taos."

"This is a private ceremony," Walk In Many Suns said. "I invented it myself. It's catching on fast though."

More Indians arrived. We were introduced and Jose and his brothers started tapping softly on their drums. The Indians squatted on the floor and drank beer and nodded as Jose and Trinidad warmed up. Neck Like A Swan brought in large bowls of mutton and rice and a huge kettle of pickled moosenose soup. Each of us ladled some of the soup into a cup and drank it. Plates were brought out by one of the daughters and we ate mutton and wild rice. The food was delicious.

"This is good food," an Indian named Face Longer Than A Stick said. "It is a long way from the mountains and this food reminds me of the mountains."

"It's good mountain food," JoJay said. "Hey, Walter, what you say?"

"Hoya hoya!" Walter cried. The Indians laughed.

After the men finished eating, Neck Like A Swan and her daughters cleaned away the dishes. Walk In Many Suns brought out his pipe. While he was filling the pipe, JoJay told what happened at the bridge. Everybody laughed. Walk In Many Suns lit the pipe and passed it around the room. Each Indian took one long toke and passed the pipe on. There were twenty Indians in the powwow room. When the pipe reached me, Walk In Many Suns reached over and turned the television set on.

"Now the Bonanza Ceremony," he said.

While the TV set flickered to life, Neck Like A Swan brought in cans of cold beer. The Indians opened their cans and gazed intently at the TV set. Jose and his brothers tapped softly on their drums and sucked from their cans. I leaned back against the wall and watched the screen. The whole room had a musky, Indian odor, an odor of sagebrush and outside. It was a good smell, reminding me of wide places and laughter. When the TV picture came into focus I peered intently at it. It was Bonanza, the western serial. Walter and I looked at one another. The Indians stared intently at the television screen. From the shadows of the powwow room I heard an eerie sound, a sound like brittle wind off the plains. I looked around and realized that it was JoJay blowing softly into his holy wingbone of an eagle whistle. Somehow the music was perfect, full and empty at the same time, like a lone bird circling high above flat tabletop vistas looking out upon the beauty and stillness of Black Mesa.

The pipe came around again and I toked from it. On the TV screen Hoss and the Cartwright Brothers rode hell for home and the Indians shouted in merriment. Beer cans emptied and others popped open and were drained in long foamswallowing gulps. Walk In Many Suns led the merriment as the Indians followed every incident on the screen with hoots and laughter. Every time Hoss or a white man came on the screen the Indians hissed and booed, throwing empty beer cans against the wall . . . .

CHARLES BUKOWSKI

FACTOTUM

an excerpt from a novel in progress

I was finally hired at another auto parts warehouse, again on Figueroa street down around 11th street. They sold retail out the front and also supplied other houses and shops from their warehouse. I had to particularly demean myself to get that one. I told them that I liked to think of the job as a second home. That seemed to please them.

I was the receiving clerk. I also walked about to 3 or 4 places in the neighborhood and picked up parts. This was the best part. I got to get out of the building and it always took some time to fill orders.

During my lunch period one day I noticed a rather intense and intelligent-looking Jewish boy looking at that day's entries.

"You play the horses?" I asked.

"Yeah," he said.

"Can I see your paper?"

He handed it over. I looked down the entries. Then I handed the paper back.

"My Boy Bobby ought to take the 8th."

"I know it. And they don't even have him on top."

"All the better."

"What do you think he'll pay?"

"Around 9 to 2."

"I wish I could bet a little on him."

"Me too."

We sat thinking a while. "When's the last race go off at Hollywood Park?" he asked me.

"5:30."

"We get out of here at 5:00."

"You'd never make it."

"I could try. My Boy Bobby's coming in."

"Luck."

"Want to come along?"

"Sure."

"Watch the clock. At 5 we'll cut, we'll run to my car."

We got through the afternoon. At 5 minutes to 5 we were both working around the rear exit. My Jewish friend, Manny, looked at his watch. "We'll steal two minutes from them. When I start running, follow me. Each second is precious."

"Right."

Manny stood there placing boxes of parts on a rear shelf. Suddenly he began running. I was right after him and we were out the rear door, the manager and the workers staring, and Manny cut right down the alley and I was after him. He was a good runner. I learned afterwards that he had been a miler in track and field in highschool. I was four feet behind him going down the alley. His car was parked at the end of the alley. He unlocked it and we were in and off.

"Manny, we'll never make it."

"We'll make it. I can tool this thing."

"Look, it's 90 blocks south and I don't know how many west. 25 maybe. We've got to go 115 blocks, park, get from the parking lot to the betting window."

"We'll make it. Only thing is we can't stop for any red lights."

Manny knew how to switch lanes and he had a fairly good car. "I've played every track in the country that exists and maybe a few that don't exist."

"Caliente?"

"Caliente too. Bastards take a 25 percent rake."

"I know."

"It's worse in Germany. In Germany the take is 50 percent."

"And they still get players?"

"They still get players. They figure all they got to do is get the winner."

"We're bucking 16, that's rough enough."

"Yeah, but a good player can beat it."

"Sure."

"Here's a red light. We can't stop."

"Whatya gonna do?"

"Take a right."

Suddenly we were in the right lane and Manny took a right. "Watch for squad cars. If you see one, tell me and I'll slow down."

"Right."

Manny was a driver. He never made a wrong move. Every move saved space and time. It was a fast motion chess game. Manny looked way ahead into developments. If Manny could bet horses like he drove, he was a winner.

"You married, Manny?"

"No way."

"Women?"

"Sometimes. But it can't last."

"Why?"

"All they want you to do is fuck 'em night and day."

"So get with one you want to fuck. That's what I do."

"Yeah but if you drink or gamble the big wail begins."

"Get one who likes to drink, gamble and fuck."

"Who wants a woman like that?"

"That's what they say about us."

Then we were into the parking lot. Parking was free on the last race and there was no admission to get in either. There was a rather minor problem of no program and no Racing Form and if there were any scratches you couldn't be sure just which horse on the tote board was your horse. You either had to find a program or ask somebody to make sure.

We parked and Manny jumped out and started running. He opened up 6 lengths on me through the parking lot but I wouldn't let him get any further ahead. We ran through the opened gate at the side and over the small length of space to the tunnel. Then we were down into the tunnel, running through the tunnel and Manny held his 6-length lead. Some stragglers from the race before were coming through the tunnel. They looked at us impassively. That tunnel at Hollywood Park is a long one. I closed down on Manny until I was only 5 lengths behind. As we ran into the park I could see that the horses were at the gate.

We sprinted toward the betting windows.

"My Boy Bobby . . . what's his number?" I yelled at somebody as we ran past. Before he could answer I could no longer hear him. Manny ran toward the 5-dollar win window. He'd opened up 7 lengths. When I got there he had his ticket. "What's the number?" I screamed.

"8! It's the 8 horse!"

I got my five down, got the ticket and the bell rang. We ran on out. Bobby read 4 to one on the board. There was a 6 to 5 favorite, the 3 horse. It was a mile and a 16th. As they came around the first turn the favorite had a 3/4-length lead and Bobby was just laying on his shoulder like a tiger, like an executioner. He was loping loose and easy, just laying on the side of the favorite.

"We should have gone ten. We're in," I told Manny.

"Yeah, we're in unless some big-ass closer comes out of the pack."

Bobby hung on the favorite's side halfway around the last curve and then he moved earlier than I expected. He came around the favorite, dropped down on the rail and used his run right then instead of later. He had 3 and one-half lengths at the top of the stretch, and then out of the pack came the horse we had to beat, the 4, he read 9 to one but he was coming. But Bobby was gliding. He won on a hand ride by 2 and 1/2 and paid $10.40 . . .

The next day at work we were questioned about our quick exit and we admitted that we had to make that last race and we were going to make it again. Manny had his horse picked and I had mine picked. Some of the guys asked if we would take bets out for them and I said no. That noon, being in the money, Manny and I went to the bar for lunch.

"Hank, we take their bets."

"Balls. We don't have time to run to those two-dollar windows."

"We don't."

"What?"

"We keep their money."

"What?"

"We just put it in our pockets."

"Uh. I see."

"It's easy."

"Suppose they win?"

"They won't win. They always pick the wrong horse. They have a way of always picking the wrong horse."

"Suppose they bet our selection?"

"Then we know we've got the wrong horse."

"Manny, what are you doing working in an auto parts warehouse?"

"My ambition is distorted by laziness."

"Suppose they win the first day?"

"We scrape up and pay off somehow. But if we get over the first day, we're in."

"All right," I said, "we're bookies."

We were then bookies, had another beer and went back to the auto parts warehouse . . . .

We ran through the tunnel again and into the infield and again they were putting them into the gate. We wanted Happy Needles and we were only getting 9 to 5 and I figured we wouldn't hit two days running so I only went 5 win but Manny went ten win. Happy won by a neck getting up on the outside in the last few strides. We got our money on the nose plus $32 in bad bets from the boys at the warehouse.

The word got around and the boys at the warehouses where I went to pick up odd parts began to lay their bets on me. I took them. Manny was right. There was seldom a payoff. People just didn't know how to bet. They bet too short or too long and the prices kept hitting in the middle. I bought a good pair of shoes, a new belt and two expensive shirts. I began to feel very wise as if I knew the secrets of the ages. And when you feel like you know the secrets of the ages you almost do.

The manager of the warehouse—the foreman—didn't look quite the powerful god anymore. Manny and I took a little longer on our lunch periods at the bar and came in smoking good cigars. But it was still a rough ride every afternoon to make that last race. The crowd got to know us and as we came running out of that tunnel every afternoon they were waiting. A big cheer would arise as we emerged sprinting from the tunnel and the cheer would intensify as we ran past them toward the betting windows. We became their joke.

Somehow this all didn't go too well for Laura. She was used to her four fucks a day and she was also used to seeing me poor and humble, and after a day at the warehouse and sprinting across the parking lot and through the tunnel and to the betting windows, there were hardly any fucks left in me, hardly four, anyhow.

So when I came on in each evening she would be well into her wine, still of beautiful leg and body, still a most interesting woman and she knew that, but things were not quite the same as before.

"Mr. Van Bilderass," she said as I walked in. She'd be all dressed up, high heels, legs crossed high, and she had the legs, those ankles, those knees; she knew she had it and she knew that I knew that she had it and she worked it for and against me and any way she felt like working it.

"Mr. Van Bilderass. You know, when I first met you I used to like the way you walked across a room. You don't walk across a room, you walk through walls, you own everything. Or you used to. Now you're a snob. You got a few bucks in your pocket and you're not natural anymore. You look like a plumber or the bread delivery man. You're shit."

"Oh, go jam it up your pussy!"

"I might as well. How long since you jammed it up my pussy?"

"Relax. Relax. I'll take care of you."

"Take care of me? You haven't fucked me for two days."

"Look, take it easy, kid. Hold still and in 6 months we'll be vacationing in Rome, in Paris."

"Look at you! Look at you! You're pouring yourself that good whiskey and you let me sit here drinking this rot-gut wine!"

I got back into my chair and wiggled my whiskey around against the icecubes. I knew it would piss her. I had on an expensive golden yellow shirt, it *blazed*, and my pants were green with thin white stripes.

"Bastard! Bastard! Bastard!"

"I give you soul, darling. I give you soul and light and music and a tiny bit of laughter. You know how hard that is to get? Besides, I'm the world's greatest horseplayer."

"You look more like a nigger pimp to me."

"Nigger pimp? Now, you see how you are? You not only lay it into me, you also lay it into the poor and the down-trodden. Ta, ta."

I drained my whiskey, got up and made myself another drink.

The arguments were similar. I understood it. Great lovers were men of leisure. I always got fucked more as a bum than as a puncher of timeclocks.

Laura began planning her counter-attack. And her counter-attack was to argue with me and then run out into the streets, the bars. All she had to do was sit on a barstool and the drinks and the advances would come. I didn't think that was fair, but then *I* had met her in a bar. So most of the evenings became similar. She'd argue, grab her purse, and be out the door. Out into the streets. She put it on me good. We'd lived and loved together too many hours; I had to feel it and feel it I did. But I always let her go and I sat in my chair and drank my whiskey and turned on the radio to a bit of classical music and drank my whiskey, and I hardly felt superior, I knew she was out there with them and I knew there would always be somebody. It wasn't easy. Yet I had to let it work. I felt I had to let the workings work . . .

But that (or this) (or whatever particular evening I am speaking of) I sat in the room and got the whiskey down between the icecubes and something just broke open in my head, I suppose I had no right but somehow something churned in me and I got up and walked down the 4 flights of stairs and into the streets and I walked along to where the bars began and I knew she was in one of the bars, there were 7 or 8, but I stuck my nose into the sky and my nose said—she's in that one. And I walked in through the winding tunnel and there she was, Laura, sitting at the end of the bar, a green and white kerchief sprawled across her hands, she was sitting between a very dumb ass of a man with a wart on the very center of his nose and a fat little mound of a thing with eyeglasses as a center of soul and I walked up to them at the end of the bar and Laura saw me coming, and she knew by the way I was walking that it meant right through the wall, and I got up to her and I said very quietly: "I tried to make a woman out of you but you'll never be anything but a god damned whore!" Then I backhanded her a good one and knocked her off her stool. She landed and screamed. I suppose she thought I was coming in to finish her off. She was wrong. I turned around and slowly walked toward the exit. When I got there I turned. Every face was looking at me and it was very silent. I said: (slowly. I speak slowly) "Now . . . if there's anybody here . . . who doesn't *like* what I just did . . . just say so."

I waited. I waited longer. There was no response. I turned and moved out of the winding exit. The moment I got to the street I heard all these voices talking at once inside there. I walked off.

At the auto parts warehouse I did less and less and less. Mr. Ignataz, the owner, would walk by and I would be crouched in a dark corner in one of the aisles and *very* lazily placing incoming parts into the shelves.

"Chinaski, are you all right?"

"Fine, sir."

"You're not sick?"

"Never felt better."

Then Ignataz would walk off. The scene repeated and repeated. My pockets were full of bookie money and the hangovers were hardly as bad, being conceived of the best whiskey that man could buy. I went along for a couple of weeks collecting paychecks for doing nothing. Then one Wednesday morning Ignataz stood at the top of the center aisle near his office and asked me forward with a motion of his right hand. I walked on up.

When I walked into his office Ignataz was behind his desk.

"Sit down, Chinaski."

I looked at his desk and saw a check in the center of it. The check was upsidedown. I reached across the desk and without turning the check over I slid it face-down along the top of the desk, and still without looking at it I picked it up and put it in my wallet. Then I sat down.

"So, Chinaski, you knew we were going to let you go."

"You people are never hard to figure out."

"Chinaski, you haven't been pulling your weight for a month. And you know it."

"That's the trouble with you people. A guy busts his ass for you and you don't appreciate it."

"You haven't been busting your ass, Chinaski, and you know it."

I stared down between my legs for some time. Then I raised my head. "Listen, Ignataz, I am going to tell you something. I've given my time and my life-blood to you on this dull, subservient two-bit beggar's job. And for a pitiful buck and a quarter an hour. That's my blood on the line so you can pay for your house on the hill and all that goes with it. I may have taken a breather now and then from placing 2-b parts on 2-b shelves but you've been buying my life with pennies and if *anybody*, if ANYBODY!!! (I stood up) has LOST on this deal, on this arrangement . . . on this whole whorehouse buy and sell of lives and bodies and profits, I AM THE LOSER, you understand—???—I, I, I, *I* . . . AM THE LOSER!"

I sat down.

"All right, Chinaski," he said.

"All right? Is that all you have to say?"

"Yes. Just please go."

"O.k.," I said, "I'll go. Just one more thing."

"Yes?" asked Ignataz. He was dressed in a conservative brown suit, white shirt, green necktie with tiny white spots, and I reached over his desk, I took a finger and flipped the necktie out.

In my mind I said, if he objects to this I am going to have to punch him. I will be in trouble but what the hell, I am going to have to punch him, no matter what it means or what happens I am going to have to punch him.

Ignataz sat there.

"I want my unemployment insurance. If I have any trouble with you from the agency I am going to have to come back and see you. You guys are always trying to cheat a man out of his rightful heritage. I am sincere, Ignataz. This is no threat but if you try to yence me out of my rights I am going to come back and talk it over with you."

"You'll get your insurance," he said, "now get the hell out of here."

He seemed to be getting angry.

"Thank you, Mr. Ignataz," I said, "I want to thank you very much."

Then I got out of there. As I walked toward my car I pulled the check out of my wallet. I was right.

MICHAEL RUMAKER

PIZZA

At the pizza parlor tonight
    the teenaged youth in the puffed navyblue jacket
  like he was wearing a mae west
    with levis or pipestems hanging down
      can't imagine how he gets into them
I've seen him around town
    tooling along on his bike.
Joking quietly with the pizza maker,
    foxy grin, eyes slits of mischief
  stain of a moustache on his upper lip
      Butterspun hair all aureoles
  about his head
    "angels are everywhere'
combed by the fierce teeth of the spring wind.
Long skinny feet in cruddy threading sneakers
  A little bit not too clean about himself,
    as it should be
    the hot odor of him
      as he does a little dance at the counter, wisecracking
      prime prime
I take my 2 slices and can of Pepsi to a back table and
thank the Great Spirit for giving us
    blood loveliness
Spring rolls in me like a river
  makes me drunk with the possibility of all earthly surprises.
    The place is crowded with fathers and mothers and kids
happily stuffing themselves with pizza
  The kids shriek and laugh and run around and
    complain and whine,
  like they own the place
    which they do.
The youth orders a meatball sandwich
    on french bread
A teen-aged girl has come in and stands close to him
  An unspoken connection between them
Something in her eyes, like she is listening
    to some pleasant song in herself
  She orders a peppersteak sandwich
    on french bread
  and Orange Crush
The small muscular pizza man
  twitching his erotically rocking behind

hands the boy his sandwich
with a smile that cracks his face
        like sun-parched hills
and watches the boy glide to an empty table.
    Knowing the best of 2 possible worlds
        he turns his smile on the girl,
            hands her her peppersteak
    his eyes all bouncing balls
        as he watches her bottom
        give her denims a real work-out as she sidles off
    to find a seat in the crowded room
            Out of the cradle erotically rocking
I expect she will join the boy
        but instead she carefully squeezes herself in
    at the long table behind him where a family of 4 sits,
        filling their faces with greasecheeked joy:
    mom dad son daughter
            the latter, maybe 2 or 3, screeching furiously
because she has burned her tongue on her slice of pizza
        Mother, father, small brother concerned,
            solicitous, making nice smiles
    ˙   but she's madder'n hell and will have none of it,
staring daggers at the pizza man tossing a pie crust
            in the air, whistling all innocence.
The teen-aged girl hasn't touched her sandwich or drink,
        she goes to the jukebox, puts in coin,
            very sure what she wants to hear, pushes the button.
Coming back, a dragstep dignity about her walk,
            brushes the young man
who is chomping hungrily on the meatball sandwich
        making more blood for those cheeks
        and bone and flesh to fill out the young body,
            as it should be.
He appears unconcerned about the young girl,
        but he doesn't miss a trick.
There's still the connection between them
in the hot cheese and tomato sauce air
    light as the sticky buds
    tossing in the trees all over the county
        gluey spring exploding itself
            sap running down
    like the meatball juice off
    the boy's chin and fingers
        A revel of eating
    all over the place
    the happy lust
the Great Spirit has seen fit to give us, gratis,
        in spite of the deadpack trying

          to stomp and maim it out
      The magic blue jukebox plays YOU ARE THE SUNSHINE OF MY LIFE
God knows, the girl is at the moment, and the boy, and the
        pizza man, and the bloodsap
racing up my limbs
     it shoots out my eyes
   and there are flowers for the world to see
       dancing asphodelly out of my eye sockets
        We happy 3, no, 4, counting the pizza guy
    I take it I take it all

  burn up and around their asphalt
      a tough flower
       Look, see
   slender leg crossed on slender leg
      his eyes blue as the jukebox,
looking out the aluminum plateglass door into the spring evening
     and rubber-hushed chrome-shiny traffic of Broadway
YOU ARE THE SUNSHINE OF MY LIFE woos the voice
     the boy's bits of sea-salt eyes focused
        on witty obscenities
         graffiti word jags
     the alert charming poise of the newly sensual.
The girl, listening in her eyes
    to the sunshine music on this juke
   of all heavenly jukes
      YOU ARE THE APPLE OF MY EYE
Her straightahead gaze
  looking into the river-tossed hair of the boy,
    ancient youthful sailor resurfaced in spring's thunder,
at the roseate flesh of his nape
  peeping between hair and acrylic collar
each looking smack ahead
       concentrated in the moment
       straightn'arrow from the skin of the broad
  world of amazing wonders
Miraculous jelly
  looking out from inside
  their fresh-seeing heads
What a world in eyes like that: the apple eye!
     The boy wipes his mouth with the back of his hand
       zips up his jacket.
The girl takes a swig of Orange Crush
  and pats a paper napkin to her lips..
With long strides and a casual wave to the pizza man,
   the boy is out the door
In the neon-lit window
  his careful eyes

flick lightly in at the girl
before he disappears
A beat, and the girl
stands up ever so casually
and moves out into the night.
Where will they go?
The Hook on the river has an ugly condominium
smothering it for the moment
no sweat
a tiny green pop cracks thickest concrete.
My legs and arms are fire
The boy, the girl and I are slips of green pushing
up out of their asphalt
Asphodels in asphalt slipping green into the land
invisible to glazed greedy eyes whose attentions
are busily intent on
ripping each other off
May they rip each other to death
We 3, the happy 3,
slip lightly in and change the world

JACK KEROUAC

POMES ALL SIZES

RUNNING THROUGH

CHINESE POEM SONG
(1961)

O I today
 sad as Chu Yuan
 stumbled to the store
 in broiling Florida October
morning heat cursing
 for my wine, sweating
 like rain, & came to my chair
 weak & trembling
 wondering if I'm crazy at last
—O Chu Yuan! No!
 No suicide! Wine please wine!
 What shall we all do
 all knowing we're dying
 without wine to guide us
 to winking at death
 & life too—
 My heart belongs
 to Chinese poets
 & their scrolls—
 We can't just die
 —Men need wine
 & poetry
 at least

O Mao, poet Mao,
 not Boss Mao,
 here in America
 wine is laughed at
 & poetry a joke
—Death's a grim reminder
 to everybody already dead
crashing in cars all around here—
 Here men & women dryly scowl
 at poets' sad attempts
 to make our lot
 a whole lot
 lesser—

I, a poet, suffer
even for bugs
I find upsidedown
dying in the grass—
So I drink wine
alone—
I shudder to think
how dead
the astronauts
are
going to a dead
moon
of no wine
All our best men
are laughed at
in this nightmare land
but the newspapers preen
in virtue—Throughout
the world the left & right,
the east & west, are both vicious—
The happy old winebibber is gone—
I want him to reappear—
For Modern China preens
in virtue too
for no better reason
than America—
Nobody has respect for the cat
asleep, and I am hopelessly
inadequate in this poem
—Nobody has respect
for the self centered
irresponsible wine invalid
—Everybody wants to be strapped
in a hopeless space suit
where they cant move
I urge you, China,
go back
to Li Po &
Tao Yuan Ming

What am I talking about?
I dont know,
I'm sick today—
I didnt sleep all night,
Walked stumbling in the field
to get wine, now I'm drinking it,
I feel better and worse—

I have something to say to Mao
& the poets of China
that wont come out—
It's all about how America
ignores poetry & wine,
& so does China,
& I'm a fool
without a river & a boat
& a flower suit—
without a wineshop at dawn
—without self respect—
—Without the truth—
but I'm a better man
than all of you—
that's what I
wanted to say

GOOFBALL BLUES

I'm just a human being with a lot of
shit on my heart

My ambition was not to be a great
lover,
but that's what I am
Even in dreams, fiancees
of other men
ball on my joint
And I am the Flying Horse
of Mien Mo
When I am an old man
my grave will rot me
The ones I loved were crazy
without knowing why
When I am old I'll yawn
in the Flannel Grave

MEXICAN LONELINESS

And I am an unhappy stranger
grooking in the streets of Mexico—
My friends have died on me, my
lovers disappeared, my whores banned,
my bed rocked and heaved by
earthquake—and no holy weed
  to get high by candlelight
  and dream—only fumes of buses,
dust storms, and maids peeking at me
  thru a hole in the door
  secretly drilled to watch
  masturbators fuck pillows—
I am the Gargoyle
of Our Lady
  dreaming in space
  gray mist dreams—
My face is pointed towards Napoleon
  —I have no form—
My address book is full of RIP's
  I have no value in the void,
    at home without honor,—
My only friend is an old fag
    without a typewriter
Who, if he's my friend,
    I'll be buggered.

I have some mayonnaise left,
a whole unwanted bottle of oil,
peasants washing my sky light,
  a nut clearing his throat
  in the bathroom next to mine
  a hundred times a day
  a hundred times a night
  sharing my common ceiling—
If I get drunk I get thirsty
—if I walk my foot breaks down
—if I smile my mask's a farce
—if I cry I'm just a child—
—if I remember I'm a liar
—if I write the writing's done—
—if I die the dying's over—
—if I live the dying's just begun—

—if I wait the waiting's longer
—if I go the going's gone—
if I sleep the bliss is heavy—
the bliss is heavy on my lids—
—if I go to cheap movies
    the bedbugs get me—
Expensive movies I cant afford
—If I do nothing
    nothing does

HOW TO MEDITATE

      —lights out—
fall, hands a-clasped, into instantaneous
ecstasy like a shot of heroin or morphine,
the gland inside of my brain discharging
the good glad fluid (Holy Fluid) as
I hap-down and hold all my body parts
down to a deadstop trance—Healing
all my sicknesses—erasing all—not
even the shred of a "I-hope-you" or a
Loony Balloon left in it, but the mind
blank, serene, thoughtless. When a thought
comes a-springing from afar with its held-
forth figure of image, you spoof it out,
you spuff it off, you fake it, and
it fades, and thought never comes—and
with joy you realize for the first time
"Thinking's just like not thinking—
so I dont have to think.
   any
  more"

POEM

I could become a great grinning host
          like a skeleton

Hung Up In Heaven

FLIES

And wasnt there ever a time when flies
  didnt seek the sun through forbidden
windowpanes?

And when men didnt pray for God
   to deliver them from mistake,
   Gesundheit?

Or when football players didnt huddle
    and plot the fall of opposing team
on chalkmark?

Who cares? God loves us all, his Own
      thought & Images in His dream,
Gesundheit.

No Jew of Torah or incantatory
    Koran was ever smarter
  than God

Loved God—all love God, themselves
—why worry about the queer in Room 3?
God bless you.

  Drink whisky sours in the Ritz
    at 3 pm Sunday talk of Tolstoy,
  quien care?

    All I want outa this persephone
    is poems instructing lovemilk thru
anemone—

GARY SNYDER

STRAIGHT CREEK -- GREAT BURN

For Tom & Martha Burch

Lightly, in the April mountains—
         Straight Creek,
dry grass freed again of snow
& the chickadees are pecking
last fall's seeds
      fluffing tail in chilly wind,

Avalanche piled up cross the creek
      and chunked—froze solid—
Water sluicing under; spills out
      rock lip pool, bends over,
      braided, white, foaming,
returns to trembling
      deep-dark hole.

Creek boulders show the flow-wear
                lines
    in shapes the same
    as running blood
    carriers in the heart's main
        valve.

Early spring dry.   Dry snow flurries;
      walk on crusty high snow slopes
—grand dead burn pine—
       chartreuse lichen as adornment
         (a dye for wool)
angled tumbled talus rock
of geosyncline warm sea bottom
Yes, so long ago.
"Once on a time."

Far light on the Bitteroots
      scrabble down willow slide
Changing clouds above,
Shapes on glowing sun-ball
Writhing,   choosing
    reaching out against eternal
                azure—

us resting on dry fern and
      watching

Shining Heaven
change his feather garments
                    overhead.
A whoosh of birds
swoops up and round
tilts back
almost always flying all apart
and yet hangs on!
together;

never a leader,
all of one swift

empty
dancing   mind.

They arc and loop & then
their flight is done.
They settle down.
End of their poem.

LMFBR

Death himself,
        (Liquid Metal Fast Breeder Reactor)
        stands grinning, beckoning.
Plutonium tooth-glow.
Eyebrows buzzing.
Strip-mining scythe.

Kālī dances on the dead stiff cock.

    Aluminum beer cans, plastic spoons,
plywood veneer, PVC pipe, vinyl seat covers,
            don't exactly burn, don't quite rot,
            flood over us,

            robes and garbs
            of the Kālī-yūgā

                end of days.

UP

Up, and up, through lower mists and clouds—
then peaks and pinnacles—the
bare rock limits—and higher yet,
lifting, leaving,   boot-tracks behind,
bird-tracks
            sky-walking
                        swimming
air-sea upward   cumulus
cirro-cumulus, horsetails,
pulses, rains of ray
            darkening,   stars and holes in the
            deepest

drawing in to
            a wheeling turbulence
            a tendril to cling to!
            in the void!
            look, the
perfume, the radiance

we have come to the feet
            of the Goddess.

            bow.

ROBERT CREELEY

ON THE BEACH

FALLING

Falling
from grace —
umpteenth time
rain's hit my head,
generous water.

SLEEP

Matrix of your legs,
charming woman,
handholds of firm

proportion—flesh figures in
the signs. Days away
from said past,

backwards "is no
direction?" Thought once,
twice—woke in night

several times as the furniture,
in the dream, backed out
the door, carried by affable

frightening people. Son-
in-law was depressed,
sitting on bed, daughter

beside how—how
had I misunderstood? Me
saying, "no, I

didn't"—little murmur
of self-content? Am
fearful, following

the couch, they have it,
into room occupied by
gang. Hence wake up

without you, bed warm,
sky grey, the day now
to come.

CIRCLE

As from afar,

through ringlet of woods,
the huntsman stares in wonder

at the sight, delight
in that light haze of circle
seems to surround you.

•

Crashing sound, the woods
move. Leaves fluttering,
birds making chatter —
your body sans error.

•

Pounds the musculature
where flesh joins bone —
hangs loose, thus
relieves.

•

Several melding persons,
one face, one
mirror in which to see it?

•

Expanse of trees
going up block
the light coming down
to us sitting here.

•

Rolls in laughter,
black hair, generous
action of your body.

•

Woods all over the place,
find them apparently forever
where you are.

•

Isolated,
to think
of you, of you —

sea's plunging forms
and sounds, rock
face, the white, recurring

edge of foam —
love's forms
are various.

•

In the circle of this
various woods,
one presence, persistent,

shines. An easy seeming
extension of her light
continually brings me to her.

•

EASE

A day's
pattern
broken,
by your love.

•

Come here
(come home)
to think

of you
(of you).

•

A bird
for you, a singing
bird.

•

I'd climb into
your body
if I could, cover

myself up entirely
in your generous
darkening body,

steal away all
senses, sleep
in the hole.

•

You, you, you —
one and only.

•

What use love —
to make me cry,
to make me laugh?

•

Flood of details, memory's
delight—the sight
of you.

•

Waves rolling over,
continuously, sound
of much being done.

Get up, for actions —
impedes the sight, hearing,
—want to walk away?

Stay here. Where I am,
is alone here, on the sand.
Water out in front of me

crashes on.

•

KID

"What are you doing?"
Writing some stuff.

"You a poet?"
Now and then.

•

Woods, water,
all you
are.

•

And the particular
warmth of you,
all asleep
together.

WATER

As much to know you,
love, to witness this changing surface
from so constant a place.

•

I'll never get it right enough,
Will never stop trying.

•

Old one-eye,
fish head,
wants his water back.

Dear friend,
bring bucket
and shovel.

•

Truly see you,
surfacing, all

slippery, wetness,
at home.

•

If I wanted
to know myself,
I'd look at you.

When I loved
what I was,
it was that reflection.

•

Color so changing here,
sky lightens, water

greens, blues.
Never far from you,

no true elsewhere.
My hands stay with me.

•

You'd think the years
would change some first sense

of whatever it is —
but it comes again and again.

•

Love's watery condition
waits only for you.

*Perfection of substance
leaps high in lacy foam.*

Deep as it goes,
entirely you.

•

Wind gets chill,
sun trying to shine.
Move on again.

In the world a few
things to think of,
a blessing.

I don't love
to prove it—love
to know it.

Bixby Canyon—July 10, 1973

DENNIS FRITZINGER

poems from

THE WAVES

airbase

toothpaste smiling senators,
airmen, republicans, officers
who sit on their hands, o base
about to close down, what of your people's future?
we need you—hah!
airbase, secrets hidden
behind wire fences, gates
reminiscent of those old ones
with barbed wire on top during the war;
camp, you are a
summer camp i was never sent off to,
but sat around playing anyway
strip poker in the dead of summer nite.
you airbase, sweltering among weeds,
whose sign announces: SAC base.
the roar of airplanes
revving up to take off
on secret missions
in the dark
is to be silenced
—at last?
watching the weeds
flicker around the lights,
the moths flying up
at nite, into them;
the guard house
at the gate, & the sign standing
blue, lit up with white,
moths flickering
into it, the heavy silence of magnolias
to be broken at last?
PEACE IS OUR PROFESSION
spelled out in big, bold letters.
the town doesn't like you;
the town
complains of broken windows

from when you fly your jets over, not even caring
enough to be gentle with the sound barrier,
but breaking it every time
or so they say.
your big, white heavy bombers
& trainers, your visitor's plane,
your fighters, piper cubs, paper airplanes
& boomerangs, all are objectionable—
go build yourself somewhere else, airbase.
we don't need your 60 million a year—ono?
i'm going to miss your
red, blinking lights,
o airbase. your runways, heavy with flowers,
will be strange, no wheels
with the big, heavy skid & bump
on them, i mean. nobody's going to
put out their hand, & say help!
i vote for this airbase,
i like its pop machines! i like its movie!
i don't like to work here!
go berserk then—
blow up, scatter grenade fragments
of yourself a mile away,
o glorious fireworks!
then you will be beautiful, o airbase!
sophia loren wouldn't be more beautiful!
a flower then—so much more than you are now,
with dreary commissary & px.
flower, o sudden rose
by the doom hiway, death of nite,
fighting the long, lost war, & shadows' hands
slip boney fingers on guns, man the long trenches

in a dream

in a bunker
spending life dug in
in a plantation of rubber trees,
i wobble to the surface
after an attack, to find
hordes of children.
they are waiting
for me to help them escape
with their elephant
who has just turned one.
they were in the midst
of a birthday party for it

in a huge, vacant house
in the back, just when
charlie began sending
mortar shells over
like party favors.
they were all lined up
outside,
waiting for me to emerge;
the sky streamed down its message
but no one screamed;
not an eyelash batted.
slowly
i got up to my knees & crawled
out of my volcano.
& there was just silence outside,
silence
& the stony children.

adepts

there are some things too secret for any but adepts to know.
there are some things hidden on the insides of rocks,
on the undersides of snails, on layers of onions
and flower pétals, in the honey of bees.
there are secret knowledges in the kingdoms of the fish,
there is perfect knowledge in the palaces of the diamond.
and everywhere are the adepts,
singing, living and dying, eating, driving their trucks.

the way

being beckoned to by a poem of someone else,
i walk off rapidly
into the utter darkness. the poem has a few friends
and more enemies. i shake my cigar at it
like a nightstick. i am justice of the peace,
my peace. i am of peasant blood
easily spilled. my world is not your world.
when i smile, it is because i remember
trees i have never seen, the dark thick trees
of germany or poland. or russia,
she who is in my blood, somewhere waiting
with a black kerchief covering her hair.
my cities are growing quiet, lighting up
few lamps; they are icecream citadels
eaten by rats.

now the trees grow quiet
and my blood, my blood grows quiet,
a few rhymes scheme
to hear themselves, to make them
selves heard, they pinch yell ouch
and will not stand in line, i call
roll call,
and the dirtiest of them comes forward,
petition in hand. why is it always thus,
they will not cease, increase
rather, out of spite, not sense,
not what is right. they elbow
me out of the way. and their demands,
troublesome, chaotic, know no peace
and no solution. it is the dream i'm in,
we're in, a dream where a revolver
makes the rules. i've never seen the face
of a word but that it reminded me of some dark place
where i've never been and yet know all about.
the poem of someone else is saying, brother,
treat me right. because it is the way.

gold doorknob

poems, like a needle,
slip under the skin
to give us a fix.
james, in the middle
of your elegant
garden of rubber giraffes,
do you meet diane
who comes there wearing
cadillac graveyard jewelry?
does she slip into your pocket
the packet of poems
saying "kool-aid" on it?
you break it open,
later, in a lavatory,
in the midst of lincoln's zoo.
the lions roar around you
while a black bat
is not so far off, thinking
thinking about what?
the chimpanzee
in his black hat,
or the blazes
locked in a cage,
gate of brass,
doorknob of gold?

the fine art

a submarine
has such intricate plumbing,
each section
watertight, efficient, smooth.
back in the days
of jules verne however,
a sub stuck out of the water,
some iron monster
with iron teeth like a buzzsaw,
and a headlight that gleamed
dull, current yellow
through the darkening waves.
its cabin was furnished
in elegant victorian
and had windows six feet thick,
glass bubbles that looked out
like lice under scales.
in the front of it
captain nemo was just standing,
trying to make out
a strange phenomenon
going on outside
when we came up on him.
the sea was liquid light.
the room throbbed like the heartbeat
of a stricken bird,
and a few leatherbound
strange volumes
fell out of the wall.
i picked one up.
sobered, i opened it,
examined the flyleaf:
it was my own handwriting.
then i remembered,
as the monster came upon me
with luminescent excrescences,
i had once written
a slim volume
on the fine art of plumbing.

my mother & the music machine

on top of the mountain
they hired a machine to make music,
they hired a man to work the machine,
they even hired an audience of birds and bees and snails.
rocks came at their bidding.
also great kings came, and emperors of rivers,
and the ocean, the sun king, even my mother before she had me.
then they turned on the music. the machine flowed like a fountain.
there were seven kinds of notes it could make, each note a precious jewel.
my mother listened. she fell asleep, and dreamed of me.
and a great cloud, the color of pearl, fell over her
like a blanket to keep her warm.

the soul's migration

a minute away
from eternity
the eyes play strange tricks.
what you thought once you had,
lo! it is gone.
you reach in your bag,
pull out
a handful of dust.
where is the money
you were saving?
the jewels got by greed?
they are gone.
all, all
are vanished,
less than the air
that shared
the bag with them.
when your soul goes,
it wheels around your body,
testing its wings
till, seeing
the new sun,
it turns and is gone.

TOM CUSON

IRON HORSE

smells of steak & whiskey
in crossroad cafes, dogs & porches,
men's dusty beer cans at gingham tables
barefoot streams, lonely women
in housecoats fading on waves of grain.
the farmhouse bent
through the windshield
shimmers in heat,
riding the plains like a whale.
a farmer pauses
to spit on his hands. laundry flutters
on the clothesline like caged birds.
pure distance nails the sky to itself.
the two lane asphalt is an
arrow aimed at the fire in the west.
some voice inside me says
it's for this you came
this is the way it was supposed to be
the innocence of wheat, buffalo skulls
& teepees, seashells
preserved inside boulders, the sound
of the sea in my gasoline blood
not so much hope
as an instinct for survival
not a destination
but a way of travelling.
sunlight pours through the windshield
& falls asleep in my lap.
dust freezes in air, reflecting flame,
my life suspended on the balance of a glance.
as if my bones
could glow i enter
through dusk the new dark
like a key.

HARVEST

morning divides
between its fingers
the living & dead.
moss curls in green joy
when the sun
with its lavender spoon
stirs the river.
dew is unbroken
yet already,
lovers without beds,
whales stretch
towards warmer seas
& I, I alone,
a juggler of wheat in the breeze,
hold in my hands
the grains of my life

THOMAS HEAD

THE TRIESTE CAFE

for there is no expression
      on their faces

they sit as they are home
      in the sun & light

of a new italy in north beach

the old men of saturday morning
      2 mandolins   2 guitars

sweet bones a breeze & sadnesses —

where does the music come from?

      the signora comes out
carrying a glaze of warmth on her face
from behind the counter to kiss
      a child

who she mistakes for an angel

      and i suppose there are
continuities like maybe two people
in the room alive to one another

      and this is america

RICHARD BRAUTIGAN

SOME MONTANA POEMS/1973

Night

Night again
again night

•

August 23

Dive-Bombing the Lower Emotions

I was dive-bombing the lower
emotions on a typical yesterday
   . . . after
I had sworn never to do it again.
I guess never's too long a time to stay
    out of the cockpit
with the wind screaming down the wings
and the target almost praying itself into your
    sights.

August 30

Nine Crows: Two out of Sequence

1,2,3,4,5,7,6,8,9

September 1

KAYE McDONOUGH

BOB KAUFMAN READING
AT VESUVIO'S BAR

Walnut doll, wind-up man
your arms and eyelids
are pulled by an epileptic puppeteer
We have seen you possessed by the invisible
madness mirrored in memory streets
Broadway blinks sad bosoms
of free women you loved
Jazz horns alive in your head
hang still in pawnshop windows
North Beach is a scavenger's museum
where the curator is Dionysus
deballed, too drunk to dream

You taught your dance to clubfoots
your vision to the blind
now walk the streets
with matted hair and maddened feet
like a dog who's been
too long without tending
Your dream was hit by a cab
at Broadway and Columbus

I saw a photograph of you and Eileen
standing in a garden
What painful apple did you eat
to hurt your eyes with such a look?
Lucifer must have turned that face to God
at his first sight of hell

But you were born before the angels
before the Christian god
You were the poet before sin
and hell is not forever

The dynamite volcano is not extinct
We heard you at Vesuvio's singing Hart Crane
You blew America from your mouth
and smiled your ancient vision
round a shocked barroom

"Die, centuries, die" you sang
and two thousand years
spilled its lava in our laps
Sodom, expecting an earthquake
was not expecting you

Jew not Jew
Black not Black
Outlaw outcast
an open sore in your own son's gut
you are the poet
of lost heavens and damned gods
Sing the dream again
that music may break the concrete you walk
and lovers rise up from their tombs

BOB KAUFMAN 1973 by PETER LEBLANC

ED BULLINS

THE PSYCHIC PRETENDERS
A BLACK RITUAL MYSTICAL DRAMA

THE PRESENCES

MIJO, The Depraved. Commanding Man.

LIBO, The Accusing Man.

RAGO, The Inspired Man.

SORO, The Serene Man.

ROTO, The Fulfilled Man.

TIHWO, The Fulfilling Man.

POBE, The Purified. Complete Man.

TELLE, The Black Witch.

Several SPIRIT PRESENCES to play their assigned roles, e.g., AUHV (The Ordinary—Human Woman), VETI (The Angelic—Female), ARIE (The Forceful—Woman of real capacity) and SANA (The Divine Woman).

These last roles are inter-changeable among the SPIRIT PRESENCES and not fixed except as the production demands.

The PRESENCES may wear different colored masks, suggesting their psychic qualities. But the SPIRIT PRESENCES should be veiled and in mystical, mysterious costume.

THE PSYCHIC PRETENDERS is the second spiritual tale in the mystic triangle/trinity/trilogy beginning with THE DEVIL CATCHERS.

★   ★   ★

THE PSYCHIC PRETENDERS opened at The New Lafayette Theatre, Harlem, in Winter/71. The production was directed by Robert Macbeth. Sets and lighting were by James and Tobias Macbeth and Alfred Smith. The cast was as follows:

Mijo	Sonny Jim Gaines
Libo	Bill Lathan
Rago	Gary Bolling
Soro	Roscoe Orman
Roto	George Miles
Tihwo	Whitman Mayo
Telle	Estelle Evans
Presences	Rosanna Carter, Helen Ellis, Yvette Hawkins, Roberta Raysor and Vaughn Reddie

★ ★ ★

ONE: DEATH

The Place of Quest

Music Light. Varied greens. Tones of yellows. Brightness. Splendid feathered creatures flit and float in the perfumed air.

The hushed shove of entrance into a peculiar reality. Sounds: water splattering among rocks. A rodent's squeal. An eagle's shriek. The shape of the vulture near. Silence.

A shadow . . . then a dim, VEILED FORM moves silently into sight. It stands and waits, looking off . . .

Then ANOTHER VEILED SHAPE moves in toward the first form with measured steps, tracing out a path. And upon the invisible path comes a RED-HOODED FIGURE that drags WOMAN, bound and gagged, dressed in black, and he ties her to a stake, and ceremoniously begins to prepare her for execution.

Meanwhile, the TWO VEILED PRESENCES prepare the death place for the tied woman, then produce an awesome knife, which the RED-HOODED MAN receives, and move away to witness the proceedings.

With the WOMAN-IN-BLACK calmly watching, HE begins an evil ritual, and unsheaths the blood-letting knife.

RED-HOODED FIGURE

(Consecration)
Zo wan-we Sobadi sobo kalisso Maitre-Carrefour . . .

(The RED-HOODED FIGURE stops his chant and listens and concentrates.

Suddenly, a sound, then a glow of color, and another VEILED FIGURE glides into view, holding a lighted candle or lantern. It guides someone with its weak light.

For behind this THIRD VEILED, spectral figure comes noises into the setting: footfalls on dried leaves, crisp crackling of broken branches and foliage. Voices.

The RED-HOODED FIGURE gestures for the WOMAN to remain silent, and holds his weapon at the ready. The THREE VEILED ONES move back into shadows; the flame'lite is snuffed/out.

MIJO and LIBO enter)

MIJO
As strangers in a strange land, my sharp tongued ally, I have a strange suspicion that this is no ordinary journey that we are on.

LIBO
It has been said by Gotama the Buddha: "It is because I see this peril in the marvel of psychic power that I am distressed by it, that I abhor it, that I loathe it."

MIJO
Is it all that you can do thusly, to quote ancient prophets and gone gods?

LIBO
If you were not so ready to use your sword, mighty Mijo, your words could have cutting edges as well.

(A VEILED FIGURE comes out of the shadows and points: MIJO and LIBO discover the RED-HOODED ONE and the tied WOMAN. The VEILED FIGURE DISAPPEARS.

Immediately, the EXECUTIONER springs at LIBO.

Stumbles, drawing his weapon)

Yyyyyyyeeeeee . . .

> (MIJO intercepts the killer; THEY fight fiercely for a
> moment, then MIJO kills him with a deft stroke)

Master Warrior . . . you saved my life . . . but did you have to do him in? We
are strangers in this strange place as well as fugitives from our own lands.

> (MIJO gestures, indicating the TIED WOMAN)

MIJO
Silence, still-living Libo! Did I have a choice? My blade bit first. Give thanks
to the Spirits of our land that your blood does not lubricate his steel at this
moment as his does mine.

> (Unseen by MIJO and LIBO, a FOURTH VEILED FIG-
> URE enters and attends the tied WOMAN, while LIBO
> soothes her.
>
> ONE of the shadowy FIGURES carefully lifts the EX-
> ECUTIONER's dropped blade, wraps it ceremonially in
> a soft cloth, and waits)

LIBO
Unfortunate elderly sister . . . oh, grayed and gracious mother/figure . . .

> The VEILED ONE unties her and removes the gag.

TELLE
(Chokes on air. Gasps)
Praise the Powers . . . praise the secret powers . . . I sent forth my vibrations
. . . and they were perceived . . .
(SHE searches about her)
Is the Sacred Sliver still intact?

> (Unknown to her the slain man's sword is placed at her
> feet by the waiting VEILED ONE)

Ahhh! . . . It is here . . . So, at last, good triumphs!
SHE picks the bundle up.

> Meanwhile, MIJO examines the body of the EXECU-
> TIONER and moves back; then the VEILED ONES
> begin to drag it from view)

No! Don't touch him? . . .

> (The VEILED ONES leave the body and exit)

LIBO

Is there something obvious to you that is unknown to us, old mother?

(TELLE begins to wail)

MIJO

Why do you cry? We must dispose of this body.

LIBO

Don't weep, queen mother . . . This thing was about to murder you . . . the disguised beast! There are limits for charitable impulses, even from one such as you, your graciousness.

TELLE

We must save him . . . he can be saved!

MIJO

Saved! . . . didn't you see him gasp his last breath, good lady? Save him? . . . Hummp, say prayers over the empty shell which is he now though his eternal salvation has already been delivered to him by my thirsty blade.

TELLE

But I hold in my hands another blade . . . the Beautiful Blade . . . the Sacred Sliver of our people's splintered psychic powers.

MIJO

(Explodes)

Nonsense!

TELLE

Rest, my savage son . . . rest as I do my work.

(SHE casts a spell upon him and HE goes into a slouching, deep but restful nod)

LIBO

Great Dracula!

(HE pulls at his weapon and moves to strike the BLACK WITCH)

What have you . . .

(SHE stops him with a gesture. HE freezes in place, though remains fully conscious)

TELLE

I do not wish to harm you, my sons . . . You LIBO, may keep your waking faculties so that you can observe me as I work . . . Brother Mijo can nod for a while . . . until we need his strong arm and fierce nature . . . But I will not tolerate any interference . . . so witness my divine work.

(SHE gestures and the FOUR VEILED ONES appear)
(Unsheathes sword)
At last you return, great shining one . . . holy Iblis beheader . . . you fell
from your father's hands in the times before these ages of slavery . . . and
our people fell with you . . . We descended into the depths of this Western
pit of hell . . . We were the lost ones . . . forever seeking our way back but
our feet are on the path now and the gleam of your razor tip points the way
. . . We follow the light in our eyes, which is you, oh Beautiful Blade . . . And
now you are back in our Black hands again to heal our people, to give
strokes of knowledge, to guide and guard us in our journey of truth!

(The VEILED ONES began a ritual of Resurrection and
dance and sing:)

THE VEILED ONES

Through the Valley of the Quest
they wander
Across the Kingdom of Searching
they cross
All kinds of Perils threaten
Most mysteries are
among these lost

Pilgrims must denounce desire
Pilgrims must denounce desire

You Wanderers came and were brave
You Wanderers came and fought
injustice
You found what could become
fame

You found death waiting
and gave the same

Pilgrims must denounce desire
Pilgrims must denounce desire

Now we Spirits must restore life that
you have taken
Now we Spirits must repair what
your warring
has destroyed
Now we must implore the earth
to bring forth a new
life
Implore nature to restore
what has been destroyed
through strife

Pilgrims must denounce desire
Pilgrims must denounce desire
Oh, yea . . . denounce desire

> (The VEILED ONES disappear; and TELLE
> stands over the inert body, as MIJO slumps
> and nods, and LIBO stares from amazed eyes,
> though his muscles can only twitch and slight-
> ly jerk)

TELLE
(Invokes)
Hear me Spirits of this land of seekers! Hear me and listen to the words of
my long/gone fathers and brothers! Hear their words:

HEAVY MALE VOICE
(Off)
. . . RISE FROM THE DEAD AND CLAIM YOUR OWN/ RISE OUT OF
DEATH TO BE AS ONE/ WITH YOUR BROTHERS/ RAISE UP OH HOLY
BEATEN DOWN BLACKMAN/ RAISE UP AND LIVE! . . .

> (TELLE passes the sword over the corpse.
>
> The sky cracks and fire and roars spew forth, as the
> RED-HOODED BODY sits up and MIJO and LIBO
> become normal.
>
> A chorus of screams is heard from the VEILED ONES
> lurking in the shadows)

MIJO
Yyyyiiiiieeeee . . . by the whites of our father's eyes . . . It can't be!

LIBO
What accursed place is this? What tragedy! That dead thing act alive? What
foul kingdom have we wandered into? Our souls will be lost in this evil place,
I fear. Old woman . . . what awful magic do you work that puts men asleep
while still awake and makes corpses rise before our eyes?

TELLE
Son . . . I work the pure magic . . . the magic given to me by my father . . .
the Black magic of life! Behold!
> (SHE reaches down and rips the hood from the head of
> the newly risen man. SHE exposes the face of a hand-
> some man)

MIJO
Ahhhh . . . what is this?

RAGO (The unhooded one)
(Feels face)
It is light . . . I see . . . and forms beyond my reach become clear and emerge from the haze of sleep . . . Oh, what a deep deep sleep I have recovered from. And this place seems so far from where I began . . . is it the same world?

(TWO VEILED ONES move forward to help him to his feet, then move off)

LIBO
Dear lady . . . your powers have given this monster an unearned reprieve . . . Allow the vigor of my blade to return this victim to his correct state.

MIJO
As if your clumsily snatched/at knife's failure aided you before, fraud! My powers made the kill!

TELLE
No quarrelling, great men . . . What you saw before was not real . . .

LIBO
Not real?

TELLE
You saw an illusion . . .

(A sigh goes up from the shadowy VEILED ONES)

. . . a dream of that which did not exist.

RAGO
It's a new day . . . a new day . . . I feel as if I've been born again.

LIBO
What new mystery is this?

MIJO
But . . . but this cannot be . . . it cannot . . . one and seven at the same instance . . . death and resurrection before our imaginations have grasped any meaning.

LIBO
What mystery!

TELLE
Only the unravelling of the unknown, the disclosure of the future and the past . . . Our handsome companion here, Brother Rago, was only a dead shell of his former self . . . a dread and dead necro/negro . . . Killing for the Unnamable beasts for his own profit. More dead than when you thrust your steel through him, Brother Mijo. More dead than a stone.

RAGO

But I am risen and am whole again. How?

TELLE

Not by my poor powers are you alive and with us, son. You have unfinished tasks to complete . . . and only through the love of a righteous Black woman can you succeed.

RAGO

Love? . . . Black woman . . . is that the answer?

> Lights alter. One of the VEILED ONES comes forward, presenting herself as:)

AUHV

Rago . . . Rago . . . I'm happy that you are yourself again . . . and are with your true companions.

RAGO

Auhv . . . my lost love . . . woman of all my women. But I had lost hope . . . and I had gone down into despair and surrendered to death . . . and I knew you were dead, my dear Auhv.

AUHV

I was only dead in your mind and memory, Rago.

RAGO

Though not my heart . . . So much has happened in an instant . . .
(HE reaches out)
What! I cannot touch you . . . What's this! This is not television. You are before me . . . I can see, smell and sense you . . . but cannot touch?

AUHV

I await you when you arrive to me at the end of your journey with your friends.

RAGO

But I need you now . . . I want you now, Auhv, love of all loves.

AUHV

(Fades)
You are one who travels through alien lands . . . a Wayfarer . . . a pilgrim in search of the future . . . I wait you when you arrive in me . . . in me . . . in me . . .

(Lights change. MIJO fights the shadows)

MIJO

HHHAAaaaa . . . HHHHAAAAaaaaaa . . . Let us leave this place of witch-craft! There is nothing to fight here but emptiness and dreams.

TELLE

In time . . . in time we leave . . . in time we shall make the journey.

(Some of them mill aimlessly and wander toward the shadows, as moans and wails come from the hidden VEILED ONES)

LIBO

(Long and drawn)

We have been traveling so long . . . and we become more lost.

RAGO

(Strained)

Is there any way out of this?

TELLE

(Precise)

We are at the first lap of our journey. From now on we must stick together and go forward . . . or we shall all suffer from . . . from the White Death.

MIJO

The White Death! . . . never!

RAGO

Cast your spell of salvation, Black mother . . . Let the sword of Salvation sing . . . We are fierce fighters all, we Black warriors . . . but what can shield us from the pure essence of evil save your magic science cast with love?

TELLE

(Softly)

You grant me too much power, my sons . . . all powers are within your minds, believe me.

LIBO

Magic Madame . . . my brother/man here, Mijo and I, come from beyond the frightening forest . . . From the evil Land of Fools. We escaped and have fought our way this far, believing that we had out/distanced the White Death . . . But you say its presence pursues us still?

RAGO

Forever . . . and ever . . . until we reach the divine place of freedom. It was the White Death that caused me to be as you first saw me . . . a nigger zombie. Its sordid veil shaded the love of my Black woman/queen, Auhv, from my eyes . . . Oh, brother/warriors we must leave this foul nest here in the West and turn east toward sun and salvation and liberation.

TELLE

Yes, make ready to go, brave brothers. We will lean upon each other . . . and with the sacred sliver we shall fight our way through every disaster together. We have begun at the exit of the Land of Fools . . . and we shall end our pilgrimage at the end of this terrible path.

(THEY assemble. Drums beat)

MIJO

I and my biting blade shall lead the way!

LIBO

I and my quick senses take up the rear. Do not fear, heads forward! . . . My eyes and sharp steel guard your backs!

RAGO

Brave bunch that you be . . . I march beside the wise Black magic mother. Together . . . our powers are equal to any encounter!

TELLE

Well said, my sons. We go!

(The VEILED ONES take up positions, lighting the way, guiding and invisibly protecting the procession. THEY sing eerily as THEY go:

VEILED ONES

Together we go
toward the
unknown
toward the
mystery of
the next cycle
into the
future . . . psychic
Pretenders
Together we are
in the past
on the path
to the future
together . . . Psychic
Pretenders
we march
strange places
we pass
awful mysteries
we discover
evil adventures

await us
together . . . Psychic
Pretenders
but we are
together . . . Psychic
Pretenders
we go forward
together
into strangeness
forward through
wonder
toward tomorrow
together
together . . . Psychic
Pretenders
our magic
imaginations
take us
take our magic
memories
forward . . . Psychic
Pretenders
forward into
the adventure
into unknowing
together

THEY pass through the Gate of the Searchers,
the first gate, and walk the bridge of Death)

TWO: PURGATORY

Place of Love

An isolated crossroads at midnight. From
afar, the hour is tolled. During the thirteen
peals the FOUR VEILED ONES enter and in
the center of the intersection place a black
cloth. At two edges of the black cloth are
placed unlit black candles. At the lower edge
of the cloth is placed a red stone, and at the
upper, a piece of iron. Upon the last stroke of
twelve a white doll is laid upon the cloth,
head pointed toward the iron, its feet not
touching the red stone, nor arms reaching the
black candles. When everything is in place the
VEILED ONES disappear.

SORO and ROTO enter.

SORO

(Solemn)
Whose crossroads are these, brother Roto?

ROTO
The devils', of course, brother. Don't they own everything?

SORO

Yes

ROTO
The Unnamable Ones give their henchmen and pets, the devils, dominion over these regions.

SORO

Will we be discovered?

ROTO
Nothing is ever certain, brother Soro. Tonight it has been whispered that those dread monsters kept by the devils, The Hunts, are not patrolling.

SORO
If those invisible and terrible beasts were abroad tonight . . . iiiieeeee . . . all would be our tragedy.

ROTO
But our plans are made. Tonight we make the pack.

SORO
Tonight . . . Is the moon full?

ROTO

The moon?

SORO
Or do we stand in the shadow of its waning wonder?

ROTO
There is no moon here, brother Soro. Only heavens.

SORO

Ahhhhh.

ROTO
Reaching boughs and broken branches above . . . with the clouded heavens hovering, brother Soro.

SORO

Ohhhh.

ROTO

No more of your nervous questioning, please. The witching hour flies almost as swiftly as death.

SORO

It is said that the shadow of the devil precedes death . . .

ROTO

Enough . . . we must act.

    (Pause)

SORO

. . . And its shadow is cast toward the West.

ROTO

Be still . . . serene sorcerer.

    (Pause)

SORO

Is everything in place?

ROTO

It appears so.

SORO

Did you bring the matches?

ROTO

I left that for you to do, my brother.

SORO

You did?

ROTO

Yes.

SORO
(Searches himself unhurriedly)

You are certain, my brother?

ROTO

That vital detail could only be entrusted to you, brother Soro.

SORO

I see.

> (SORO concentrates. A VEILED ONE appears and hands him matches)

You are exactly as you always are, brother Roto. The matches are in my hand.

ROTO

Well done.

> (The VEILED ONE disappears.
>
> SORO lights each candle as ROTO touches the iron, then the red stone.
>
> Then SORO produces a small American flag which HE ties about the middle of the white doll.
>
> THEY make hypnotic gestures and speak:)

SORO

Be you gone and may you rot in the grave *Devilman*. Damballah, curse him as I curse him and spoil him as I spoil him.

ROTO

By the fire at night, by the dead black hen, by the bloody throat of the strangled blackmen hung in Southern night, by the goat, by the rum on the ground, by the rapes of black madonna/queens in the boat, by the cursing drum, by the six fingered hand, this ouange be upon him, the *Devilman*.

SORO

May he not have peace in bed, nor at his food, nor can he go and hide.

ROTO

Waste him and wear him and tear him and rot him as this white wanga rots beneath the roots of our dead trees.

> (The FOUR VEILED ONES have come out and taken up positions about the pair, representing the four corners of the universe. THEY chant:)

VEILED ONES
L' APPE VINI, LA GRAND ZOMBI
L' APPE VINI, LA GRAND ZOMBI

L' APPE VINI POUR FE GRIS-GRIS
L' APPE VINI POUR FE GRIS-GRIS

(THEY shift in unison and dirt and water is produced
for SORO and ROTO)

CARREFOUR, CARROFOUR, CONGA NOUNE DE LE
CARROFOUR, CARREFOUR, CONGA NOUNE DE LE

(SORO lights three matches at this point, and HE waves
them together flaming over the doll)

BARON CIMITIERE, BARON CIMITIERE, CONGA BAFO TE
BARON CIMITIERE, BARON CIMITIERE, CONGA BAFO TE

(ROTO sprinkles dirt upon the doll, covering the flag)

AIA BOMBAIA BOMBA, GHEDE, GHEDE, CONGA DO KI LA
AIA BOMBAIA BOMBA, GHEDE, GHEDE, CONGA DO KI LA

YOUR NAME AND YOUR LIFE AND YOUR SUFFERING
SHALL BE THAT OF THE DEVILMAN

YOUR NAME AND YOUR LIFE AND YOUR SUFFERING
SHALL BE THAT OF THE DEVILMAN

THE DEVILMAN
THE DEVILMAN
THE DEVILMAN

(Together, SORO and ROTO deliberately take daggers
from their belts and raise them over the white doll.

Suddenly, a crashing sound of breaking bushes and
branches, and a voice shouts:)

MIJO
(Rushes in, weapon drawn)
HALT! . . . Stop this blasphemous performance!
(Stunned silence)

SORO
(Recovering)
What hidden pit of hades have we summoned you from, freakish fiend?

MIJO
(Hateful)
No poetry, you swine! Satan did not issue me forth . . . I am not his kin nor
of his clan . . . I stand here the son of noble Devil Catchers!

SORO

So be it, phantom fool!

MIJO

Enough now . . . prepare to die.

ROTO
(Dagger at the ready)
Whatever womb you clambered out of will soon shrivel when it senses your doom.

SORO

Evil Intruder . . . I shall slay you and hang your soul at this crossroad for the bats to bite the edges from.

MIJO
(Feints)
Cursed devil worshippers . . . defend yourselves!
THEY feint, move and parry.
More entrance sounds)

LIBO
(Enters)
Wait, brother/warrior . . . Why do you attack these brothers?

MIJO
(Still pressing attack)
Did you come to fight, Libo . . . or only to die.

ROTO
(Challenges LIBO)
Hahhh . . . another assassin! He's mine!

LIBO

Why do you want to kill without a hearing, brothers?

TELLE
(Enters)
Hasty men . . . hasty men . . . so ready to destroy your own brothers.

RAGO
(Enters)
Careful, great Black lady . . . these are savage swordsmen . . . and their steel is sharp.

SORO

Is this some kind of crazy carnival? Before we shed your blood . . . confess . . . what klan do you hail from?

RAGO

We are of the . . .

MIJO

Quiet all! . . . if there is explaining to be done . . . only I have the correct knowledge to render the truth.

ROTO

If there be any truth in a nightmare such as you, devil protector.

MIJO

(Lunges)

Cursed coward! . . .

(ALL break away)

TELLE

Young gentlemen . . . why don't we sit down like the super intelligences that we are and discuss this unfortunate dilemma.

(SHE makes a magical gesture. The lights change. And THEY ALL take ritual positions in a circle.

The VEILED ONES appear and bring fruit and wine. And TELLE, the black witch, produces a long pipe with a small bowl, lights it, and they pass the pipe among themselves.

Music begins. The VEILED ONES dance.

TELLE throws a pinch of magic powder into a lighted urn. Perfumed, colored smoke spews forth)

TELLE

(croons and hums)

Great Spirit of the Black tribe . . . visit our efforts and endow them with your righteous magic.

SORO

(Sings spirit song)
How do we find ourselves here
far from heaven
on the far side of hell
How are we the way
we are
                when
in the way
in the way
                of seeking

but far from heaven
haven   Oh
Once ago
oh, once ago
we were cast
from our homes
from our homes
and left to wander
these woods
and do cursed deeds
against the devils
of our memories
of our memories
Once ago
Oh, once ago
the sun people conquered
the moon people
the sun people conquered
the moon people
and we wanderers appeared
yes, we wandering woodsmen
appeared
Oh, how do we find ourselves
here
far from heaven
on the far side of hell
Oh, had wanderers inhabited
these forests
before time
or were they too journeying
through
yes, journeying through
through
through

(TELLE throws another pinch of magic powder upon the fire, producing a different colored smoke)

TELLE

Great Spirit of the Black tribe ... visit our efforts and endow them with your righteous magic.

(THEY pass the pipe among themselves. THE VEILED ONES dance a magic love movement as SORO sings and TELLE croons and chants.

SORO completes his song .. the song, spirits and pipe having placed all but TELLE into a divine stupor)

TELLE
(chants)
Secret spirits of the soul
Secret spirits of the soul
steal these warriors
shadows
steal these warriors
shadows
so I may enslave
their/selves to
a sacred cause

Silent spooks of the shade
Silent spooks of the shade
stealthy now
stealthy now
snatch away
their spirit shapes
snatch away
their spirit shapes
seduce their souls
release their lusts
oh, secret spirits
see my sorcery done
see my sorcery done

(TELLE tosses a third colored powder into the fire)

Great Spirit of the Black tribe . . . visit our efforts and endow them with your righteous magic.

(The VEILED ONES change into SHADOW SPIRITS as the MEN rise in a zombie-like Dance of Horpheus.

During the rites the SHADOW SPIRITS take away the shadows of MIJO, LIBO, RAGO, SORO and ROTO.

The lights change. The MEN awake in a lustful state.

The WARRIORS are enslaved within TELLE's spell and undergo a lust/rite: THEY dance, make bawdy and sensual movements, and sing to the "invisible" female spirits who have stolen their shadows.

TELLE observes them from the center of a magic circle that SHE has drawn with the sacred sword, for at times the MEN lewdly attempt to attack her, as THEY would ravage any woman in their drugged, carnal state, if THEY had power to do so)

WARRIORS
(Together. Freeform, like a wet dream)

Women . . . women . . . sexy, sensual, soft, warm, wet women . . . ssssssuuuuuuuhhhh . . . to be in them . . . deep inside their holes . . . to be upon and within them . . . suck . . . burrowing burrowing . . . lick . . . down deep deep inside . . . bite . . . women women . . . give me some . . . we must have women . . . give it to us . . . honey/pot . . . oh, my love . . . titties . . . my beloved . . . ass/hole . . . my darling . . . pussy . . . my dear . . . nipples . . . sweetie . . . short hairs . . . sugar . . . eyelashes . . . honey . . . lips . . . soft, warm, wet . . . kiss . . . sooo gooooo . . . baby . . . sweetcake . . . ummmmmmm . . . darling . . . oh, I must have you . . . ooouuucccchhhh . . . I love you so much, woman . . . oh, jesus . . . can't get you out of my mind . . . Gawd! . . . can't do nothin' without you . . . holy moly . . . can't eat sleep think fight work play dream build without you woman of my sexy dreams and fucking fantasy schemes . . . oooooohhhhhhh . . . women . . . give me some . . . oh, please . . . just a little bit more, baby . . . i want some . . . i need some . . . i need you, baby/dooolll . . . can't do wit'out it . . . just one more time . . . can't stop lovin' you, baby . . . gimme some . . . goin'a go out of my mind without you, girl . . . o, baby baby baby . . . ah, so good . . . so good . . . yes, yes . . . just one more time . . . that's right . . . do that number . . . yeah . . . do it once again . . . oh you know how . . . yeah yeah . . . I loves you baby don't you know that with your fine little foxy sexy self yeeeaaaaahhhhhh . . . so good gracious . . . sock it to me honey baby sugar sweetcake mine . . . uuuuummmmm . . . mine own and only . . . hey, desirable . . . hi, pleasure . . . mine own . . . mine . . . mine own woman of my desires and lusts . . . oooooeeeeeeee . . . make it funky . . .

> (THREE of the VEILED ONES take the identities of the spirit women, AUHV, VETI and ARIE, and tantalize the MEN with their bodies and words.
>
> The MEN are unable to make physical contact with them, due to the SPIRITS' incorporeal states and their own incapacities)

AUHV
(Tantalizes)
I am here . . . I am here . . . come and take me.

RAGO
(In somnolent pursuit)
Again . . . again I suffer . . . What horror is this? Seeing you . . . smelling your sexy scent . . . but unable to reach you?

AUHV
(Weirdly)
Come and get me, Rago.

MIJO
Out of the way, weakling . . . she is a man's woman . . . here . . . I'll take her!

> (HE reaches out, stumbles and falls upon his face, for AUHV is not there)

VETI AND ARIE
(Together)
Ha ha ha ha . . . why do you brave men fall all over yourselves for us mere women?

LIBO AND SORO
(Together)
Demons . . . devilish women of our wet dreams . . . stop your dancing . . . stop your crooning siren songs and stay awhile. . . . Our third legs are stiff and ready for you . . . our leg that has no shoes is ready to walk into your female opening.

AUHV
Come take me, Rago.

RAGO
Wait a minute, baby . . . wait a minute . . . I'm comin' . . . I'm comin' . . .

MIJO
(Recovering)
Mighty men . . . savage swordsmen of flame, blood, death and the future . . . What cruel witchcraft has taken your senses . . . What demonology is this that turns you into creeping curs behind a pack of undisciplined bitches! . . . Get yourselves together, brother/men, or by the sword of my great ancestor Seniag the Mighty I shall sever your crazed heads from your lust filled bodies.

> (A strange light falls over MIJO. The wind rises and thunder is heard.
>
> Smiling from her refuge within the magic circle, TELLE speaks:)

TELLE
You have recovered, my sons . . . you are ready to lead our journey even farther . . .

> (HE approaches her. THEY reach out with their swords, pierce the barrier of the magic circle and touch blades; the sky opens, the shadow spirits vanish, and the MEN recover with their shadows intact)

LIBO, RAGO, SORO, ROTO
Free! Free from this curse! Free! Free!

MIJO
But we have far to journey . . . and each stage we pass through brings us wisdom . . . but more loss of our former selves.

RAGO
It is our future selves that we seek, risen master.

TELLE
(Steps from circle)
We said, holy men. But now we must kiss the sacred sliver, pointer-of-the-way-that-it-is, give thanks to the great Black presence that guides every action . . . and move on in unity.

> (THEY do a brief ritual of kissing the sacred sword and offering thanks for their salvation and deliverance from hell, then instantly THEY are transported through the Gate of Love, the second gate and across the Bridge of Purgatory)

> The tinkle of tiny bells. A warm, richly colored place.

> A MAN, hooded, dressed in black, is seen kneeling, meditating; HE plays a string instrument and chants:

TIHWO
Kindness to the Young
Generosity to the Poor
Good counsel to Friends
Forebearance to Fools
Respect to the Learned

Fasting is only the saving of bread. Formal prayer is for old men and women. Pilgrimage is a worldly pleasure. Conquer the heart—its mastery is conquest indeed.

(HE repeats)
Kindness to the Young
Generosity to the Poor
Good counsel to Friends
Forebearance with Enemies
Respect to the Learned

Fasting is only the saving of bread. Formal prayer is for old men and women. Pilgrimage is a worldly pleasure. Conquer the heart—its mastery is conquest indeed.

(HE kneels upon a path, in front of a huge gate.

MIJO enters. HE follows the path until HE meets TIHWO, the kneeling man)

MIJO

Greetings, solemn worshipper . . . I pray that your prayers are over so that I may pass you by and enter the gate and cross over the bridge to the land of Ooo Blah Dee . . . the land of the future.

TIHWO

Greetings to you, lordly leader . . . my whispers with eternal wisdom are never ended . . . but I must inform you that this gate is not for you to pass through . . . not at this moment.

MIJO

What! . . . you would hinder me on my path? . . . You, gatekeeper, move aside or be a martyr to your ignorance and duty.

THREE: HEAVEN

Place of Intuitive Knowledge

TIHWO

My only duty is to bring you truth, brother Mijo.

MIJO

(Taken aback)
You know my name? . . . what kind of spy are you?

TIHWO

A divine spy, brotherman . . . Now turn away from this point in reality . . . you will transverse your destiny soon enough . . . but not now. There are numerous gates fixed upon the path of knowledge . . . and the knowledge that one knows to be his own knowledge . . . is the true knowledge . . . There are paths leading to life . . . and there are those leading to death . . . but this path for you leads to nothingness . . . have patience, my friend.

MIJO

(Draws his weapon)
If I had patience . . . I would not be who I am. Move aside, blocker of the path . . . or defend yourself.

TIHWO

There is little defense against ignorance.

MIJO

So be it!

> MIJO lunges. TIHWO stops him short with a psychic stab of his forefinger to MIJO's forehead; MIJO freezes, caught in an energy field, and TIHWO takes his sword from him and severs his head from his body)

MIJO'S HEAD

(Gasping and choking)

Wait! . . . what is this? A new dream? . . . What seemed to happen couldn't have happened . . . could it?

> (MIJO's body stands confused, lost, its arms moving randomly, its legs slightly jerking, finding no direction.

Fearful and fearsome)

My body . . . my body . . . I can't find it! . . . I don't have it with me any longer . . . What curse has befallen me? . . . Ohhhh . . . I cannot move my arms! . . . My sturdy, swift legs that carried me to the fight . . . where are you? What has happened? . . . I have lost my way in this lost land . . . Where are you neck? Where are you neck from where atop I swiveled myself and wound my big white goo goo eyes in the springtime of my youth at every curving ankle and full/back/shaped African female behind.

(Crying)

. . . Oooooeeeee . . . where are you shoulders? . . . Oh oh oh . . . shoulders . . . where once I carried the world and the weight . . . the weight of the people's burdens that were entrusted to my keeping . . . Iiiiieeeee . . . what if I should tilt over in my roundness like a football and become prey for tom cats? . . . Where are you chest from whose inner cavity a heart thumped and thudded . . . as generous as an elephant's! . . . Where are you me . . . let me be whole again . . . not split and parted, divided, like the nation of Black groping forms that I am a soldier of righteousness to . . . What is a warrior without a body to be his fighting machine . . . ooooohhhhhhh . . . Why don't I die? How can I be here but not dead like this? . . . This sorcery is beyond my understanding . . . ooooohhhhhhh . . . if I could pinch myself I would wake myself from this dread and unfunny dream.

> (TIHWO places the head back upon the body.

> Immediately, MIJO falls to his knees in supplication)

MIJO

Great Master . . . I . . .

> (TIHWO strikes him gently with a touch of power and HE falls into a coma)

TIHWO

Rest ... rest ... sincere savage ... Rest and heal and become even stronger.

    (LIBO enters)

LIBO

What! ... Ho! ... what simple mystery is this that lies across my path? ... I see my warrior leader, Mijo, lying still, as if the finger of death had traced his brow ... And there is this strange, dark aspected dude. Here, you! Speak now ... what is the meaning of this?

TIHWO

Your eyes have told you all you need to know, my friend.

LIBO

My eyes! ... yes ... My eyes ... what have they told me? That my Ace Boon Coon, Brother Mijo, lies dead at your feet .. that my A.B.C. has been bushwhacked ... that you stand over him like a satanic vulture ... for what purpose? ... To pick the flesh from his settling bones being the cannibal that you are? ... To breathe the last whiffs of his escaping soul/spirit breath rising through his nostrils, expelled by the vacuum of his having left this gruesome place?

TIHWO

Your eyes tell you very little truth, Warrior Libo!

LIBO
    (Frightened)
Who told you my name? ... It must have been Mijo before you struck him from behind.

TIHWO

Your accusing tongue is no keener than your intelligence or eyesight, foolish fool. Mijo is in deep slumber ... he only awaits my call to be with us again.

LIBO
    (Draws sword)
Awaits your call! ... but who will call you from the place of darkness that I shall now send you, disgusted monster!

        (LIBO advances upon TIHWO. When HE is within strik-
        ing range, LIBO lifts his weapon, and TIHWO makes a
        sudden magical gesture, igniting LIBO's sword into a
        brilliant cold flame.

        LIBO stares at his glowing sword and becomes blinded.
        HE drops the fiery thing and clutches his eyes. Blood
        squirts from between his fingers and HE tries to hold his
        melting eyeballs back inside his skull)

AAAAAĀAAAAAAAAGGGGGGG ... AAAHHHH ... AHHHHHHH ...
I've BEEN PLUNGED THIS SECOND TO THE DEPTHS OF HELL! ... Oh
pain ... oh pure black lightless pain ... What suffering this ... iiiiieeeee ...
my brain is afire ... but there is no light ... the pain of my melting eyes is
beyond belief or faith ... even in the rescue of death! ... gory gory gory is
this story where I find myself in agony for glory ... and eyeless ...
eeeeaaaahhhhhh ... god god god god god god! SAVE ME!

> (TIHWO passes his hand over LIBO's covered face.
> LIBO stops his writhing, lowers his hands, looks out of
> clear eyes and smiles. Then TIHWO stuns him with a
> touch)

TIHWO
Your vision will be clear when I awaken you.

(RAGO enters)

RAGO
You there, Black Cloaked Stranger ... have you seen ...
> (HE spies MIJO and LIBO)
Holy Moly! ... my strong-fisted road buddies seem to be sleeping on the job
... I'll approach them cautiously and awaken them with my ridicule and
scolding ... but as I draw close I see that the deepness of their sleep lies
somewhere on the far side of dreams ... And this black-hooded figure that
stands near them fills me with awe.

TIHWO
You, Brother Rago ... Stop where you are!

RAGO
I see that you know me.

TIHWO
I know many things, young lover of unattainable females ... and I know
that you are not ready to take this path ... unless I guide you.

RAGO
> (Points)
Is this what you call guidance, evil one? ... The slaying of my comrades in their
sleep!

TIHWO
Youth is so impetuous and your ears have not opened to truth.

RAGO
I follow the path set for me by my brother warriors. I follow the teachings
and direction of our clan.

(HE draws his sword and slowly advances upon TIHWO)
I follow the way of my elders; I follow the right and correct path laid down
by history and convention; I follow the way that my fathers and their
fathers set for me to follow; I follow . . .

TIHWO

Then follow you must.
(HE makes a mysterious motion)

RAGO

. . . I follow the way that . . . ba ba ba ba ba . .

(At TIHWO's gesture a strange light covers RAGO, and
HE is seen to bend down on all fours and begin bleating
like a sheep.

SORO and ROTO enter)

SORO

Hark! . . . we must be approaching mountains . . . I hear the bleating of
bighorns.

ROTO

Bighorns? . . . Bleating? . . . But, brother, we have not ascended a moun-
tainous incline . . . Bleats as such come from sheep not goats that stroll
across the mountain tops, my misguided missionary.

(THEY see RAGO walking on fours and bleating)

SORO AND ROTO

(Together)
SAAAAY WHAAAT!

SORO

What is this? . . . Have we lost our way and stumbled upon another illusion?

ROTO

Impossible! . . . We are the scouts of this divine expedition, are we not, foe
to deception? . . . And we are in the lead . . . as well as behind any hoax to
make us appear less than we are.

SORO

Yeabo! . . . to that, ready Roto. Be heroic . . . come, let us gaze closer into
this enigma.

(THEY discover MIJO and LIBO.)

SORO AND ROTO
(Together)
UUUUUUUUUUUUUHHHHHHHHHH . . .

(At this sight THEY draw their weapons and frantically
search about for an adversary.

(TIHWO steps from the shadows; at the sight of him,
SORO and ROTO panic, having backed into one another, spin about and engage in a furious bout with one
another.

TIHWO casts a strangely colored cloud over them. And
SORO and ROTO become invisible)

SORO AND ROTO
(Together. Invisible, walking about)
We're lost . . . gone . . . poof! . . . disappeared from our own sights. To be
without substance or content . . . to be without shadow or shape . . . We
can't see ourselves, be ourselves . . . But how did we become nothing? . . . a
space in air . . . an empty circle . . . a nothing . . . a blank . . . a vacuum . . .
Should we think ourselves ghosts? . . . Spirits? . . . when we are still flesh and
juices and feces turned colorless, though still smelly, but without form? . . .
ohhhh . . . save us, master of all men. Save us from this living problem of
being unseen, unfelt, unknown, uncared for, unnoticed . . . as only mysterious footprints left in the sandy road, mornings after midnights of misgivings
and doubts.

TIHWO, the hooded master, assumes a position of meditation, as SORO and ROTO bemoan their fate, RAGO
bleats and acts like nervous goat, and MIJO and LIBO
lay still in coma and from being stunned.

TELLE, the Black Witch, enters with her entourage of
four SPIRIT PRESENCES which hum her praises, strew
flower petals in her path, and fan away from her any
unpleasantness.

SHE stops, taking in the scene fully. The stage becomes
still. The SPIRIT PRESENCES drift away. And TELLE
fixes her gaze upon TIHWO and carefully approaches
him, the Sacred Blade held at the ready.

Within striking distance of him, SHE halts, and begins to
raise the mighty sword. TIHWO slowly looks up, pulls
his hood back, revealing his startling face, and silently
TELLE sinks to her knees in front of him, places her
sword in his hands and kisses his feet.

At this MIJO, LIBO, RAGO, SORO and ROTO become normal, and THEY and the SPIRIT PRESENCES sing:)

TOGETHER

Kindness to the Young
Generosity to the Poor
Good counsel to Friends
Forebearance with Enemies
Indifference to Fools
Respect to the Learned

Fasting is only the saving of bread. Formal prayer is for old men and women. Pilgrimage is a worldly pleasure. Conquer the heart—its mastery is conquest indeed.

(Having kissed TIHWO's feet and tapped the ground with her forehead three times, TELLE withdraws to the ranks of her escort after the song, and the GROUP forms a magic circle about the MASTERFUL MAN. HE speaks:)

TIHWO

Power expressed is more profound than power spoken of. Forgive me, my brothers and sisters . . . for power expressed is more complete than power spoken of. Have mercy upon your lowly servant.

(The circle closes in upon him, and THEY give him a thorough beating.

Beating him just short of unconsciousness, THEY pull away, allowing him to rise, then with him THEY ALL dance in harmony)

ALL TOGETHER
(As THEY dance)
THE ATTAINMENT OF HARMONY IS KNOWN AS HEAVEN! THE ATTAINMENT OF HARMONY IS KNOWN AS HEAVEN! THE ATTAINMENT OF HARMONY IS KNOWN AS HEAVEN!

(THEY lift TIHWO upon their shoulders and in a kingly procession THEY march through the Gate of Intuitive Knowledge, the third gate, and cross the Bridge of Heaven)

THE END

MICHAEL McCLURE

MR. PLUMM

HEY, MR. PLUMM,
YOU'RE A BUM.
DON'T BE DUMB.
Get off your ass —
put down that glass.
You are going to get
big soft beer tits
underneath your tie-dyed shirts.
Are you going to eat strawberries till you come?
What about the war?
Are you a kind of whore
who complains about it
while you live in a sticky dirty house
and smoke your joints?
Put down that glass
and shake your ass
till you really are some kind of Tyger
and not a frothy pussy
soaking up
the Dairy Queens.

Man, you can really eat a burger
and I know your fridge is full.
Anybody who says you are dull
must be crazy.
You've got sweet wine,
and cigarettes,
cat-piss bathtub acid,
and everything is fine.

You fight the revolution
and you are in a state of evolution
because you know the solution
is to live on welfare,
unemployment,
and to do some panhandling too.
You can even deal a ki
and get a hundred extra sixpacks.
That's your war against the state!
You don't fight with any simple hate.
You are going to get a great big car
and drive it far

(*you're lookin' good, man!*)
to hear a transvestite whacking a guitar.
—And every fume
that you exhume

from the gas tank
will kill another pig.

Why,
you are really big!
You are the STUFF!
Man, there's no guff
to you,
except that little bit of psychic fat
that hangs down from your lower chin —
or sometimes you're a little thin
from sucking drano up your nose
or sticking needles in your arm.
It's true, man, you almost glow
(you've got charm!)
you're so wonderful!

When there's thunder
and it shakes the street with rain
then you don't have to move
—it's all the same
whether things are dry or wet,
or smeared with dog shit,
'cause, man,
you are a revolutionary,
a poet,
and a mystic!

•

WE ARE ENTHUSIASTIC
about how you strut
and shake your butt
(man, you've got so much of it).
You've got lots of bottom!
You tell us about everything that's rotten.
You are *the* authority.
You chant your mantra
twice a month
and then you point your finger
like the stinger
of a bee turned all gold and noble

at those who do not do their duty
to the revolution!
REVOLUTION!
Why you tell them, man!
There are not enough free double feature movies!
the world doesn't bring you raspberries and country ham
—you have got to walk to the store to get them.
Your dope won't stay lit
and sometimes you're forced to skip a hit
of the latest alphabetic psychedelic.

You have to get up at noon
and stumble 'round your room.
How sad!
MAN, YOU ARE ONE OF THE PEOPLE!
PEOPLE IS WHAT YOU ARE!
You are the Natural Leader!
Why don't they listen?
Once,
you read Marx
and slept in the parks.
You got extra dirty fingernails,
and your breath smells like stout malt liquor ales.
.You have been around
and know the secret ways
to run the ship of state aground.
You left the wife and kids with the folks
in Cincinnati.
Then you came here
to quell our fear
and give us a steer
towards the Revolution,
'cause man,
you are an environmentalist,
a revolutionary,
a poet,
and a mystic!

CHARLES UPTON

FUCK MYSTICISM

Robert Graves said: "Yoga is the most refined solitary vice imaginable." Even when I categorically disagreed with this statement, I still *loved* it.

I think yoga is a profound science and a valuable tool—but to immerse yourself in the whole value-system of yoga without questioning & criticising at every point is to embark upon an incredibly one-sided course of development. Take for example the little pamphlet I read the other day, in which this crazed old Sikh guru, Kirpal Singh, actually said: "Sexuality is death." Well *this* guy let the cat out of the bag. I can just see those shrewd old yogis sitting up there in the foothills of the Himalayas for a thousand years: "Hoo-boy, look at those Americans, they fucking themselves silly over there—they have turned sex into amusement park beginning to get a little tired out—so go, bring them the message brother Kirpal—the Americans are getting ripe . . . ."

This dirty old man and his ilk are perpetuating one of the worst crimes the human race ever perpetuated upon itself—the denial of sexuality—again! To say sex is death is like saying it's a sin to have a left arm. This sick attitude makes only two courses of action possible: To hide from sexuality forever in the heaven of the spirit & sever all contact with the world, or to immerse yourself in brutal exhausting lust. Heaven & Hell—*again*! Because sexuality so cruelly deserted by the human spirit *is* Hell—and the spirit cut off from the lifegiving embrace of the senses is simply *nowhere*. Yoga uses the spirit to break the tyranny of the senses—fine—but who will break the tyranny of the *spirit*? The healthy function of the spirit is to *free* sensuality from its smoky self-intoxication, to enlighten it & let it soar—and the healthy function of sensuality is to bring spirituality down out of its cold & windless places, embrace it & make it real! *Fuck* these cowards who have neither the courage to live nor the courtesy to die, but try to make slow death a lifetime career. Leave death to the dead!

It's unhealthy to spend your whole life cultivating a single experience, even if it's an infinite one. The mystic vision should be the crown of a full & vigorous life—otherwise it becomes a foul hidingplace, a voyeuristic trance. Heaven is a home to the warrior; to the refugee it is a prison. Nor is the true paradise even attainable to someone who has squashed himself to get it—God never yields himself to those who seek God alone. Any "spirituality" which is based upon escape from anything or denial of anything is a *fake*.

Now in the science of yoga, especially kundalini yoga, the attempt is to send the life-energy, the kundalini or Shakti, up the spine & unite her with her Lord or Shaktiman in the Sahasrara, the "thousand-petalled lotus." As she ascends the ladder of the chakras (the energy-centers which give life & consciousness to the body) they dissolve—they *die*. Finally, in the last ecstasy, the body becomes stiff, corpselike—actually *cold*. If this ecstasy is not terminated, the result is death. Now does this sound like a healthy practice? How'd you like to catch your husband or wife in this condition? Well, let's be fair. The yogis don't actually recommend death; rather, after the two life-principles have consummated their love, the kundalini is urged to return to her seat at the base of the spine. As she does, the chakra-centers are rekindled & filled with the Amrita, or nectar, which was produced during the ecstasy—the God-come of the mystic fuck. So the full process is not a death, but a death-and-resurrection—which I have no quarrel with, because death-and-resurrection is the way all real growth happens. But how many people who start out on this path ever reach the end? Too few. Most simply spend their lives leaning away from life in the direction of death, always fading but never quite gone.

Wilhelm Reich found that the natural sensual energy-flow in the human body is not up, but *down* the spine. He discovered that people who couldn't have full orgasms had energy blocks, muscle armor, which interfered with this downward flow. He even traced the origins of the fascist mind to this kind of thwarted sensuality.

Yoga seeks to reverse the natural flow of life-energy, to divert it away from sensuality & use it to energize the higher centers, the lotuses of the mind & spirit. Which is good—no human being can reach his full potential, if there is such a thing, unless these centers are awakened & fed—but watch out! Watch out for the kind of yoga which claims that the higher centers are *better* than the lower ones! That's absurd! Is my head better than my loins? Beware of fascist yogis who come on with: "Don't be a penis all your life kid. Grow up. Be a Brain." That's a failed sensualist talking if I ever heard one. Beware of the kind of yoga which fills the head with light and the belly with ice! And who wants that dumb Platonic heaven anyway?

The function of yoga & related arts should be to energize all the centers equally, introduce them to one another & let them fall in love. Because to prefer one center over another is to subtly *identify* with it—and that's just another trick to maintain the ego. So before you start doing yoga & sending all that energy up your spine, be sure that you have no blocks in the *downward* flow—be sure you aren't using yoga to deny & escape some wound to your natural sensuality. And don't *ever* let that energy desert your lower centers, unless you are prepared to go the whole way of tantric death-and-resurrection.

And listen girls—a lot of "spiritual" trips are nothing more than male chauvinism, a kind of psychic homosexuality. Yoga was *invented* by men in one of the most sensual female cultures that ever existed, as a method of *escape.* They didn't want to *mess* with you, so they choked off their semen & split for the high Platonic Brahmanhood of the isolated Male spirit. Nirvana is like a pub where all the male Buddhas sit around getting drunk on the nectar of bliss & rapping about how glad they are to get away from the Wife—a little woman called Maya.

Now in the history of consciousness, such a move was necessary—the male consciousness always has to depart from the female consciousness, the mother-consciousness, into a totally male space in order for the male power to come into its own—otherwise, if the young man shifts his connection directly from his mother to his mate without this intervening rite of passage, his mate becomes just another mother to him—and we all know *that* problem . . .

But the human race has already departed too far from the Mother. We've already *gotten* off. We're so far away from the Earth now that we can gouge & slash her with merciless cruelty and not even *know* it, or treat the whole thing like a fantasy, like it was all happening on TV. It's the Jesus Freaks, never masters of subtlety, who best reveal this mentality. They say: "The Earth is Hell. It is here to be burnt. Get off with Christ, brother, while there's still time." Get off? We've *already* gotten *too far* off. What we've got to do is *come back*. If we don't love this beautiful Earth & love the beautiful bodies with which we walk this Earth & love the beautiful senses through which she streams into us, we're gonna set this place afire, & all "get off" for good.

There's a new Puritanism sneaking through this country today under a smokescreen of porno-flicks & free love. We're profoundly weary of our own cruel adolescent self-indulgence, & so we're closing down—how many tight hard angular people walking down the streets!

Come Holy Spirit, fill the loins of your people, give us back to one another again.

SOME BACK TALK FROM MA KALI

something broke a few years ago . . . . in fact everything broke . . . . the absolute inconceivability of future time shattered society . . . . we had tried the obvious, through psychedelics, but we found we could not withstand the obvious . . . . all our dreams came true, left us, then the Abyss opened, vast colorless stretch of empty time . . . . we remembered eternity's unspoken hour in diagrams . . . . now swamis spring up & flourish to service droves of wetbacks & defectors from the physical plane . . . . sly & mysteriously healthy young men prance down the street in Hindu garb, eyed with contempt by sharp neat Indian exchange students . . . young kids with blown wordminds de-sert the English language forever . . . . our mythology is shattered, blowing back in time like scrapped leaves, who grabs one is holy . . . . so he forms a cult of course . . . . mystery cults who creep you with the smell of secrecy & power . . . . Christian Street Gangs who creep you with guilt & sentimentality, walk in with their old cooked-down ancestral symbols & appropriate all the Good in the area so as to use it for extortion & blackmail . . . . or you can always take a course in Industrial Magic . . . . more & more opportunities opening up, each one smaller & screwier . . . . like a friend of mine said: Everything is possible—but nothing is likely . . . .

and the hungry female magnet sucking images to the center of this world, is Kali—she rips off every mask, strips us to the deathless rind—this is her age & her stomping-ground—mad, dancing, pounding the broken flesh of history .... the years pass by like months, they age us like decades .... remember the obvious? remember the Clear Light when there wasn't anything there? then came memory ten-thousand feet per second so it looked like it was really happening .... and we bore down through that ocean, cars on the street people on the sidewalks look like hot fish in a slow green current undersea .... all going the same way: toward a hole in the ocean .... six thousand years of time pouring across our eyes, draining away .... they've appropriated everything, every memory .... time is the only commodity, & there's inflation on the market .... so unweave the old Universe & let it drop .... groan no more under the weight of your name

.... your name is a luxury item & as such is heavily taxed .... drop those Call Letters, outlive them .... only the naked are invisible, and only the invisible shall survive ....

otherwise, as the radiant sky fills our skulls, the earth beneath our feet grows unsteady .... the more trees you see on television the more real trees begin to look like television trees, ghostly, unsure .... they have yoked the Coca-cola image to every blazing distance in the Big Sky Country, pierced by a rocket-sled's fiery track in the yellow-orange sunset .... because memories, like stars, go through Redshift .... the farther the faster they move away the redder they get, leaving a cold blue hunger in the eye of the Sun .... those dreams that peel off your body like smoke, don't follow them! all dreams are going back now to the Moon where they began—and the Moon is red with blood ....

DESTINY MANIFEST

What happened was, the journey ended. And some of us, Americans to the bone, had to die to keep on going.

Always we were looking back, into the yellow sunset radiance of the Past, or forward, into the electronic future ozone blue Dawn. We were never *here* before. It is this present reality of things which makes everything look so unreal to this nation of mythic travelers.

The Beat Generation was on a mythic journey in physical terms. When I was younger I remember how the road ahead & the hum of the engine used to open up like great Paradise Gates. That trip ended about five years ago on the coast of California. Time ended here, dissipated West, poured out through a hole in the physical shape of our destiny, through LSD and the Vietnam War, the clear current lost forever in an Asian vortex, destiny unmanifest. Passage to more than India ended too; the American Dream the Greek Dream the Hebrew Dream gone back to the Moon where all dreams start. Nixon to China to complete that circle, a faceless entity simply blown there by history's last wind . . . . and Johnnie come drifting home again without a face, we catch him like a balloon & place him in a child's hand at a middleaged birthday party.

And if many are tired now? We are tired from jogging in place. The journey—is ended. The Future—is over. The Past— blown out like a flame. Arrived.

So Mother Necessity comes now & taps us on the shoulder: "Wake up Sonny, stop Mooning over the ancient Sunlight by the shores of Galilee & all yr sweet country wine. Turn off that TV set, get up & find yourself something to eat—Mother Hubbard's been here & gone.

LAWRENCE FERLINGHETTI

RIDING NOTES

or *Zen and the Art of Riding to a Buddhist Ceremony*
Honoring an Anglican Casuist East-West Philosopher
One Hundred Days After His Death

Circumambulating Mount Tamalfuji on horseback and thinking that the best position for deep meditation must certainly be the foetal position in a warm bed with covers over head since the foetus is doing perfect Buddhist Breathing or Yoga Yinhalation in its warm womb not with its lungs but through the umbilical cord breathing with the very rhythm of the Great Body of Being in a steady state of meditation rapt in satori or numb in nirvana like my horse or the animals of the field (cows mooing *om* backwards) as if each knew in its gut or cud that there cud be no single answer to any Zen koan but rather a myriad of possible enlightened answers so that the sound of one answer cancels out the sound of another thus leaving only the silence of 'dumb' beasts who can't clap with one hand or hoof

So riding around and down to Muir's Beach and up Green Gulch to the Zen Center I chanted to my horse on the weigh of Zen but found he responded not nor snorted any sutra since he was in fact far into his own profound meditation in which responding to any Other was irrelevant if not pedestrian

And so caught up together in tantric tether we rode up together to that Green Gulch ranch and passed one Zen Robin Hood practicing archery and one Friar Tuck of Zen snoring under a greenwood tree and thus proceeding on did come upon by chance the beginning of a Buddhist ceremony celebration of the death of one enlightened East-West philosopher Watts his name one hundred days after the Emptying of his body into the Buddhist void

And there was good Richard Baker-Roshi at the head of a little silent procession in sunlight in that green valley just entering into the semi-dark of the barn made over into a zendo where exactly one hundred humans sat in half-lotus positions and Richard Baker-Roshi looking like the white King of a chessboard or the Wizard of Oz wearing a huge sunshiny silver cone on his head as if his high hard head had been made over into the Transamerica Pyramid with blue sky and gulls flying and the sun a gold coin

And the One Hundred Humans crouching there in the semi-dark the One Hundred Transitory Imaginary Sentient Beings just sitting there breathing together as one Being half-lotus half-enlightened half-approaching the satori state of my sixteenyearold dog now underground or my horse standing now with head high ears forward in his constant state of meditation in which trying to get his back legs folded up into the full-lotus position was definitely not his Bag though Ganesha the elephant-god had done it at least in statues

And I sitting there in half-lotus half-ass position on him the horse in all of us peering into the dark zendo through a barn door and every once in awhile the horse stretching his neck and also peering inside to shake his high head yet never say neigh

And anyway they were all now chanting the Great Prajna Paramita Sutra slowly and solemnly and with great force and beauty and I was thinking this should surely change the world as when they chant it altogether at the Zen Center in San Francisco I hope it changes at least the nearby Fillmore ghetto into a place of light & enlightenment where no more hunger or evil will ever exist

But anyway in the Great Prajna Paramita the great untainted mantram we were all a part of that Emptiness in which there is no form, no sensation, thought or consciousness, in which there is no eye, no ear, no nose, no tongue, no body and no mind, and also no annihilation of it all, and so also no old old age, nor death nor suffering, and we were all a part of that great cycle made of meat Great Chain of Being, all beings being one O wheel of meat made of us turning and turning

And I was on a cycle made of meat on which I peddled in Western saddle And that cycle of a sudden turned and whirled and reared and in that whirring then I heard far off the sea's long long withdrawing *om* and heard not the voices still so beatifically chanting and saw not the zendo transcend itself nor heard at a later date the Board of Directors of the Society for Comparative Philosophy telling me that the transcription of the tape of that One Hundred Days Celebration couldn't be published in this Anthology since the Board felt the original thrust of the Celebration should not be blunted by publication elsewhere than in the book of it they were preparing to sell for imaginary money, the philosopher having maintained himself and the Society on a great barge which took a thousand silver dollars a month to keep afloat (and in a comix-strip balloon above my head just then I saw the famous great Stone Boat of an oriental Emperor plunging suddenly straight down to the Buddhist bottom) so that I was forced to fabricate instead this dumb profane account to honor Watt, a light, a hundred Watts

After the above was set in type, Baker-roshi prevailed upon the Society for Comparative Philosophy to allow the transcript of the ceremony to be published here, and it follows.

ONE HUNDREDTH DAY CEREMONY
FOR ALAN WATTS

Green Gulch Farm
February 2, 1974
Led by Baker-roshi

Yu Zan Myo Ko, Great Founder,
Opener of the Zen Samadhi Gate of Enlightenment
for so many beings throughout these many worlds;
Great Hero, you have crossed over,
completely taken refuge in the Buddha,
Buddha's child shining in everything.

Now we will come back from grief, come over from grief, and find you in all things, in the flow of our own heart wisdom, as you found us in your great mercy; O Kanzeon, Avalokitesvara, one thousand arms, eleven heads. You showed us the many ways.

Gary Snyder wrote:
"(You) blazed out the new path for all of us,
and came back and made it clear. Explored
the side canyons and deer trails, and
investigated cliffs and thickets.

Many guides would have us travel single
file, like mules in a pack train, and
never leave the trail. (You) taught us
to move forward like the breeze—tasting
the berries, greeting the blue jays, learning
and loving the whole terrain."

Now we have rested your ashes. Found your new home. Acknowledged the great stupa of your pure body, difficult to see, neither big nor small, found nor lost. O Alan, wide joyous loving mind, we enter your field anew.

[Together everyone chants the Maha Prajna Paramita Hridaya Sutra.]

Dedication:
　　May we awaken the true compassion of Buddha
　　having chanted the Heart Sutra of well-gone wisdom
　　We offer the merit of this life to
　　the great original teacher, Shakyamuni Buddha,
　　the first master in China, Bodhidharma,
　　the first master in Japan, Eihei Dogen,
　　The Bodhisattva of perfect wisdom, Manjusri,
　　and all the Buddhas and Patriarchs.
　　May their true compassion be with all beings.

[Together everyone chants the Dai Hi Shin Dharani (mantra).]

Dedication:
　　We have chanted many things for you, O Alan,
　　and there have been many offerings from friends
　　fellow Buddhists and fellow teachers. From you,
　　we have learned to turn toward emptiness, seeing
　　the transiency of this life, and yet seeing your
　　nature in all things, the great merit of your
　　spirit. Thus we now offer ourselves in this
　　resolve to all beings to continue your work.

Everyone chants:　　JI HO SAN SHI I SHI HU
　　　　　　　　　　　SHI SON BU SA MO KO SA
　　　　　　　　　　　MO KO HO JA HO RO MI

ALLEN GINSBERG

JAWEH AND ALLAH BATTLE

Jaweh with Atom bomb
    Allah cuts throat of Infidels
Jaweh's armies beat down neighboring Tribes
Will Red Sea Waters close & drown th'armies of Allah?

Israel's tribes worshipping the Golden Calf
    Moses broke the Tablets of Law.

Zalmon Schacter Lubovitcher Rebbe what you say
      Stone Commandments broken on the ground
  Sufi Sam whaddya say
      Shall Prophet's companions dance circled
        round Synagogue while Jews doven bearded
          electric inside?
Both Gods Terrible!   Awful Jaweh Allah!
      Both hook nosed gods, circumcised.
Jaweh Allah which unreal?
         Which stronger Illusion?
          Which stronger Army?
     Which gives most frightening command?
       Which God tribe more numerous?
What God maintain egohood in Eden? Which Nameless?
      Which enter Abyss of Light?
The worlds of Gods, Warriors, Humans, Animals & Flowers,
    Hell Beings, even Hungry Ghosts all die.
All Jews all Moslems'll die all Israelis all Arabs
    Pig Snake and cock eat each other & Perish
Cairo's millions and Jerusalem's multitudes suffer Death's
      dream Armies in battle!
Yea let tribes wander to tin camps at cold Europe's border?
Yea let the Million sit in desert shantytowns with tin cups?
I'm a Jew cries Allah! Buddha circumsized!
     Snake bringing apples to Eden—
  Alien, Wanderer, Caller of the Great Call!
What Prophet born on this ground
        bound me Eternally to Palestine, circled by Armies
          tanks, droning bomber machines, radar
           electric computers?
What Mind directed Irgun Stern Gang Al Fatah Black September?
  Meyer Lansky? Nixon Shah? Brezhnev Hussein one-eyed Dayan
    Golda Meir & Kissinger bound me with arms?
HITLER AND STALIN SENT ME HERE!
  WEITZMAN & BEN-GURION SENT ME HERE!
    NASSER AND SADAT SENT ME HERE!

ARAFAT SENT ME HERE!   MESSIAH SENT ME HERE!
GOD SENT ME HERE!
Hungary sent me here!
Buchenwald sent me here! Vietnam sent me here!
My Lai sent me here!
Lidice sent me here!
My mother sent me here!
I WAS BORN HERE in Israel, Arab
circumcised, my father had a coffee shop in
Jerusalem
One day the Soldiers came & told me to walk down road
my hands up
walk away leave my house business forever!
The Israelis sent me here!
The Sphinx & Pyramid sent me here!
JAWEH AND ALLAH SENT ME HERE!
Abraham will take me to his bosom!
Mohammed will guide me to Paradise!
Christ sent me here to be crucified!
BUDDHA WILL WIPE ALL THIS OUT AND DESTROY THE WORLD!

The New York Times and Cairo Editorialist Heikal sent me here!
Commentary and Palestine Review sent me here
The International Zionist Conspiracy sent me here!
Syrian Politicians sent me here! Heroic Pan-Arab
Nationalists sent me here!
They're sending Armies to my side—
The Americans & Egyptians are sending bombing planes
tanks
Russians help me battle for my righteous house
my Soul's   dirt Spirit's Nation body's
boundaries & Self's territory my
Zionist homeland my Palestinian Inheritance
The Capitalist Communist & Third World Peoples
Republics Dictatorships Police States Socialisms
& Democracies
Are all sending Deadly Weapons to our aid!
We shall triumph over the Enemy!
Maintain our Separate Identity! Proud History
evermore!
Defend our own bodies here this Holy Land!   This hill
Golgotha never forget, never relinquish,
inhabit eternal
under Allah Christ Jaweh forever one God
Shema Yisroel Adonoi Eluhenud Adonoi Echad!
La Illaha Illa 'llah Hu!
OY! AH! HU!   OY! AH! HU!
SHALOM!   SHANTIH!   SALAAM!

January 13, 1974

REINHARD LETTAU

THE ENEMY

translated by A. Leslie Willson & the author

OUTSIDE IT IS RAINING. THE GENERAL COMES BACK.

"Did you win?" he is asked.

"I did not find the enemy," the general replies. The men who have come in with him stand in dripping overcoats next to him. Puddles on the floor.

"The adversary did not show up. We did not find him anywhere," says the general.

Meanwhile the field marshal has entered; they woke him up. He sits down on a chair which is pushed over for him. There he buttons his uniform jacket from bottom to top; then he says: "Report on the battle."

The general casts down his eyes. "I informed the gentlemen just now that locating the adversary was difficult. For instance, once we thought we had come across an enemy patrol. With the fog it's hard. Phantoms all over." He points behind him.

The field marshal has gotten up now and walked to the window. Creaking of the floor, the field marshal shifts position at the window. Those present watch him there. A soldier steps up next to the field marshal and holds the curtains aside so that the field marshal can look out. The field marshal presses against the glass. In the room quiet prevails. After a while the field marshal says, "Really, you can't see anything outside." The general sighs with relief. Still at the window the field marshal asks, "I suppose you didn't hear the enemy either?"

"Once the enemy was in a tree and imitated a bird," answers the general. "We went over and heard it twittering from up there. Distinct twittering in the foliage. Real birds would have flown away at our approach."

The field marshal goes back into his room. The general points at the doorway.

"Is he alone in there?"

"He is alone a lot. He is always in there."

A colonel enters with two soldiers. Still at the door, he calls out before it is closed: "Where are my troops?" Only then does he notice the general present, salutes.

"Explain that question," says the general.

"Sir, it is raining hard. Last I saw the troops, they were on the road running behind an enemy. The enemy in front, my troops behind. I myself stopped on a rise so I could get a good look. The troops all ran past me. Finally, in the distance, where the road goes uphill, I watched them for a long time, running more slowly. Worn out, they ran like losers behind the enemy."

The field marshal is standing in the open door again.

"Did the enemy turn around at times?" he asks.

The colonel salutes the field marshal, stands vibrating.

"Sir," he says, "the enemy often turned around while running."

"What does the enemy look like?" asks the field marshal.

"This enemy," says the colonel, "how can he be described?"

"Does his appearance correspond to the idea that is held of him back home?" asks the field marshal.

The colonel reflects.

"Describe the appearance of the enemy," says the general. "Does it correspond to our expectations?"

"This enemy is a fairly small man and runs very fast. You can tell by where my troops are. For instance, he has pimples. Through the binoculars I saw pimples on his face."

"So he has pimples?" asks the field marshal. "Yes, go on. I'm listening."

"And he's very small and runs fast, but lop-sided."

"And?" asks the field marshal.

"When he runs, he raises his knees high. Did you win your battle?" he now asks the general.

"Did you hear shooting? Am I singed? My features blackened with smoke?"

"Naturally," says the colonel, "it makes you feel bad when whole companies run after a single enemy."

"Aha," cries the field marshal. "And why? Just because we outnumber him, can't we be in the right? Have I got to stay here alone? Humble myself, run around stooped over? Are dwarfs always to win? You put ten men here, one there; then suddenly the one is right because he's alone, has skin eruptions; but are we devils because we are healthy, tall, ten in number?"

Later, at night, the field marshal is again standing in the room. He is buttoning up his jacket still, and he says: "I've thought it over and I believe we'll beat the enemy today."

Turmoil in front of the house. A major enters the room.

"Why, you have flowers in your hand," says the field marshal.

"Of course, a bouquet," answers the major. He looks at his hand. "Wild flowers."

Then, upon being queried, "You know how the people come out of their houses when we go through a village. We hardly had the village behind us, flat land ahead of us, there in the distance we see men marching toward us, about a thousand. I'd hardly told my men to take cover and they're already on us, go past, on a mass stroll into the village. I push through their columns to the first one, where I expect the leader, take up a position in front of them, and yell out: 'Halt!' 'Why halt?' they shout, and keep marching, so I'm forced to run backwards in order to keep an eye on their forward march. 'Aren't you the enemy?' I yell, whereupon they laugh, toothy grins appear, they grimace, shouting out: 'So you won't be afraid,' and are already past, up the hill, and disappear behind it."

"Are they still behind that hill?"

"We had to decide either to take a look or come here first and make a report."

"All your troops?"

"My troops wanted to see how the report was received here." The major now notices the general. "Didn't you want to have a battle?" he asks him.

Briskly, with shining eyes, the field marshal enters the room in the early morning.

"We shall beat the enemy today," he says.

The adjutant responds.

"Why today?"

Then a lieutenant enters the room. He salutes all sides.

"A man," he says, "said he would show us the place where the enemy is staying, if he isn't underway. Then he said: 'Wait here,' disappeared, came back: 'Maybe somewhere else,' he said. Arriving at somewhere else he called out: 'Behind here.' There: 'No, where we were before.' There: 'now follow me.' Suddenly: 'Now wait,' we waited."

"He didn't come back while you were waiting?"

"No. Not while we were standing there."

"You saw no more of him?"

"On the way back. He was fighting, but there was no one else there. 'Where's your opponent?' we asked him. 'Over there, last I saw,' he said. 'Say, what are you doing?' we asked him then. 'This punch, he'll feel it,' he cried out."

"Did you touch the enemy?" asks the field marshal.

"I grabbed him myself."

"How did he feel to you?" asks the field marshal.

The lieutenant grabs the gentleman next to him.

"Like this gentleman here. Only you have to bend over to touch him."

"About how far?"

The lieutenant goes to his knees.

"This far," he says.

The men now squat below the windowsill, heads level with the table, and take hold of one another.

"And how did you get along here?" asks the lieutenant.

A soldier stumbles in. The men straighten up quickly and turn around toward the door. The soldier stands wavering.

"You have a nice medal there," the field marshal says to him.

"We have never seen a medal that size," says the colonel.

"Where did you get that medal anyway?" asks the adjutant.

The soldier shifts from one foot to the other.

"This medal," he points at the medal, "is my medal."

"Of course," says the field marshal. "Come on over here."

The soldier takes two staggering steps toward the field marshal.

"I suppose the medal is heavy?" asks the field marshal.

"You can hardly wear this medal," says the soldier.

"And where did you get the medal?" asks the field marshal.

"In front of the house. Right by the statue."

"What statue?" cries the field marshal and hurries in front of the house.

The field marshal stands before the house, the officers in a semi-circle behind him. Sun out there.

"Where is the statue?" asks the field marshal. "I do not see a statue."

"There never was a statue here," says the adjutant.

"But over there are many statues," says the general and points to the horizon.

"Those statues are new to me," says the adjutant.

"The variety of poses," says the colonel.

"One next to the house," says the adjutant. He points to the side. In a flash they all are in the room.

The field marshal now issues orders to guard the statues by posting a couple of men about each one. After this has been done, the field marshal stands again at the window. He looks out. Gloomy, foggy day, silent groups in the field, high on the slope, an arm's length away from the window. The field marshal turns back into the room. "One fellow winked," he whispers.

Bleak morning, spent silently. The men sitting around along the wall. The room: small-flowered wall paper, white mantle, ship picture. Brown floor, shining like a mirror. Single, distant, muffled cries from outside. The general looks at a map, which is thickly folded many times; the major holds a book in his hand, stares at the wall. Occasional trips across the room by the field marshal. He steps out of his chamber, motions for the men who are ready to jump up to remain seated, and hurries through the room, watched by them from below, from heel to head. Once, in passing the general, he whispers to him: "Well, did you win the battle?" and is already past the blushing man. He hurries into the dining room to see if the table has been set. He comes back. "Are the statues still there?" he asks. "All still there, sir," whispers the adjutant.

Midday, together next door, quiet lunch. "Reports?" the field marshal asks later. "Queries from home," answers the adjutant. "What do you think of the queries from home?" asks the field marshal. "Proof of impatience," says the adjutant. "Of curiosity," says the general. "Well put," says the field marshal.

Numbing midday quiet, creaking of the field marshal's bed audible from inside. They hear the field marshal jump up, put on his accoutrements. Again trips through the room by the immaculately dressed field marshal, while outside it grows dark. The shivering men have a fire built in the fireplace. Meanwhile the field marshal enters the room, the men rise only to a hunched position from their bent knees and flop right back.

"Did I give you permission?" cries the field marshal. When all get up immediately: "Haha, fine, sit down," he cries.

Later, gloomy afternoon. Close by from outside, cries. "Now you've got your teeth in the enemy," says the field marshal. "Bite deeper and deeper, till he's destroyed."

Then, after an exchange of words in front of the door, two men enter the room and salute together.

"What kind of uniforms are those?" asks the field marshal.

The newcomers inspect one another, then the men in the room.

"Our uniforms? What about yours? What kind of uniforms do you have?"

"We have proper uniforms," says the adjutant.

"No nasty green jackets," says the general. "Ours are correct."

"Our uniforms," says one of the newcomers, "are worn by every one of us."

"I am a field marshal," says the field marshal and points left and right to his epaulets.

"Let's get out of here," says the first man to the second man, and both withdraw.

Quietly spent night. The field marshal had books brought into his room again. The adjutant, the only one still up, soon heard him yawn next door and heard the light snapped off.

The field marshal appears promptly at breakfast. "Statues still there?" he asks aside, as he sits down. When all nod: "I'm in a good mood," he says. He surveys the breakfast table.

Afterwards, in the living room, the men stand in a semi-circle before him. The adjutant closest, next the general with the colonel, to the left the major and the lieutenant, at the door a soldier.

"How are the troops today?" asks the field marshal. "Has anybody seen them?" he asks. "How do they look today?"

"There's no action," says the adjutant.

"We've got to take a new tack," says the field marshal. "Arrive here again and make the most of it. Or stay here and start over again."

"Start from where?" asks the adjutant.

Expectation in the room. The field marshal assumes a decisive posture.

"All the way from the beginning," he says. "Sit down, take notebooks and pencils out, and write!"

The men sit with poised pencils.

"I, you, he, she, it, we, they," says the field marshal.

"All the way back to there?" asks the adjutant.

"Did you write that?" asks the field marshal.

All nod.

"Then read what you have written," says the field marshal.

He points to the adjutant.

He rises.

"Sir, in the name of the men, I beg you to begin with a coherent dictation."

"For instance, a sentence about a picnic," says the general.

"First, the genders," says the field marshal. "Decline!"

The colonel called upon rises. He stares at the notebook which he holds in front of him. The men wait.

"He, him," he says.

"Fine," says the field marshal.

"She, her," says the colonel.

"Go on," says the field marshal.

"It, him," says the colonel.

"Good," says the field marshal.

"False," says the adjutant.

"What do you mean false?" asks the field marshal.

"Sir," says the adjutant, "you say *it* for child, not *him*. For instance: I see it. It's another gender."

"I see the child, I see it," murmurs the field marshal. He lowers his head, puts his hand on his forehead. Finally the field marshal raises his head high with a jerk.

"You can also say *him* for child," he says.

"*Him* for child, *him* for child," all murmur and shake their heads.

"*Him* for child also sounds good," says the field marshal. "*Him* for ship you can say, too, I go on board *him*, how does that sound?"

"*Her* for tree," says the general and sits down immediately.

"I foliage," says the lieutenant.

Now the major stands up. He waits until all the men have recovered. Then he raises his index finger up, looks at it, and says: "O hat." Applause from all sides.

"Quiet!" roars the field marshal. "Li, lu, a, o." all the men nod.

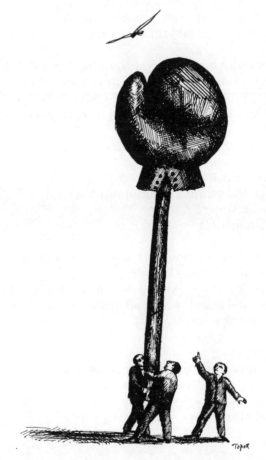

TOPOR

HAROLD NORSE

GREECE ANSWERS

for Nanos Valaoritis

Greece answers with rape and sodomy, a good answer
to all those xtian centuries poisoned with
conscience for having warped the bacchic kicks
of the soul

Greece answers with cold cells and swill for pot adventures
and cisterns full of microbial woe
olive trees condemn red tape
the umbilicus of the world at Delphi is a rotten egg of stone
who touches the egg touches the origins of madness

Greece answers with shipowners
mystic poets lost in bureaucratic offices
choked with crimes of customs officials
legally stealing cars from impoverished invalids
in nightmare cubicles of labyrinthine ledgers

Greece answers with lyrical lawyers quoting fiscal strophes
jacking up fees while tenderly requesting an old photo
falling upon your bed to the strains of ouzo voodoo
extorting the last drachma of devotion from trapped clients

Greece answers with iron rods smashing footsoles
crushing kneecaps and ankles
freedom gags on a colonel's moustache
electroshock to the genitals brings down the classics
lobotomy on the Winged Victory
deranges the Discobolus

Greece answers thru the mouth of Medusa, paralyzing
with concrete stars, flinging her serpent sting
into the eyes sput and the eyes go dead as the black hole
at the center of the galaxy where all matter ends
in the cosmic garbage can

Greece answers with junta tanks and tommy guns nursed by the CIA
answers with screams of peasant pain, drowned
in fabulous sunlight and jasmine, strangled
in galvanised gulfs of amethyst, glazed
in grottoes and olive groves, guillotined

by dances in tavernas, fingers snapping
mustachioed murder official as passports
by horny secret police insatiably dreaming of orgies
answers with short hair, long skirts, dead newspapers,
dungeons, broken statues, torn pacts,
battered remains of civilisation, destroyed works,
poets howling from ruins of bleeding parthenons,
tragic muse in a bomber, gods in the sixth fleet

Greece answers with a Texas accent
with a tongue of tungsten with a larynx of gas
with orange smog with lizards in the agora
with computers wrestling the abacus in wineshops
with a heart of missiles
with blood of marble
with 8 million electric eels
entire population of Greece
writhing under 3 or 4 miserable minds
U.S. agents in Constitution Square
investigating sex habits for sexless files
bugging dolma vine leaves and cocktail cherries
books armpits genitals
so that not a thought shall be free from New York to Piraeus
and the rubber octopus of steel and oil shall inherit the earth

Greece answers with islands with suicide
wells of loneliness white walls of flowers
myths of monsters prowling everyone's labyrinth
memory overwhelms us in Greece the statue falls forever thru time
abandoned Delos aims Apollo's broken cocks at eternity
Rhodes hurls cockroaches large as sparrows at the coast of Turkey
the frogs of Aristophanes croak in the brakes of Crete
Plato's boys roam hissing and snapping their fingers in rhythmic dance
the minotaur flirts with the trojan horse in the fleamarket of Athens
the dollar has raped the drachma on the abdicated throne of Constantine
and now little draculas are the debased currency of Greece
Tsaruchis the painter says 'There are no men anymore'
he should know, he has had them all
Minos has fled to London to play Che Guevara in his imagination
Zina has gone to Nepal to become Madame Blavatsky
Nanos in Oakland exile plots the surrealist overthrow of the junta by
                                                                    poetry

nobody's left in Greece except American Express
what good are the cafes now only the dead inhabit them
corpses reading guidebooks
cadavers aiming cameras
mummies poking in ruins
the Acropolis bored with skeletons
Caryatids consider moving to Hollywood
they will rival Melina Mercouri in personality ratings

I don't want to lose you Aegean
o amethyst sea come back
what will we do without you
where can we go anymore
I am desolate grief bites the air
who will comfort me who will magic me

Greece answers Know Thyself

PHILIPPE WEISBECKER, "GREECE"

VOICES OUT OF JUNTA GREECE
GREEK POETS TODAY

Translated by Eleni Fourtouni & Bertrand Mathieu

RETURN

The statues were the first ones to leave. After that
it was the turn of the trees, of people, of animals. The place
became competely deserted. There was nothing left but the wind.
Some newspapers, some weeds blowing in the streets.
At night, the lights lit up by themselves.
A man came back, took a look around him,
took out his key, buried it in the ground
as if he were giving it to an underground hand,
or as if he were planting a tree. Then he stood up, climbed
the marble stairs and looked at the city a long time.
One by one, cautiously, the statues were coming back.

27. IX. 68

—*Yánnis Rítsos*

OUR COUNTRY

We've gone up the hillside to look at our country—
some worn-out land, some stones, some olive trees.
Some grapevines that go down along the sea. Near the plough,
a little fire's smoking. The grandfather's clothes,
we've used them to make a scarecrow. Our days
have come a long way for a little bread and lots of light.
Under the poplars a straw hat's glowing.
The bird on the fence. The cow in the dry grass.
How come with a hand of stone we've managed to furnish
our houses, our lives? All over our doorsills,
there's still smoke from the Easter candles—
tiny little black crosses traced there, year after year, by the dead
coming back from the Resurrection. It's a country you love a lot,
patiently, proudly. Every night, from the dried-out wells,
the statues come out cautiously and climb up the trees.

Léros, 13. XII. 67

—*Yánnis Rítsos*

KASTANIÁ

Up there, just like yesterday, they shot forty.
Twenty years have gone by. Nobody's spoken their names.
You understand our life. Each year
on a similar day, they've been finding in hiding places
a ripped canvas, two extinguished braziers, a little incense,
a basketful of grapes, a candle
with a black wick. It's been almost impossible to light it.
    The wind's been blowing it out.
That's why, in the evening, the old women are sitting
    in the doorway like ancient ikons,
that's why the eyes of our children have grown
    large so quickly
and why our dogs pretend to look elsewhere
    when policemen pass by.

—*Yánnis Rítsos*

WE'RE RESPONSIBLE

To build a hut
we take red clay and water and knead the mud with
    the feet throwing in bunched-up hay so the
    bricks will harden when they put them in the sun.
The only thing we had was ashes blood and rusty
    barbedwire.
For years and years I've been trying to make
    my little bricks harden with those ingredients
for years we've been trying to build the world
                to transform things
we knead the mud and it keeps dissolving
from the bigotries the downpours the betrayals.
We're responsible for the ingredients
for our gutlessness
we're responsible for going right on
kneading the ashes and the blood
with bare feet.

—*Áris Alexándrou*

. . . .

never allow sacrilegious mouths
to take the schooners out beyond safe waters,
especially when they're unhinged by a fit of fanaticism
in bad weather.
most of all never allow the dreams,
in a lull to be towed away by an armed naval fleet
undetected by you, while Reason
walks past, walks right past you sadly.
and while a breeze blows from the land of the phaeacans
while a breeze blows . . .
never allow the sacred land of the greeks
to be sacked by their admirers with the single eye
in the middle of their foreheads,
the civilizers . . .

. . . .

—*Ektor Kaknavatos*

VISIGOTHS

All of a sudden our door sprang open.
First the emperor stepped in
        in his new clothes
then the new archbishop
the minister of education and religious affairs
(the worker Dúmpyova has turned out
        fifteen thousand drinking-glasses)
the field marshal hero of the battle of Saro
further back the court Kiss-assers
all the clerks and their wives
the presiding justice of the supreme court
at the tail-end a boy who performed as jester.

I myself represented the armed forces of Korea
the French resistance
the Spanish exiles
the closed-down newspaper "Freedom of Opinion"
and the other one with only its masthead left.
The poets who carried the banners were composing
        hymns in their heads
they naturally held their breath in the presence
        of the dignitaries
they went on and on applauding
        all the speakers.

Now what caused this unappetizing crowd
    to start bunching up against the fence
what caused
the builders' union to authorize
a unanimous vote
in favor of spreading out carpets for that procession
is anybody's guess.
It's the person next to me who's to blame
for whispering into the silence
    at a crucial pause:
The mayor's wife's right tit makes one think
    of geography.

What happened next is indescribable.
The rumor circulated in the lackadaisical crowd
the ministers exploded
the boxer who'd become a policeman put up his dukes
the firemen rushed towards the side exits
the president filled the whole hall with the sound
    of his little bell
the candles went out in the temple
and in the middle of this confusion I succeeded
with one tiny sidestep in suddenly finding myself
    admiring the view.

When the lights came on again
the bronze door slammed shut seemingly without a sound
and all around me the women were howling loudly
were tearing their hair and *screaming*
not so much because they were missing out on the procession
    of the assembled dignitaries
but because they were misplacing their husbands
    in the dark.

The sidestreets leading to the platforms
to the doors of the temples and the prisons
to the patios of the summer spots
to the people's parks
to the government-operated schools
to the sweat shops
to capital punishment
everywhere everywhere everywhere
even lackadaisical me
had been surrounded in secret police style
    by the Visigoths.

Please don't be rough on the Visigoths
they're just a big bunch of funny-looking screwballs
    who masquerade as invaders.

Anyway you're bound to've figured out the ancient temple
what the jester represented
what even a ridiculous person like me really meant
who the Visigoths are and the archbishops
    and the magnificent emperor.

We can all look forward to a *nice* Spring.

                    —*Mikháli Katsarós*

ODE TO MARILYN MONROE

Tattoo on my body all the craters
of all the volcanoes on earth, the kudos of all the dockworkers
    of New York
Tattoo on my body all the eunuchs of the new
fuhrer, the voice of the cranes of Evikos
Tattoo on my body my mother Ethel
—Was that her name? Ethel?—my last lover who
was killed on a motorcycle in Chicago
Tattoo on my body the ecstacies of JAZZ
of ROCK 'N ROLL, hashish and barbiturates
Tattoo on my body the dreams
of Kinsey's homosexuals and of the prostitutes of New York
Etch on my body that lady
on TV who says that "mushrooms from Tibet are preferable
for a Wednesday dinner"
Etch on my body my voice on 78 rpm records
singing the National Anthem of the United States
Then circulate my face at night on pennies
on toilet paper
on school looseleaf holders
and on cheap underwear.

That's what Marilyn Monroe said
that morning
when she walked into the restrooms of New York
holding in her hands her womb
her false eyelashes and her lovely head.

                    —*Yiórgas Khronás*

("Hellas for Christian Hellenes!")
—slogan of the Greek military dictatorship

THESSALONÍKI, DAYS OF 1969 A.D.

On Egypt Street—the first road to the right—
Stands the palatial building of The Bank of Exchange
The Bureau of Tourism and The Department of Emigration.
And the kids can't play there any more because of all the
        motor vehicles passing through.
Anyway the kids've grown up, the old days are gone
These days they don't laugh much, they don't whisper secrets,
        they don't trust—
Floods, tidal waves, earthquakes, mechanized soldiers,
They're remembering their fathers' words: You'll know
        better days
It doesn't matter in the end that they haven't known them,
        they go on repeating the lesson by rote to their kids
Hoping against hope someday the chain will break
Maybe for their children's children or their children's children's
        children.
For the time being, on that old street we're talking about,
        there stands The Bank of Exchange
—I exchange, you exchange, he exchanges—
    The Bureau of Tourism and The Department of Emigration
—We emigrate, you emigrate, they emigrate—
    Wherever I travel Greece wounds me, said the Poet
    Greece with its lovely islands, its lovely offices, its
        lovely churches

The Hellas of the Hellenes.

                                        —Manólis Anagnostákis

YOUNG MEN OF SIDON, 1970

Actually we really shouldn't complain.
Your warm and zestful circle, brimming with youthfulness
Bright-eyed girls—tough-bodied boys
Full of feeling and love of life and drive
So nice, the style and content of your songs
So deeply human, moving,
About children who're dying on a nearby Continent
About heroes who were killed in some former time,
About revolutionaries Black, Green, Yellowish,
About the anguish of suffering Man in general.

What does you credit especially is your involvement
In the problems and struggles of our time
You favor a quick and drastic availability—in view of this
I think you have an absolute right
To play, to fall in love, in twosomes, in threesomes,
And to take things easy, brother, after such exertions.

(They've made us old before our time Yiórgo, do you read me?)

—Manólis Anagnostákis

SAFE CONDUCT

Statue of a woman with hands tied

Right away they all call you a statue.
I see you right away as a woman.

You're an adornment in some park.
From a distance, you're a bit misleading.
You seem to be slowly sitting up to remember
a lovely dream you've seen,
collecting all your strength to live it out.
From close up, it's clear what the dream is:
your hands are tied behind you
with a rope of marble
and your whole bearing's taut with quiet desire
to break out
of your beautiful captive's *eclat.*
But that's the way their commission to the sculptor read:
captive.
You're not able
to weigh even a few raindrops in your hand,
to pick a tiny daisy.
And the marble itself isn't your only Argus.
If changes were to take place
in the malleability of marble, if statues
were to start struggling
for freedom and equality—
like wage-slaves,
like the dead,

like our inner feelings—
wouldn't you *still* exist
inside this intransigent cosmogony of marble
with your hands still tied: captive?

They all call you a statue right away.
Right away I call you a woman.
Not because you surrendered
like a woman
to some sculptor's need for marble—
allowing the shapeliness of your thighs
to grow into this rock's fertility,
this clean harvest of immobility.
But because your hands are tied.
Everywhere I turn, I see your hands are always
tied.
That's why I call you a woman.

I call you a woman
because you always end up

          a captive.

                    —Kikí Dhimoulá

THE BLOOD CRIMINAL

I'm the priestess of a blood cult,
a law-breaker *made famous* by her crime—
freeing the riffraff gauchos from my soul!
Sisters, women, victims,
press your hands against my gash!
Smear the white walls, smear the kitchens,
smear the fading faces of lovers,
smear the whole world trying to escape the dark
witness of its birth!
When you lie on my altars, stripped,
skewered by the mandrake thrusts—
let the blood-struck cunt gape wide,
let out the vivid stenches, the quickening flow,
the bruisable pulp—
No love's ever shameful.
The only perversion's *being afraid*!

                    —Líli Bíta

OUTLINE OF A POEM FOR A BEGINNING POET

Make sure you start out with the three deserters
soldiers in September at night
half-stripped under the dusty yellow moon
smoking the last cigarette the three of them had behind the bushes
Out there in the city their faces are being flashed
on the TV sets and the WANTED notices
Leave out, deliberately, the size of the reward and the surrender
  terms
Leave out, deliberately, the image of the mother in tears
telling the reporters: "Turn yourselves in, my children!"
Make sure at the close you don't leave out
their names
Nikólaos
Konstantínos
Ioánnis

—Yiórgos Khronás

17

It's time we got accustomed to holocausts.
If a house catches fire
or someone in a moment of despair
decides to immolate himself
or some racketeer walks towards us
disguised as a respectable homeowner or a pimp
we have one hand held out for a handshake
the other one on the trigger
and that's how we while away our lives.

—Tákis Karvélis

Z

—Is Alexander the Great still living?
the mermaid asked the sailor
And while he tried to tie his lines up
    high in the masts
he yelled
—He lives!
Maybe he lived maybe he didn't, how did he know
He was just a sailor by himself at sea
    and the lines were
rough with salt and the wind was blowing.

—Yiórgos Khronás

REZA BARAHENI

TWO POEMS

Autobiographical Sketch

1. Born in a very poor family, poorer than beggars, worked from the age of six to eighteen (now thirty-eight) with his hands, in factories of all kinds with his father and older brother—packing tea, knitting socks, dirty, humiliated, worked his way up to part-time melon merchant, part-time shoeshine boy to those entering a mosque for prayer. Groomed his father's cadaverous cart-horse, helped him carry bricks from Tabriz to various factories. Saw the Russian march into his home-town when seven, loved their big horses, hated their machine guns and loved their fat faces. Watched. Experienced one year of a local brand of Turkish Democratic Republicanism, then the Iranian army. For years, before, then, and after heard shooting, saw men on gallows. Suffered without knowing, in silence.

2. Sent to school by a rich philanthropic *hadji*, studied hard, worked hard outside. No time to clean his nose or scratch his ass. Sang his head off in the dark narrow streets of Tabriz. Watched his mother clean wool and make thread for a factory. Mother got 25¢ a day. Fought in the streets with the children of the rich. Ordered, by the Iranian government, along with five million other Turkish-speaking people, not to read or write Turkish. Books in Turkish burnt to ash in the squares. A linguistic orphan, took revenge on Persian. Through learning the literature and mastering it began criticizing Persian and the Persians for watery, romantic (contemporary) diction. Breathed solid masculinity into the veins of this contemporary Persian, made it a weapon. Took a Ph.D. in English Lit. to which he attaches the importance of flushing his completed thesis down the toilet. Has written 20 books of prose-poetry and added the art of criticism to the literature of the Persians. Loves Lenin and Trotsky on the one side, Nietzsche and Beckett and Genet on the other. He considers those vacillating in between mediocre. He proves this in his teaching, writing and conversation.

3. Poetry is everything for him. If prose is not poetry it is not prose. If drama is not poetry it is not revolution. Poetry is the measure, the yard of Being. Both Heideggerian and Marxian. Poetry is the praxis of being.

EVENTS AND PARENTS

The horse's whinny gleams again in the mirror.
Two closed clocks dream in the mirror.
Two dumb locks.

(Father says, "The Russians have come." Mother says,
"The Russians are gone.")

and then like a storm coming up
a machine gun attacks the street
and all the leaves fall.

Two closed locks dream in the mirror.
Two dumb locks.

(Father says, "The Democrats have come." Mother says,
"The Democrats have gone.")
The horse's whinny gleams again in the mirror.
An officer's cap passes behind the window.
And again machine guns;
and then soldiers.
Two closed locks dream in the mirror.
Two dumb locks.

(Father says, "The Persians have come." Mother says,
"The Persians have gone.")

The horse's whinny gleams again in the mirror,
and then the roaring of an airplane
shakes the windowplanes.
Thousands of colorful leaflets fall to earth.

(Father says, "I have no education. I don't understand. Let me go
and close the gate to the courtyard." Mother says,
"First throw your Party card into the coals.
That's more important than the gate.")

The horse's whinny gleams again in the mirror.
Two closed locks dream in the mirror.
Two dumb locks.

(Father says, "The Russians have come. The Democrats have come.
The Persians have come." Mother says, "Only the Turks haven't come.")

THE MASK OF TURK I

I am the 46th brother of the Turkoman general who ran barefoot
from the Wall of China to the cliffs 'round the Danube.

I am Turk I.
My 6th uncle received tribute from Siberian bears.
My cousins split the bosoms of Eskimo women like apples.
My tribe was womanless.
We married all the men and women of the world.
The sprung eyelids of the Chinese,
the prominent cheekbones of the Copts,
the mighty wrists of the Magyars are the heritage of my tribe.

My tribe married horses
and their children at birth were heavy as anchors.

We don't like museums. We made history and museums are for tribes
with no history.
My grandfather thrust ships at the sea from mountains tops,
broke the thunderbolt of Zeus and handed him the bits.
My 12th uncle's kick at the Caliph's dimpled guts dumped Baghdad
into Euphrates.
The pupils of the Caliph's eyes, and his balls, turned into water.

We sang to horse-whinny and drumbeat, and the waters of the Caspian and the
Mediterranean waved.

The kings of Egypt, Rome, Persia and China were our clowns.

We ate the meat of bull camels and does.

Our teeth were whiter than the stars.

I never had an aunt or a sister, and my 24th brother was my mother.

I am Turk I.
I will not bow at the grave of my tribe.

I keep no scribes, sculptors, engravers.
I carve this script on Alburz mountains
with my own two hands and in two tongues.

Record me!

I hate shrines and tombs. A man should not build a shrine of his bones.
Let the hyenas eat my corpse.
Hang the poet who writes my elegy! My shining eyes watch the world
and my heart
turns round the axis of history.

I am Turk I.
I do not finish.

Translated from the Persian by the Author & Harris Lenowitz

VICENTE HUIDOBRO

EQUATORIAL

Translated from the Spanish by William Witherup & Sergio Echeverria

It was the time in which my wingless eyelids were opened
And I began to sing about the storm-wracked distances

Leaving their nests
             The flags thunder in the air

MEN
        IN THE GRASS
                LOOKED FOR BORDERS

The world is dying
            on such a banal field
Burning wings
            sprout from premature heads
And in the equatorial trench
                 broken at intervals
Soldiers sang in the hard afternoons
Under the shadow of live airplanes

Cities of Europe
            Burn out one by one

On the way to exile
The last king wore a chain
Of dead lamps around his neck

      The stars
          that fell
      Were fireflies of moss

And strangled posters
            were strung along the walls

A shadow rolled down the mountain slopes
Where the old organ grinder makes jungles sing

        The wind stirs horizons
        Hung with tackle and sails

A bird was singing
                    Over the rainbow

          Open the mountains to me

I have seen swallow's wings
Everywhere on the ground
And the Christ who rose and flew away
Forgot his crown of thorns

                    Let us look at our time
                    Sitting on the parallel

CENTURY CHAINED TO AN ANGLE OF THE WORLD

In the grass
                    the locomotive that crossed the winter
Whistles in heat

The two strings of its tracks
Remain behind it singing
Like a rebellious guitar

Its naked eye
                    Cigar of the horizon
                                        Dances among the trees
It is Diogenes, with the burning pipe
Searching among the months and days

I started to walk
Over the path of the equinox

Each star
          Is an exploding bombshell

The feathers of my throat
Warmed themselves near the sun
                              which lost a wing

The divine airplane
Brought an olive branch in its hands

Nevertheless
                    wounded sunsets are bleeding
And in port the departing days
Were carrying a cross in place of an anchor

We are sitting on the beaches as we sing

The bravest captains   Captain Cook
Went on an iceberg to the Poles   Hunts aurora borealis
To leave their pipes in the lips   In the South Pole
Of Eskimos

Others stick fresh spears into the Congo

The heart of sunny Africa
Opens like pecked figs

And the divine race
              of blacks
    slaves of Europe

Were wiping from their faces
              the snow that stained them

Men with short wings
          Have been everywhere

And a noble Norwegian explorer
Brought the four cardinal points
To Europe
         along with rare animals
And exotic trees
I have also embarked
Leaving my reef I came to see you

Sea gulls were flying around my hat

And here I am
         on my feet
             in other bays

The captive cities
Sewn one by one with telephone wires
                    pass slowly
Beneath the soundless cluster of trees

And words and gestures
Fly around the telegraph
Burning their wings
          like unskilled gods

Tired airplanes
Went to rest on lightning rods

Pregnant biplanes
         give birth in the fog

They are loved birds
That have sung in our cages

It is the bird that sleeps among branches
Without putting its head under its wing

During nights
                    Airplanes flew near the lighthouse
The lighthouse that suffers at the bottom of years

Someone bitter
                    Eyes empty
Throws his sad days into the sea
He takes the ship

To leave
                    And there far away
To look at lighted windows
And shadows crossing mirrors

The emigrants sang
                    Over the inverted waves
Like a flock of young swallows
                              SEA
SEA OF GREEN SMOKE

I would like that sea for my old thirst
Full of floating hair

My true desires disappeared over those waves

A shipwrecked Angel
                    Makes wreaths from weeds
                    Under the gassy waters

The new moon
                    anchored at Marseilles this morning
With broken tackle

And the oldest sailors
Found living pearls
In the depths of their pipe smoke

The submarine captain
Forgot his destiny in the depths

As he returned to earth
                    He saw someone else carried his star

Feverish exiles from the old planet
Killed in flight at random
By anti-aircraft cannons

A blind emigrant
                    Brought four tame lions
And another was carrying an untuned nightingale
To the port hospital

That child pilot
                    who forgot his smoking pipe
Near the extinct volcano
Found men on their knees
                    in the city
And saw pregnant virgins give birth

Far away
                                        Far away

Gold prospectors come
                    in a pensive mood

They pass singing among the leaves
Carrying California
On their shoulders

Half naked beggars
Came in the depths of the evening twilight

A praying whisper
                    Bent the trees

                    Summer flew
                    Over the seas

HOW MANY THINGS HAVE I SEEN

Beggars in London streets
Stuck like posters
Against the cold walls
In the thick vegetable fog

I remember well
                    I remember

That Spring afternoon
A sick girl
Entered a hospital
Leaving her two wings by the door

That same night
              beneath the oblong sky
Ten Zeppelins came to Paris
And one wild boar hunter
Left seven bleeding
On the wild dawn

Inside the cloud that rubbed the roof

A green clock
              Announces the year

1 9 1 7

IT IS RAINING
                    They buried the dead
                    Under water
        Someone who wept
        Made the leaves fall

The bearded astrologer
Says there are signs in the sky
                        An apple and a star
                        Are pecking like owls

Mars
        passes through
              Sagittarius

THE MOON RISES
                    A battered star
                    Is sliding

Ash flakes fell from beards
Of astrologers with pointed mitres

And here I am
              In jungles tuned
More truly than old harps

In the house that hangs in the void
                              The Magi
Tired of searching
              have gone to sleep

Elevators rest in a squatting position

And in all the rooms
Each time the hour strikes
A serious page came out of the clock
As if to say
        The coach is waiting
               milady
By the living door
The black slave
          quickly opens his mouth
For the master pianist
Who makes his teeth sing

This afternoon I saw
The latest phonograph posters
It was a confusion of cries
And songs as different
As in foreign ports

Men of the future
will come to decipher the hieroglyphs
That we now leave
Written backwards
Among the girders of the Eiffel Tower

We arrive at the end of the skirmish
My watch lost all its hours

I go over you very slowly
Century cut in two
         And with a bridge
Over a bloody river
One afternoon
          in the depths of life
On the Western Road
A horizon of camels passed by
On their mute backs

Men of Egypt
Weep like new crocodiles
Between two bony pyramids

And the saints on board the train
           got off and on at all the stations
Looking for other regions
My soul   sister of trains

        A train can be said like a rosary
        The smoking cross perfumed the plains

Here we are travelling among the saints

The train is a piece of city pulling away

The station announcer
Has cried

                          Spring
                          To the left
                          30 minutes

The train passes filled with flowers and fruit

Niagara has wet the hairs of my head
And a mist grows around them

The rivers
              All the rivers of sprouting hair
The badly braided rivers
Burning summers have kissed
A lost steamer coasted
Golden islands of the Milky Way

The Andean range
                  Crosses Latin America
As swiftly as a convoy

Love   Love

I have found it in very few places
And all unexplored rivers
Have passed through my arms

One morning
              Alpine shepherds
Played the violin over Switzerland

And in the neighboring star
He who had no hands
Played the piano with his wings
Century on board drunk airplanes

WHERE WILL YOU GO

Walking to exile
The last king wore a chain
Of dead lamps around his neck

And yesterday I saw the amethyst
Of Rome among the roses

ALPHA
OMEGA
DELUGE   RAINBOW

How many times has life started again

Who will say all that has happened on a star

Let us move on
Carrying the ripe head in our hands

THE MECHANICAL NIGHTINGALE HAS SUNG

That multitude of rough hands
Carries funeral wreaths
Toward the battlefield

Someone went by lost in his cigar
WHO IS IT

A cut hand
Left the newly sprouted equatorial line
On the marble

Century
        Submerge in the sun
If it's evening
        Land on an airfield

A flock of hands
Will rise from the years
Toward the only airplane
That will someday sing in the sky

SOUTHERN CROSS

SUPREME SIGN   CHRIST'S AIRPLANE

The rosy-cheeked child with naked wings
Will come with the trumpet in his fingers
The still new trumpet to announce
The End of the Universe

(1918)

VICENTE HUIDOBRO

Fragments from

ALTAZOR

VIII

Enough lady harp of the beautiful images
Of the secret lighted cosmos
Something else we are looking for something else
We know how to put down a kiss like a look
To plant looks like trees
Cage trees like birds
Water birds like heliotropes
Play a heliotrope like music
Empty music like a sack
Cut a sack's throat like a penguin's
Cultivate penguins like vineyards
Milk a vineyard like a cow
Unmast cows like sailing ships
Comb a sail like a comet
Unload comets like tourists
Bewitch tourists like snakes
Harvest snakes like almonds
Undress an almond like an athlete
Carve up athletes like cypresses
Light up cypresses like lighthouses
Nest lighthouses like larks
Breathe larks like sighs
Embroider sighs like silks
Shed silks like rivers
Wave a river like a flag
Pluck a flag like a rooster
Put out a rooster like a fire
Row in fires as in seas
Mow seas like wheatfields
Ring wheatfields like bells
Bleed bells like lambs
Sketch lambs like smiles
Bottle smiles like liquor
Set liquor like jewels
Electrify jewels like twilights
Man twilights like ships
Remove a ship's shoes like a king's
Hang kings like dawns
Crucify dawns like prophets

IX

There's no time to lose
The one-time swallow is coming
She brings an opposite accent of approaching distance
The swallow is coming like a swallowgondola

To the hortain of the mountizon
Violinswallow and swallocello
Unfastened from the moon this morning
It comes at full gallop
The swallow is coming coming
Swallofine is coming
Swallotrill is coming
Swallopeak is coming
She is coming swallochina
She is coming swallowclimate
Swallorhyme is coming
Swallolaughter is coming
Swallogirl
Swallogyre
Swallolyre
Swallobreeze
Swalloscream
The swallowday is coming
And night contracts her nails like a leopard
The swallotrill is coming
Who has a nest in each of two heat waves
As I have in each of four horizons
She is coming swallolaughter
And waves rise on the points of their toes
She is coming swallowgirl
And the mountain's head feels dizzy
She is coming swallogyre
And the wind becomes a parabola of orgiastic sylphs
The telephone wires are filled with musical notes
Dusk goes to sleep with its head hidden
And the tree with its feverish pulse

But the sky prefers the nighgale
His beloved child the nightale
His flower of joy the nightpetal
He tear-like skin the nightfangale
His nocturnal throat the nightsungale
The nightingale
The nightengale

X

There's no time to lose
Icebergs that float in the eyes of the dead
Know their way
Blind would he be who wept
The darkness of the boundless coffin
Abolished hopes
Torments changed into cemetery inscriptions
Here lies Carlota eyes of the sea
One of her satellites was broken
Here lies Mathias two spiny dogfish beat in his heart
Here lies Marcelo sea and sky in the same violincello
Here lies Susana tired of fighting against oblivion
Here lies Teresa that is the land her eyes ploughed
        today occupied by her body
Here lies Angelica anchored in the harbor of her arms
Here lies Rosario river of roses to the infinite
Here lies Raimundo his veins are the world's roots
Here lies Clarisa clear laughter cloistered in light
Here lies Alejandro cavern removed in the wing
Here lies Gabriela the dikes broken going up with sap
        to dreams waiting for resurrection
Here lies Altazor, goshawk thundering with height
Here lies Vicente anti-poet and magician
Blind would he be who wept
Blind as a comet going off with its cane
And his mist of souls following him
Obedient to the instinct of his senses
Paying no attention to the meteorites that stone down from far away
And live in colonies according to the season
The insolent meteorite crosses the sky
Meteosilver meteocopper
Meteostones in the infinite
Meteosticks in the glance
Watch out for the stars pilot
Watch out for dawn
So the air sailor doesn't become dawn's killer
Never had a sky as many roads as this
        nor was it so dangerous
The wandering star brings me greetings from a friend
        who has been dead for ten years
To hurry to hurry
Planets ripen in the planetation
My eyes have seen the birds' roots
That which is beyond water lilies
And that which is before butterflies

Do you hear the noise mandolins make before they die?
I am lost
There is nothing else but to give up
Before the war that gives no quarter
And the nightly ambush of the stars

XI

The tomb opens and in the background you see a herd lost in the
    mountain
The shepherdess with her wind cape beside the night
Counts the footsteps of God in space
And sings to herself
The tomb opens and you see a parade of icebergs
    in the background
That shine beneath the storm's searchlight
And drift by in silence
Solemn procession of icebergs
With large hatchets of light buried in the flesh
The tomb opens and you see autumn and winter in the background
An amethyst sky comes down slowly slowly
The tomb opens and you see an enormous wound in the background
Growing greater in the earth's depths
With a noise of summer and spring
The tomb opens and you see a jungle of faeries fertilising
    in the background
Each tree is tipped with an ecstatic bird
And everything stays within the enclosed ellipse of their songs
In those whereabouts a nest of tears must be discovered
Rolling around the sky and crossing the zodiac
From sign to sign
The tomb opens and you see boiling nebulae burning out
    and flaming up in the background
A star shoots by without answering anybody
Lanterns dance on the limited scaffold
Where the stars' bloody heads
Leave a halo that grows eternally
The tomb opens and a wave leaps up
The shadow of the universe splashes
And everything that lives in the shadow or on shore
The tomb opens and sobbing comes from planets
There are broken masts and whirlpools of shipwrecks
The bells of all the stars are tolling
The persecuted hurricane whistles through the infinite
Over flooded rivers
The tomb opens and a bunch of flowers leaps up loaded with
    hairshirts
The impenetrable fire grows and an odor of passion invades
    the world
The sun tries the last corner where it is hiding
And the magic jungle is born
The tomb opens and you see the ocean in the background
A song rises about one thousand ships that are sailing away
Meanwhile an avalanche of fish
Slowly hardens

                                          (1931)

Isabelle Eberhardt

Isabelle Eberhardt at 20 in Algeria

"Si Mahmoud" shortly before her death

BIOGRAPHICAL NOTE

Born in Geneva, 1877, illegitimate daughter of Russian mother and Armenian father, A. Trophimovsky, a nihilist who had known Bakunin. At age 19, she went to Algeria, where in male attire and going by the name of Si Mahmoud, she studied and mastered classical and colloquial Arabic. Married an Algerian soldier in Moslem rite. Set about to learn the secrets of Sufism and partake of the mystical ecstasy she believed its adepts attained. In El Oued a holy maniac attempted to cleave her in two with a sword. Upon recovery from her injuries, she was expelled from Algeria by colonial authorities who disapproved of her alleged anti-French activities. Landed in Marseilles where she worked as a stevedore. Later returned with her husband to Algeria where she was accepted as an adept in the cult of the Djilala. Traveled extensively in mountain and desert regions where no European presence was tolerated, keeping precise notes on her journeys and writing stories and poems. Died in Ain Sefra, Algeria, in a flash flood at age 27.

ISABELLE EBERHARDT

THE CONVERT

A ruined stone farmhouse, a rocky field in the rough French Piedmont highlands, hopeless poverty in a family of twelve children. The early years of apprenticeship under a brutal master. A few images, vaguer, scarcely etched into his illiterate's memory, a few times when the sunlight had lighted up the blue peaks, a few quiet spots in the dark woods, on the banks of streams among curling ferns. That was about all that Roberto Fraugi could recall at the moment when he set sail for Algiers, with his comrades, who were all itinerant workers like him. Over there in Africa he would be working on his own, and could put aside a little money. Later he would go back to Santa Reparata, buy some good land, and there, raising what corn and rye he needed for himself, finish out his days.

But he felt lost, perhaps almost afraid, here on this burning land with its dreary horizon. Everything was so different from what he had ever known.

He spent several years in the cities along the coast, where he found countrymen of his and where he could still be reassured by certain understandable facets of the social life around him.

The men in burnouses, who walked slowly and spoke an incomprehensible tongue, were to be avoided. He distrusted them and so, although living in their midst, he remained ignorant of them. Then one day a native chief from the edge of the Sahara offered him a construction job in his bordj. The pay was good. There was no work to be found in Algiers. Roberto ended by agreeing to go, but only after long deliberation. The idea of travelling so far, of being in the desert and living for months on end with Arabs, frightened him.

Full of misgivings, he set out. After a trying trip in a carriage that creaked, he found himself at night in Msila. It was summer. The heat seemed to come up from the earth and enfold him. An indefinable odor hung in the air. He felt strangely uncomfortable standing there all alone in the square only faintly illumined by the great pale stars. Far off, in the country, the crickets were singing, and their immense sound filled the silence broken only now and then by the nearby croak of frogs from the ditches that lined the streets. In the distance there were the black silhouettes of young palm trees against the greenish-blue sky. Vague forms in white lay stretched out on the earth around him, men who had not been able to sleep inside their houses for the heat and the scorpions.

The following morning in the sparkling clarity of dawn, a tall sunburned Arab with sombre eyes, came for Fraugi in his little hotel room.

I work for the caid. Shall we go?

The cool air of the open countryside was delicious. A vague, fresh scent rose from the earth. Behind them silence lay over the still sleeping town. Fraugi, perched on a mule, followed the bedouin, who rode a small shaggy grey horse that bounded joyously at each step. They crossed the river in its deep-cut bed. The new-born day gave color to the adobe houses and the unlikely shapes of the saints' tombs.

After the palm gardens of Guerfala, they came out onto the plain. It stretched before them, pink, empty, infinite. Far away to the south the Mountains of the Ouled Nail were barely visible, a diaphanous blue.

This plain is called the Hodna, said the native. And over there by those hills is Bou Saada.

Far out on the plain, at the bottom of a saline depression, they came upon a few ruined greyish walls and a crumbling mausoleum with a high, narrow dome. Farther up, on a stony swelling of the earth, stood the caïd's bordj, a sort of square fortress with cracked walls that once had been whitewashed. They passed a few stunted figtrees around a fountain. The warm pink water trickled into a canal lined with crooked piles of reddish salt and stacks of white saltpetre.

The mason was given a bare little bedroom, all white. In it there was nothing but a reed mat, a chest and a skin of water hanging from a nail. Here for six months or so Fraugi lived, far from all contact with Europeans, among the bronze Ouled Madbi with their eagle-faces and eagle-eyes, and around their heads the high *guennour* with its black cords.

Seddik, the young man who had gone to Msila to fetch him, was the foreman of the gang of laborers working under the mason. They were slow in their movements, and as they worked they intoned long, plaintive chants.

In the solitary bordj there was silence, broken only faintly from time to time by the gallop of a horse, the squeaking of the well, or the savage growl of the camels when they arrived to kneel in front of the main gate.

In the evening at the red hour when everything grew still, the men assembled on the heights above and prayed. Their gestures were all-embracing, their voices solemn. Afterward, when the caïd had gone inside, the khammes and the servants squatted on the ground to chat or sing.

The people at the bordj were friendly and polite to Fraugi. Above all, they demanded practically nothing of him. Little by little, lulled by the pleasant monotony that life had assumed there, the desire to return to his homeland left him. He grew used to the slow rhythm of a life without care or haste, and since he now was beginning to understand Arabic, he found the natives simple and sociable, and as a result enjoyed living among them. He sat with them now on the hillside at the end of the day, and questioned them about their lives, or told them about his country. Ever since his first communion he had neglected to practise his religion, because it left him indifferent. Seeing these men so calm in their belief, he asked to hear about their faith. What he heard sounded to him a great deal simpler and more humane than the religion he had been taught to believe, with its deliberately confusing mysteries.

Winter came, and the work at the bordj was finished. Fraugi began to think disconsolately of his approaching departure. The farm-workers and the laborers did not want to see him go. Here was a foreigner who was not proud, who did not look down on them. He was an *ouled-baba-Allah*, they said—a good man.

And one evening, as Seddik and Fraugi lay stretched out side by side in the courtyard near the fire, listening to a blind singer from the Ouled Nail, Seddik said to the mason: But why are you going? You have a little money and the caid likes you. Abdelkader ben Hamoud has left now for Mecca. You could rent his house. It has figtrees and a plot of good land. Besides, the men in the tribe have decided to build a new mosque and a mausoleum for Sidi Berrabir. That work would pay your living expenses, and everything would go on the same as before.

And in order that things might go on "the same as before," he agreed to stay.

In the spring, when they learned of Abdelkader ben Hamoud's death at Jiddah, Fraugi bought the small property, without even reflecting that this would mean the end of his dream of returning home. No longer afraid of the hot rude earth, he signed a pact with it for all time. He let himself fall so voluptuously into the languid tempo of events that he no longer bothered even to go into Msila. It was enough for him to stay where he was. His European clothing became ragged, and one day Seddik persuaded him to put on native dress. At first he felt as though he were in disguise. Then he found it practical, and grew used to it.

The days and the years passed uneventfully in the sleepy village. No trace of homesickness for his native Piedmont remained with him. Why should he want to go anywhere else when he was so well-off at Ain Menedia? He spoke Arabic now, and even knew a few songs with which he accompanied the ever slower motions of his work.

One day, talking with Seddik, he unthinkingly called to witness the "god beside which there is no other," and Seddik exclaimed: *Ya Roubert!* Why don't you become a Moslem? We're friends now. If you did, we'd be brothers. I'd give you my sister, and we'd stay together.

Fraugi remained silent. He could not analyze his feelings, but he was convinced that in some way he was already a Moslem, since he found Islam more satisfying than the faith of his fathers. He went on thinking about it. A few days later, in front of Seddik and the elders of the village, he testified of his own free will that there was no god but Allah and that Mohammed was His envoy. The elders praised the Eternal. Seddik, in spite of his calm exterior, was deeply moved. He seized the mason and kissed him.

Roberto Fraugi was now Mohammed Kasdallah, and Seddik's sister, Fatima Zohra, became the convert's wife. Simply, with no display of religious zeal, Mohammed Kasdallah performed the duties of prayer and fast.

They waited in vain for him in Santa Reparata, but he never went back. Thirty years later, Mohammed Kasdallah, now a pious elder, regularly praised Allah and His all-powerful *mektoub*. For it had been written that the cottage and the field he had dreamed of owning were to be granted him, only they were not to be in Santa Reparata. He would find them under another sky and on different soil, in the Hodna country among Moslems, and surrounded by the vast sad horizon of the wasteland.

JEAN GENET

an excerpt from

THE STUDIO OF ALBERTO GIACOMETTI

translated from the French by Daniel Peri Lucid

In the café. While Giacometti reads, a wretched, nearly blind Arab causes a bit of a scandal by treating a customer like a queer . . . The insulted customer stares at the Arab wickedly and moves his jawbone up and down as if chewing his rage. The Arab is skinny and stupid. He beats against an invisible but solid wall. He understands nothing in a world in which he is blind, puny, and idiotic, he insults it in each and every of its manifestations.

— If you didn't have your white cane! yells the Frenchman the Arab treated like a queer . . . I rejoice secretly that a white cane renders this blind man holier than a king, stronger than the most athletic butcher of bullcocks.

I offer the Arab a cigarette. His fingers fumble for it and come across it almost by chance. He's short, skinny, unclean, also a little drunk. He stammers and drools. His beard is thin and poorly shaven. One can't picture legs inside his trousers. He's barely able to stand upright. A dalliance with his finger. I say a few words in his language:

— Are you married?

Giacometti goes on reading and I don't dare disturb him. Perhaps my attitude toward the Arab irritates him.

— No . . . I don't have a wife.

At the same time he tells me that, the Arab makes a to-and-fro motion with his hand to let me know he's masturbating.

— No . . . no wife . . . I have my hand . . . and then with my hand . . . no, there's nothing, nothing but my towel . . . or the bed sheets . . .

His white eyes, discolored, expressionless, are in constant movement.

— . . . and I'll be punished . . . the good lord will punish me . . . you don't know all I've done . . .

Giacometti has finished reading, he takes off his cracked spectacles, puts them in his pocket, and we leave. I'd like to discuss the incident, but what would he reply, what would I say? I know he knows as I do that this wretch retains, maintains—with furies and frenzies—this feature which makes him the same as everyone and more precious than the rest of the world: that which subsists when he has drawn back into himself as far as possible, as when the sea recedes and leaves the shore.

I've told this anecdote because it seems to me that Giacometti's statues have receded—leaving the shore—to this secret spot which I can neither describe nor specify, but which makes each man, when he takes shelter there, more precious than the rest of the world.

"Rimbaud, Cool Impudence on his Part" by Jim Dine

ARTHUR RIMBAUD

A SEASON IN HELL

Translated into American by Bertrand Mathieu
For Anais Nin & my daughter Rachel

A while back, if I remember right, my life was one long party where all hearts were wide open, where all the wines kept flowing.

One night, I sat Beauty down on my knees. —And I found her galling. —And I roughed her up.

I armed myself to the teeth against justice.

I ran away. O witches, O misery, O hatred, it's you I've turned my treasure over to!

I managed to squelch from my mind every trace of human hope. On every joy I leaped, sneakily, like a wild animal eager to strangle.

I called for the executioners so that, while dying, I could bite on the butts of their rifles. I called for plagues to choke me with sand, with blood. Bad luck was my god. I stretched out in the muck. I dried myself in an air of crime. And I played some fine tricks on insanity.

And Spring made me a gift of the frightening laughter of the idiot.

So just recently, when I found myself on the brink of the final *quack*! it occurred to me to look again for the key to that endless party where maybe I'd find my appetite once more.

CHARITY is that key. —This stroke of genius proves I was dreaming!

"You'll continue to be a hyena . . ." etc., yells the devil who'd crowned me with such marvelous poppies. "*Deserve* death with all your appetites, your selfishness, and all the capital sins!"

God! I've *had* it now: —O sweet Satan, I beseech you, a less blazing eye! and while waiting for the few little cowardly gestures yet to come, since you *like* an absence of descriptive or didactic skills in a writer, let me rip out these few ghastly pages for you from the notebook of one of the Damned.

BAD BLOOD

I've got my Gallic ancestors' light-blue eyes, their narrow skull, and their clumsiness in combat. I consider my clothes as barbaric as theirs. Only I don't butter my hair.

The Gauls were the most ungifted skinners of beasts and scorchers of grass of their time.

From them I get: idolatry and the love of sacrilege—O all the vices, anger, lust—magnificent, this lust—and especially lying and laziness.

I despise all trades. Foremen and workmen—all of them, peasants, riff-raff. The hand that writes is the same as the hand that ploughs. —What a century of hands! —I'll never own my hand. Next, domesticity goes too far. The honesty of begging sickens me. Criminals are disgusting like castrates; myself, I'm intact, and I don't give a damn.

But! who made my tongue so tricky that it's managed to guide and guard my laziness up till now? Without even using my body for a living, and loafing around like a toad, I've lived everywhere. Not a family in Europe that I don't know. —I mean families like my own which owe everything to the Declaration of the Rights of Man. —I've known every mother's son of such families!

If only I had ancestors at some point in French history!

But no, nothing.

It's very obvious to me I've always belonged to an inferior race. I can't figure out revolt. My race never rose up except to loot: like wolves after beasts they haven't killed.

I think over the history of France, the Church's eldest daughter. I once made, as a serf, the journey to the Holy Land. My head's full of roads through the Swabian plains, views of Byzantium, ramparts of Jerusalem: the cult of Mary, compassion for the Crucified One wake up in me among a thousand profane fantasies. —I'm sitting there, a leper, among smashed vases and nettles, at the foot of a sun-frazzled wall. —Later on, as a trooper, it seems I bivouacked under German stars.

Ah, once again! I'm dancing the witches' sabbath in a reddish clearing with old women and children.

I can't remember farther back than this old earth and Christianity. I'll never have my fill of seeing myself in that past. But always alone. Without family. Still, what language was I speaking? I never see myself in the councils of Christ. Nor in the councils of the Nobility—the representatives of Christ.

What was I in the last century? Only today I find traces of myself. No more vagabonds, no more vague wars. The inferior race has covered everything—the people, as we put it, reason, the nation, knowledge.

O Knowledge! Everything's been taken care of. For the body and the soul—the last rites—there's medicine and there's philosophy—old wives' remedies and new arrangements of popular songs. And the pastimes of princes and the games they've outlawed! Geography, cosmography, mechanics, chemistry . . .!

Knowledge, the new nobility! Progress. The world moves ahead! Why *shouldn't* it turn?

It's the vision of numbers. We're going towards the SPIRIT. What I'm saying is absolutely sure, it's oracular. I *understand*, and since I don't know how to explain things without using pagan words, I'd rather shut up.

Pagan blood comes again! The Spirit is near. Why doesn't Christ help me by giving my soul nobility and liberty? Too bad, the Gospel's *passé*! the Gospel! the Gospel.

I wait for God with terrific *hunger*. I belong to an inferior race throughout eternity.

Here I am on the Brittany beach. Let the cities light up in the evening. My own day's done, I'm quits with Europe. Sea air will burn my lungs. Far-out climates will tan my hide. I'll swim, I'll trample the grass, hunt, smoke especially. I'll drink liquor hard as boiling metal—like my grand old ancestors around their fires.

"Rimbaud at Harrar in 1883"
by Jim Dine

I'll come back with limbs of iron, the skin darkened, a furious eye. Seeing my mask, they'll think I'm from a tough race. I'll have gold: I'll be lazy and brutal. Women love to look after these fierce invalids who come back from hot countries. I'll get mixed up in politics. Saved.

Right now I'm an outcast, I loathe the homeland. The best thing for me's a boozy sleep on the beach.

We can't take off. —Back again to the local roads, lugging my vice, the vice that's grown its roots of suffering at my side since the birth of reason—that rises to the skies, clobbers me, knocks me down, drags me along.

The ultimate innocence and the ultimate shyness. So they say. Never to show the world my disgusts and my betrayals.

Let's go! The march, the burden, the desert, the boredom, and the flare-up.

Who needs a paid hand? Which beast do I worship? Which holy ikon do we attack? Whose hearts do I break? What lie do I cover up? —In what blood do I stomp?

Instead, steer clear of justice. —The tough life, un*com*plicated brutishness—just lift the coffin's lid with a withered fist, sit down, suffocate. This way no old age, no dangers: Terror isn't French.

—Aaaaaah! I feel so godforsaken that I offer my yearnings for perfection to any divine image *whatever*.

O my abnegation, O my marvelous charity! here on *earth*, however!

De profundis, Domine, what a jackass I am!

When I was a kid, I admired the uncompromising convict the prison gates were closed on forever. I visited the taverns and rooming houses he'd consecrated by his stay. I looked *with his mind* at the blue sky and the flower-patterns in the countryside. I could smell his downfall in the cities. He had more strength than a saint, more horse sense than a traveler—and he, he alone! as a witness of his renown and his rightness.

On the highways on winter nights, with no roof, no clothes, no bread, a voice would clutch at my frozen heart: "Weakness or strength: there you *are*, it's strength. You don't know where you're going, or why you're going. Go everywhere, answer everything. They won't kill you any more than they'd kill a corpse." In the morning I'd have a look so lost and features so dead that those I met *probably didn't see me*.

In the cities the mud suddenly seemed to me reddish and black, like a mirror when the lamp moves around in the next room, like a treasure in the woods! GOOD LUCK, I shouted, and I saw a sea of flames and smoke in the sky. And on the left, on the right, all sorts of fabulous riches blazing like a billion thunderbolts.

But orgies and the comradeship of women weren't available to me. Not even a side-kick. I could see myself in front of an infuriated mob, facing a firing squad, weeping over the misfortune they wouldn't have understood, and forgiving! —Like Joan of Arc! —"Priests, professors, masters, you're making a mistake by turning me over to justice. I've never belonged to this people. I've never been a Christian. I'm of the breed that *sang* under torture. I can't figure out laws. I've got no moral sense, I'm a wild man: you're making a mistake . . .!"

Sure, I shut my eyes to your light. I'm a beast, a nigger. But I can be saved. You're all phony niggers, you maniacs, zealots, misers. Businessman, you're a nigger. Judge, you're a nigger. General, you're a nigger. Emperor—Old Itchiness—you're a nigger, you've drunk untaxed liquor from Satan's distillery. —This people is uplifted by fever and cancer. Cripples and old people are so respectable they *cry out* to be boiled. —The smartest thing would be to cut out from this continent where insanity goes prowling around to supply these wretches with hostages. I'm moving on to the true kingdom of the children of Ham.

Do I know Nature yet? do I know myself? —*No more words*. I bury the dead in my belly. Shouts, drum, dance, dance, dance, dance! I can't even imagine the time when, after the white men've landed, I'll plunge into Nothingness.

Hunger, thirst, shouts, *dance, dance, dance, dance*.

The white men are landing! The cannon! We've got to submit to baptism, getting dressed, work.

I just got a stroke of grace through the heart. Ah, that's something I hadn't expected!

I've done no evil. My days'll be light, I'll be spared repentance. I won't've known the torments of the soul that's almost dead to goodness from which a light glows through as grave as funeral candles. The fate of sons of good families: the premature coffin covered with limpid tears. Naturally debauchery is stupid, vice is stupid. What's rotten's to be swept aside. But the clock won't've managed to strike anything but the hour of pure pain. Am I going to be picked up like a child to play in Paradise and forget everything painful?

Quick! are there *other* lives? Sound sleep's impossible for those with wealth. Wealth has always been public property. God's love alone confers the keys of knowledge. I see now that Nature's nothing but an extravaganza of goodness. Goodbye daydreams, ideals, misdeeds.

The reasonable song of angels rises from the rescue ship: it's God's love. —Two loves! I can die of earthly love or die of devotion. I've cast aside the souls whose pain will increase by my going! You're choosing *me* among the shipwrecked. Aren't those who are left behind my friends?

Save them!

Reason's born in me. The world is good. I'll start blessing life. I'll love my brothers. These aren't childish promises any longer. Nor the hope of escaping old age and death. God's giving me strength and I praise God.

Boredom's no longer my love. Rages, dissipation, insanity—I've known all their excitements and disasters—my whole burden's laid down. Let's consider coolly the extent of my innocence.

I wouldn't be able to ask any more for the comforts of a thrashing. I don't consider myself setting out on a wedding with Jesus Christ as father-in-law.

I'm not a prisoner of my reason. I said: God. I want *freedom* in salvation: how do I find it? I've lost my taste for the frivolous. No more need of devotion or divine love. I don't miss the century of bleeding hearts. Each has its charms, contempt *and* charity. And I reserve my place at the summit of this angelic ladder of good sense.

As for conventional happiness, domestic or not . . . no, I just can't. I'm too worn out, too weak. Life flourishes only when you *work*, an old cliché! As for me, my life doesn't weigh enough, it flies off and floats high up above ACTION—that point the world measures you by.

What an old maid I'm getting to be because I lack the courage to fall in love with death!

If only God granted me heavenly aerial calm and prayer—like the ancient saints. —The saints, tough types! anchorites, such artists we don't *want* any more!

Never-ending joke? My innocence makes me want to weep. Life's the joke each of us keeps on playing.

Enough! here's the punishment. —For*waaaaaaaaaaaard*, MARCH!

Agh! the lungs are on fire, the temples groan! The night rotates inside my eyes in this sunlight! The heart . . . the limbs . . .

Where are we heading? to battle? I feel weak! the others are moving ahead. Tools, weapons . . . time . . .!

Shoot! shoot me! *Here*! or I'll surrender. —Cowards! —I'll kill myself! I'll throw myself under the horses!

Ah . . .!

—I'll get used to it.

—That would be the French Way of Life, the path of honor!

HELLISH NIGHT

I've swallowed a terrific mouthful of poison. —Blessings three times over on the impulse that came to me! —My guts are on fire. The poison's violence twists my limbs, misshapes me, flings me down. I'm dying of thirst, I'm choking, I can't scream. It's hell, endless pain! Look the fire flashes up! I'm burning nicely. *Go to it, hellcat!*

I'd caught a glimpse of conversion to goodness and happiness, salvation. Can I describe the vision? hell's atmosphere won't allow hymns! There were millions of charming people, an enchanting spiritual concert, strength and peace, noble ambitions, and so forth.

Noble ambitions!

And this is still life! —What if damnation's everlasting! A man who wants to mutilate himself is pretty well damned, right? I think I'm in hell, therefore I'm there. It's the catechism come true. I'm the slave of my baptism. Parents, you've created my tortures and yours. —Poor nitwit! Hell can't wield power over pagans. .

This is still *life*! Later on, the delights of damnation will be much deeper. A crime, quick, so I can plunge into Nothingness in accordance with human law.

Shut up, will you shut up . . .! There's disgrace and reproaches here: Satan who keeps saying the fire's contemptible, who keeps saying my temper's desperately silly. —Enough . . .! Lies and more lies they're whispering to me, magic, misleading perfumes, childish music. —And to think I'm dealing in truth, I'm looking at justice: my reasoning powers are sane and sound, I'm ready for perfection . . . Pride. —My scalp is drying up. Help! Lord, I'm scared. I'm thirsty, so thirsty! O childhood, the grass, the rain, the lake water on stones, *the moonlight when the bell was striking twelve* . . . The devil's in the tower right now. Mary! Holy Virgin . . .! —The *horror* of my blunder.

Out there, aren't those good people who're wishing me well . . .? Come . . . I've got a pillow over my mouth, they won't hear me, they're ghosts. Besides, no one ever thinks of others. Don't come near me. I smell like I've been roasted, I'm sure.

No end to these hallucinations. It's exactly what I've always known: no more faith in history, principles forgotten. I'll keep mum: poets and visionaries would be jealous. I'm a thousand times richer, let's be miserly like the sea.

Well now! the clock of life stopped a few minutes ago. I'm not in the world any more. —Theology's a serious thing, hell is certainly *way down*— and heaven's up high. —Ecstasy, nightmare, sleep in a nest of flames.

What tricks of attentiveness out in the country . . . Satan—Old Nick— goes running around with the wild grain . . . Jesus is walking on the blackberry bushes without bending them . . . Jesus used to walk on troubled waters. The lantern revealed him to us, standing, pale, with long brownish hair, on the crest of an emerald wave . . .

I'm going to unveil all the mysteries: religious mysteries or natural, death, birth, future, past, cosmogony, nothingness. I'm a master of hallucinations.

Listen . . . !

I've got all the talents! —There's no one here and there's someone: I wouldn't want to waste my treasure. —Do you want nigger songs, houri dances? Do you want me to disappear, to dive down for the *ring*? Do you want that? I'm going to make gold . . . remedies.

Then have faith in me, faith is soothing, it guides, it cures. Come, all of you—even the little children—and I'll comfort you, I'll spill out my heart for you, the marvelous heart! —Poor men, workers! I don't ask for prayers. Just with your trust I'll be happy.

—And what about me? All of this doesn't make me miss the world much. I'm lucky not to suffer more. My life was nothing but lovely mistakes, it's too bad.

Shit! let's make every possible ugly face.

We're out of the world, for sure. Not even a sound. My touch has disappeared. Ah, my castle, my Saxony, my willow woods. Evenings, mornings, nights, days . . . I'm so tired!

I should have my hell for anger, my hell for pride—and the hell of laziness: a whole collecton of hells.

I'm dying of tiredness. It's the grave, I'm going to the worms, ordeal of ordeals! Satan, you joker, you want to take me apart with your charms. I appeal. I appeal! a poke of the pitchfork, a drop of fire.

Ah, to come up to life again! to feast my eyes on our deformities. And that poison, that kiss a thousand times *damned*! My weakness, the world's cruelty! My God, mercy, hide me, I always misbehave! —I'm hidden and I'm not.

It's the fire flashing up again with its Damned.

DELIRIUM

I

The Foolish Virgin

The Hellish Bridegroom

Let's listen to a hell-mate's confession:

"O heavenly Bridegroom, My Lord, please don't reject the confession of the saddest of your servant girls. I'm lost. I'm drunk. I'm impure. What a life!

"Forgive me, heavenly Lord, forgive me! Ah, forgive me! Lots of tears! And lots more tears later on, I hope!

"Later on, I'll get to know the heavenly Bridegroom! I was born to submit to Him. —The *other* one can give me beatings for the time being!

"Right now, I'm at the bottom of the world, O my friends! . . . no, not my friends . . . Never been such delirium and tortures as these . . . How idiotic!

"Aaaaaaa, I'm suffering, I'm screaming. I'm really suffering. Still, everything's permitted me—burdened with the contempt of the most contemptible of hearts.

"Anyway, let's make this admission, doesn't cost anything to repeat it another twenty times—as dreary, as insignificant as ever!

"I'm a slave to the hellish Bridegroom, the one who ravished the foolish virgins. He's *that* devil, all right. He's not a fantasy, he's not a ghost. But I who've lost all control, who've become damned and dead to the world—they won't kill me! How do I describe him to you? I can't even talk any more. I'm in mourning, I weep, I'm scared. A bit of coolness, Lord, if you wish it—only if you wish it!

"I'm a widow . . . —I *was* a widow . . .—well yes, I used to be serious once, and I wasn't born to become a skeleton . . .! As for him, he was almost a child . . . His mysterious delicacies had enticed me. I forgot all my human duties and followed him. What a life! Real life doesn't exist. We're not in the world. I go where he goes, I've *got* to. And many times he gets screaming mad at me, *me, poor thing.* The *devil*! —He's a devil, you know, he's *not a man*.

"He says: 'I don't like women: love's got to be reinvented, that's obvious. All they're able to grasp is the need for security. Once they've got security, feelings and beauty are put aside: all that's left is cool disdain, the food of marriage these days. Or else I see women with the earmarks of happiness, with whom I could have been close friends, swallowed up right away by pigs with the sensitivity of oak logs . . .'

"I listen to him turning disgrace into glory, cruelty into grace. 'I belong to a faraway race: my forebears were Scandinavians. They used to pierce their sides, drink their own blood.—I'm going to gash myself all over, tattoo my whole body, I want to be as hideous as a Mongol: you'll see, I'll be howling in the streets. I want to become insane with rage. Don't ever show me jewels, I'd crawl and writhe on the floor. My wealth, I'd like it splattered with blood all over. I'll never work . . .' Many nights his devil would lay hold of me, we'd roll on the floor. I'd wrestle with him! —Many times at night, soused, he hides there waiting for me in the streets or behind houses to scare the daylights out of me —'They're really going to chop my head off. It'll be disgusting.' O those days when he likes to swagger around in an air of crime!

"Sometimes he talks, in a kind of touching dialect, about death which can make you repent, about the miserable people who certainly exist, about irksome jobs, about separations that rip out the heart. In the dives where we'd get drunk, he used to weep just looking at the people around us—down-and-out livestock. He'd pick up drunkards in dark streets. He had the pity of a rotten mother for little kids. —He walked around with the gentleness of a little girl going to catechism. —He made believe he knew everything there was to know about everything—business, art, medicine. I followed him, I *had* to!

"I saw the whole décor he surrounded himself with in his own mind: clothes, sheets, furniture. I lent him weapons, another face. I looked at everything in relation to him, as he'd have liked to create it for himself. Whenever he looked absent-minded, I'd follow him into freaky and complicated strategies, far out, good or bad: I was sure I'd never get into his world. Next to his gorgeous sleeping body how many hours I used to spend awake at night, wondering why he wanted to escape from reality so badly. No man ever had such a wish. I realized—without any fear for him—that he could be a serious threat to society. —Maybe he's got secrets to *change life*? No, he's only looking for some, I'd say to myself. His charity's bewitched, in short, and I'm its prisoner. No other soul would have the strength—the strength of despair!—to endure it, to be protected and loved by him. Besides, I couldn't imagine him with another soul: you see your Angel, never someone else's Angel—I think. I was in his soul like in a palace you've vacated so nobody plebeian like yourself can be seen: that's the size of it. But God, I was *really* dependent on him! Yet what did he need my dull and spineless existence for? He wasn't making me any better—when he wasn't killing me outright!

Out of sadness and spite, I'd sometimes tell him: 'I understand you.' He'd shrug his shoulders.

"So, since my grief was always being renewed and since I looked more hopeless than ever in my own eyes—like in the eyes of everyone who would've watched me if I hadn't been condemned to oblivion forever by everyone!—I kept hungering more and more for his kindliness. With his kisses and his loving hugs, it was really a heaven—a dark heaven—which I entered and which I'd have liked to be stranded in, poor, deaf, dumb, blind. I'd become completely hooked. I saw us as two good children, free to walk around in the Paradise of sadness. We got along fine. Deeply moved, we worked together. But after a penetrating caress, he'd say: 'How queer it'll all seem when I'm no longer here—what you've gone through. When you don't have my arms around your neck any more, or my heart to lie down on, or this mouth teasing your eyes. Because I'm going to have to go some day, pretty far. After all, I'm going to have to help the others: it's my duty. Even though it's not terribly appetizing . . . sweetheart . . .' Right away I could see myself, with him gone, in the clutch of vertigo, plunging down into deepest darkness: death. I'd make him promise never to leave me. He made it twenty times, that lovers' promise. It was as flip as when I used to tell him: I understand you.'

"Look, I've never been jealous of him. He'll never leave me, I keep thinking. What would he do? He doesn't know a thing. He'll never work. He wants to live a sleepwalker's life. Do his goodness and charity alone give him the right to live in the real world? At times, I forget the depths I've fallen to: he'll make me strong, we'll go gallivanting, we'll hunt in deserted places, we'll sleep on the sidewalks of unknown cities, with no worries, no griefs. Or else I'll wake up and the laws and customs will've changed—thanks to his magic powers—or the world, while staying the same, will leave me to my desires and joys and carefree ways. O the life of adventure that's found in children's books, will you give it to me to reward me for all the things I've suffered? He can't do it. I don't know what his aims are. He told me he's got regrets, hopes: it's none of my business. Does he talk to God? Maybe I should check with God. I'm in the lower depths of the abyss and I don't know how to pray.

"If he explained his sorrows to me, would I understand them better than his mockeries? He assaults me, he spends hours making me feel ashamed of everything that ever touched me in this world, and gets furious if I cry.

" 'Do you see that elegant young man going into the nice refined house: his name's Duval, Dufours, Armand, Maurice, how should *I* know? A woman devoted her whole life to loving that filthy jackass: she's dead, she's a saint in heaven now for sure. You'll kill me the way he killed that woman. That's what happens to loving hearts . . .' Agh, there were days when all active men seemed to him grotesquely ridiculous playthings. He'd laugh out loud in a ghastly way, long whiles. —Then, he'd switch right back to the manners of a young mother or a big sister. If he were less wild, we'd be saved! But his sweetness too is deadly. I'm his slave. *Aiiiiiiie*, I'm insane!

"One day maybe he'll disappear in a miraculous way. But I've simply got to find out if he's due to go up into some heaven so I'll be sure to catch a glimpse of the ascension of my luscious little lover!' "

A queer twosome!

DELIRIUM

II

Alchemy of the Word

My turn. The story of one of my screwy ideas.

For a long time I'd boasted of knowing all possible landscapes inside out and liked to poke fun at the celebrities of modern painting and poetry.

I loved idiotic paintings, door panelings, stage sets, back-drops for acrobats, street signs, popular prints, old-fashioned literature, church Latin, erotic books with terrible spelling, the novels of our grandmothers, fairy tales, little childhood storybooks, old operas, nincompoop refrains, naive rhythms.

I dreamed up crusades, voyages of discovery that haven't been recorded yet, republics with no history, hushed-up religious wars, revolutions in folk customs, displacements of nations and continents: I believed in all kinds of witchcraft.

I invented the colors of the vowels! —*A* black, *E* white, *I* red, *O* blue, *U* green. —I regulated the form and movement of every consonant and with instinctive rhythm, I prided myself on inventing a poetic language accessible to all the senses sooner or later. I reserved translation rights.

In the beginning it was trial and error. I was writing silences, writing nights. I scribbled the inexpressible. I pinned down vertigos!

Far from birds, from herds, from home-town girls,
what was I drinking on my knees in the bushes
with hazelnut trees all around me
in the lukewarm green of an afternoon mist?

What was I able to drink in that young Oise—
trees with no voices, grass with no flowers, sky with no sun!—
to drink from those yellow gourds, far from the cabin
I like? Liquors of gold that make you *sweat*.

I made a pretty poor sign for a tavern.
—A noisy storm was hassling the sky. At night
virgin sands were sucking up the wet of the woods,
God's wind kept shoving icicles in the ponds.

I wept when I looked at gold—and couldn't have a drink.

At four in the morning, summers,
the sexual sleep still lasts.
Under the trees, the love-feast's smells
      evaporate.

Out there, in their huge lumberyards,
under occidental sunlight,
already busy as bees—in shirtsleeves—
      the carpenters.

In their Deserts of Foam, quietly,
they're preparing fabulous ceilings
where the city will paint
    fraudulent skies.

For the sake of these workingmen,
eager slaves of a Babylonian king—
Venus! leave for a while the Lovers
    whose souls are crowned!

  O Queen of Herds,
 bring the workers a little brandy
 so their strength will feel no hurt
while they wait for their swim in the sea.

Out-dated poetic trickery played a big part in my alchemy of the word.

Every day I practiced easy hallucination: I actually saw a mosque where there was a factory, a corps of drummer-boys made up of angels, pony-coaches on the highways of heavens, a living-room at the bottom of a lake—monsters, mysteries—the title of a vaudeville show would suggest horrors to me.

Then I'd justify my magic sophistries with the hallucination of words!

I ended up viewing the disorder of my mind as sacred. I was passive, the victim of a heavy feverishness: I envied the happiness of animals—the caterpillars that represent the innocence of limbo—the moles, the sleep of virginity!

My temper turned sour. I said goodbye to the world in this kind of light-hearted love-song:

SONG OF THE TALLEST TOWER

Let it come, let it come,
the time we've all been dreaming of.

I've been waiting for such a while,
I've lost track of my own past.
All my fears and all my guile
have gone to heaven at last.
And a terribly unwholesome thirst
proves my blood is cursed.

Let it come, let it come,
the time we've all been dreaming of.

Like the meadows and the hills
sticky with purposefulness,
my cocksure heart *knows* and *wills*
its odors and its wildness
and breeds its gorgeous lies
like filthy flies.

Let it come, let it come,
the time we've been dreaming of.

I loved the desert, dried-up orchards, musty shops, tepid drinks. I hung around the stinking alleys and with eyes closed, I gave myself to the sun, god of fire.

·"General, if there's an old cannon left on your demolished ramparts, fire away with lumps of dried-up muck. At the mirrors of the magnificent department stores! at the living-rooms! Make the city eat its own dust. Oxidize the gargoyles. Fill the bedrooms with the red-hot powder of rubies . . ."

O the tipsy little fly in the tavern piss-pot, in love with diuretic smells, liquidated by a sunbeam!

HUNGER

If I've got taste, it's not
strictly for dirt and stones.
My breakfast's always air,
rocks, charcoal, steel.

My hungers, *turn*! Hungers,
nibble on a field of sounds.
Suck in the gorgeous poisons
of the prickly plants.

Eat up the crushed pebbles,
old stones from churches,
gravel from archaic floods,
bread scattered in gray ditches.

The wolf howled under the leaves
while spitting fine feathers out
from his feast of fowl:
like him, I devour myself.

Lettuces and fruits
are waiting there for the picking.
But the spider on the fence
eats only violets.

Let me sleep! let me boil
at the altars of Solomon.
The broth drips down the mildew
and blends with the Kedron.

At last—O happiness, O reason—I wiped out of the sky the blue which is blackness, and I lived—a golden spark of *pure light*. Out of sheer bliss, I put on an air as oafish and unhinged as possible:

It's found again!
—What? —*Eternity*.
It's the sun merging
with the sea.

My eternal soul,
stick to your desire—
despite the nights alone
and the day on fire.

This way you'll be free
from human idiocy,
from humdrum longing!
You fly according . . .

Not a trace of hope,
never any *praying.*
Knowingness and patience,
pain's a sure thing.

No more tomorrows,
bright ashes, sorrows—
        your *eagerness*
        is the key.

It's found again!
—What? —*Eternity.*
It's the sun merging
        with the sea.

I became a fabulous opera. I saw that everybody's born with a fatal need for happiness: action isn't life, but a way of maiming some power, a mere irritant. Morality's the blind spot of the brain.

Everybody seemed to me to deserve lots of *other* lives. This taxpayer doesn't know what he's doing: he's an angel. This family's a litter of puppies. With lots of people, I talked aloud with one split second of one of their other lives. —That's how I came to love a pig.

I never forgot any of the trickeries of madness—madness fit to be locked up: I could repeat them all, I'm holding on to the key.

My sanity was threatened. Terror was near. I'd fall into deep sleep for days and when I got up, I'd go on dreaming the gloomiest dreams. I was ripe for death—and on a road brimming with risks, my weakness drove me to the outer limits of the world and of Kimmeria: land of shadows and whirlwinds.

I needed to travel, to sidetrack the witchcraft that crowded my brain. Over the ocean, which I loved as if it'd been about to cleanse me of filth, I saw the cross of consolation rising up. I'd been damned by the rainbow. *Happiness* was my fatal need, my remorse, my worm: my life would always be too immense to be devoted to strength and to beauty.

Happiness! Its tooth, sweet enough to kill, warned me at the crowing of the cock—"in the morning," in the words of the hymn *CHRIST IS COM-ING*—in the darkest of cities:

O seasons, O castles!
What soul's without hassles!

Happiness was my pursuit
and I've never touched its root.
To *it* and to *you*: GREETINGS!
every time the French cock sings.

No need to keep on craving:
it sees which way you're aiming.

Its force could clinch the body and soul
and make a perfect whole.

O seasons, O castles!

The time of its ultimate flight
will be the hour of *blight*!

O seasons, O castles!

That's over now. These days I know how to say hello to Beauty.

THE IMPOSSIBLE

Ah, that childhood life of mine, the open road in and out of season, supernaturally sober, not giving a damn like the best of beggars, proud to have no country, no friends: what stupidity that was! —And I've just begun to realize it . . .

—I was right to despise those old fogeys who never lost out on a chance for a little ass-grabbing, parasites of the cleanness and healthiness of "our women," now that women seldom see eye-to-eye with us.

I was right in all my disdains—because I'm escaping!

Am I escaping?

Let me explain.

Even yesterday, I was saying: "Good grief! aren't there enough of us damned ones down here! I've already spent so much time in their camp myself! I know them all. We always recognize each other—we disgust each other. Charity's unknown among us. But we're polite. Our relations with people are quite correct." Is this stunning? People! Businessmen, nitwits! —We're not disgraced. —But the elect, how would *they* receive us? Look, these are types who are bad-tempered and blissful, the phoney elect, since you've got to have guts or humility to approach them. They're the *only* elect. They're not used to blessing!

Since I've picked up two cents' worth of smartness—*that*'s soon spent!—I can see that my anxieties come from not having figured out soon enough that we're in the Western World. The Western swamps! Not that I think the light diminished, the forms anemic, the momentum slowed down . . . Shit! look how my spirit insists on taking the blame for all the brutal developments which the Spirit's suffered since the eclipse of the East . . . My spirit's really *willing*!

. . . My two cents' worth of reason's spent! —The spirit's in charge, it wants me to be in the Western World. I'd have to silence it to end up with my own conclusions.

I said *to hell* with the glories of martyrs, the sparkle of art, the cockiness of inventors, the efficiency of exploiters. I was going back to the East and to the first and everlasting wisdom. —It seems it's a dream of crass idleness!

Still, I hardly dreamed of the pleasure of escaping the modern aches and pains. I didn't have the bastard wisdom of the *Koran* in mind. —But isn't there genuine torture in the fact that ever since that manifesto of science, Christianity, man's been *kidding himself,* convincing himself of the obvious, inflating himself with the thrill of repeating the *proofs,* and just can't live any other way? Finicky torture, stupid—the root of my own psychic meanderings. Nature might get bored, perhaps! Mr. Play-It-Safe was born the same day as Christ.

Isn't it because we're cultivating fog? We eat fever with our watery vegetables. And drunkenness! and tobacco! and ignorance! and self-sacrifice! —All that's a long shot from the wit and wisdom of the East, the primieval fatherland, isn't it? What good's a modern world if poisons like that are invented?

The clergymen will say: We see your point. But you're talking Eden. Not a thing in the history of Western civilization for you. —That's true. It's *Eden* I was thinking of! What's that got to do with my dream, that purity of ancient races!

The philosophers: The world is ageless. The human race, quite simply, moves around. You're in the Western World but you're free to live in your East, as ancient as you care to be—and quite comfortably. Never say die. —Philosophers, you're stuck with your West.

O my soul, watch out. No violent schemes of salvation. Get busy! —Ah, science doesn't move fast enough for us!

—But I notice my soul's asleep.

If it kept staying wide awake from now on, we'd soon reach the truth which may be surrounding us with its weeping angels . . .! If it'd been awake up to this point, I wouldn't have given in to my devastating instincts at a moment I'll never forget . . .! If it'd always been awake, I'd be *flying high* on the breeze of wisdom . . .!

O purity! purity!

It's this moment of awakening that's given me the vision of purity! —We come to God through the spirit!

—Tough bit of bad luck!

LIGHTNING

The work of the human race! that's the explosion that lights up my lower depths from time to time.

"*Nothing*'s vanity. Move ahead with science!" shouts the modern Ecclesiastes, which is to say EVERYBODY. And yet the corpses of the bad guys and the lazy-bones plop down on the hearts of others . . . Quick! shake the lead out! Out there, beyond the night, those future rewards, everlasting . . . are we going to miss them?

—What can I do? I know what work is. And science is too slow. Prayer gallops along and the light rumbles . . . I see that too. It's too simple, and it's too hot. They'll do without me. I've got my job. I'll take pride in it the way others do—by laying it aside.

My life is used up. Come on! let's shirk, let's gold-brick, for pity's sake! And we'll go on enjoying ourselves, dreaming up monstrous loves and fantastic universes, griping and criticizing the world's disguises—acrobat, beggar, artist, outlaw—priest! On my hospital bed, the smell of incense came back to me so potent: custodian of the sacred aromatics, confessor, martyr . . .

I recognize in that the filthy education of my childhood. So what . . .! Here's my twenty years, since others put in twenty years . . .

No! no! I revolt now against death! Work looks too lightweight to my pride: being betrayed to the world would be too *brief* a torture. At the last minute, I'd attack right and left . . .

Then—agh!—my miserable soul, wouldn't eternity be lost for keeps!

MORNING

Didn't I *once* have a lovely boyhood—heroic, fabulous, worth writing about on golden sheets, with good luck to spare! Through what crime, through what mistake did I deserve my weakness now? Those of you who tell us that animals sob with grief, that sick people despair, that the dead have bad dreams, try *please* to explain my fall and my sleep. Myself, I can no more make you see my point than the beggar with his endless *Our Father*'s and *Hail Mary*'s. *I don't know how to talk any more!*

Yet today I think I'm all through telling about my hell. It was really hell. The old hell, the one whose doors were thrown open by the Son of Man.

From the same desert, towards the same night, my tired eyes always wake up to the silver star, always, without ever managing to move the Kings of life, the three magi—the heart, the soul, the mind. When are we going to take off, past the shores and the mountains, to greet the new task, the new wisdom, the defeat of tyrants and devils, the end of superstition—to worship—*the first to do so*!—Christmas on this earth!

The singing in the heavens, the marching of the peoples! Slaves, let's not curse this life.

GOODBYE

Autumn already! —But why worry about everlasting sunshine since we're hell-bent on discovering the divine light—far away from those who get all hung up on the seasons.

Autumn. Our boat, lifting up in the motionless mists, turns towards the port of misery, the enormous city in a sky splotched with fire and muck. Ah, the rotten rags, the rain-soaked bread, the drunkenness, the thousand loves that've crucified me! She'll never be *through*, then, that ghoulish queen of a million dead souls and bodies *which are going to be judged*! I see myself again—skin eaten away by muck and plague, hair and armpits full of worms and much larger worms in the heart, bedding down with strangers of no status, no feelings . . . I could've died there . . . NIGHTMARE MEMORY! I *despise* poverty.

And I dread winter because it's the comfortable season!

—Sometimes in the sky I see limitless beaches covered with white countries full of joy. A huge golden ship, high above me, waves its many-colored banners in the morning breezes. I've created all the holidays, all the triumphs, all the dramas. I've tried to invent new flowers, new stars, new flesh, new tongues. I thought I'd acquired supernatural powers. O well! my imagination and my memories've got to be buried! A grrrrrreat artist's and story-teller's fame blinked out!

Me! *me* who've called myself magus and angel, above every moral code, I yield to the earth—there's duty to dig out, there's a harsher reality to get the hang of! PEASANT!

Was I wrong? Is charity death's kid sister for the likes of me?

Anyway, I'll ask forgiveness for having gorged myself on lies. Move along.

But not *one* friendly hand! and where do you turn for help . . .?

Yeah, the new hour's at least pretty harsh.

Because I can say victory's been won: the gnashing of teeth, the hissing of fire, the stinking sobs are all simmering down. All the filthy memories are fading away. My last regrets are skedaddling: feeling jealous of beggars, of thieves, of death's friends, of the maladjusted of all kinds. —*Damn* you! if I ever get revenge!

We've got to be *strictly* modern.

No more odes: hang on to what's been won. Hard night! dried blood smoking on my face, and I've got nothing behind me except that horrible bush . . .! Spiritual combat's as brutal as combat with people, but the vision of justice is the pleasure of God alone.

But now it's the vigil. Let's welcome all the inflows of vigor and genuine tenderness. And at dawn, armed with a terrific patience, we'll walk right into the magnificent cities.

Why talk about a friendly hand! One benefit is that I can now ridicule the old fakeries of love and heap scorn on all the two-faced couples—I saw the hell of women down there!—and now I'll be entitled *to enjoy the whole truth in one soul and one body.*

April-August 1873

The
SURREALIST MOVEMENT
In The United States

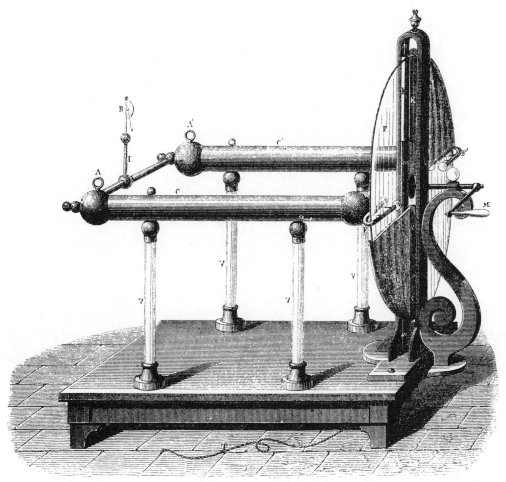

Fig. 307. Scheibenelektrisirmaschine.

In response to the sympathetic invitation of the publisher, this separate section was entirely compiled and edited by members of the surrealist movement. It appears here as an exception to their refusal to participate in projects outside their own origination, since such projects are generally incompatible with surrealism's revolutionary aims and principles.

The Surrealist Movement in the U.S.

Table of Contents

ILLUSTRATIONS BY: Thom Burns, Robert Day, Jean Jacques Jack Dauben, E. F. Granell, Robert Green, Louise Hudson, Timothy R. Johnson, Wayne Kral, Ronald Lee Papp, Franklin Rosemont, Penelope Rosemont.

Robert Green: *Blind Railroad*

Manifesto

Lighthouse of the Future

Death to Miserabilism!

Pessimism exists only to be carried as far as it will go.

Whatever else we may be, we are not mourners of false steps along the endless escalators of lost time.

Life is boring, society is boring, art is boring; above all, boredom is boring.

Only by despairing, and then despairing of despair, can mankind begin truly to *see* and to act consciously in the service of the marvelous. This preliminary violation of the rules prepares the way for an entirely new game, *our* game, known as subversion, sublime love, the exaltation of freedom.

Notwithstanding the whimpering objections of art critics and museum necrologists, the surrealist game is, in essence, the *crime of the century*. It can be played only by those who know that it can be played only for keeps.

All or nothing is the watchword of this absolutely modern and ever-renewed *crime of crimes* that magnetizes our thoughts and deeds and guides them through the ubiquitous fog of dissimulation like the blackest raven seized from the left eye of the reddest lion.

To those who ask why surrealism has eluded the attention of criminologists we reply: for the same reason that it repels every recuperative effort of every *specialist* — the feverish or clammy grasp of the political dilettante, the art clown, the "psychedelic"/mystical lackwit, all seeking historical justification for their miserable impotence. Like the Great Invisibles surrealism is beyond the reach, beyond even the *scales of reference* of these atomized gnats whose ambition is only to replace the stoolpigeons, "intellectual" or otherwise, who continue to serve the wardens of the universal dungeon of everyday life.

Specialization, to the extent that it fails to exceed a restricted domain, is a kind of soul of the soulless system of human isolation, a form of self-crucifixion on the cross of commodity fetishism. Unalterably disdainful of this contemptible system of mass mutilation, the surrealists demand nothing less than the fullest development of the unfettered imagination, the expansion of the human personality, the triumph of the human spirit.

It is no accident that all the shadow-boxers in the stupefying half-light of competitive ideology, apparently having nothing better to do than to perfect the abject thrusts and parries of vain "intellectual" equivocations, recognize us precisely as their *worst enemies*.

Report to the Council of Salamanders

Five hundred years after the birth of Copernicus there still exist such things as priests, cops, landlords. While the number of kings has diminished, the number of *cash registers* increases beyond belief. These facts alone suffice to make us wonder how it is that so many people manage to refrain from running amok.

From the headlines of the daily papers to the footnotes of academic journals it is rats and more rats who are in charge of "Reality." On this score we have passed beyond the point of argument:

Salvador Allende's "revolution" collapses like a balloon before a putrid alliance of the military and the petty-bourgeoisie.

Zionism colludes with a cenacle of Arab politicians with all the usual atrocities and hypocrisies.

The Pope, having unfortunately survived a heroic attempt on his life in 1970, confers with the Dalai Lama.

The suicide rate soars.

The leading bureaucrats of the United Auto Workers in Detroit hire a legion of club-swinging goons to assault union auto workers on a wildcat strike; a high-ranking police official remarks "I'm glad the union is on our side."

The infamous "power blocs" career over the globe like the immensely bloated creatures in Tex Avery's magisterial 1947 cartoon *King-Size Canary.* The repressive organization of alienation and reification, the regimentation of leisure and confusion, proceeds in all directions with its insidious technical refinements under the various and more or less interchangeable labels of entertainment, literature, tourism, politics, mysticism, pornography, diplomacy, sports, patriotism, law, advertising, speculation, psychology, etc.

In the last seconds of *King-Size Canary* the empty bottle of Jumbo-Gro unmistakably poses the question: where do we go from here?

Revolution x Revolution x Revolution = Revolution³

Nothing could be more obvious: we are not free, you are not free, no one is free.

Almost as obvious, however, is the fact that those who pretend to embody the cause of freedom, the maudlin "left"— and we refer to the entire U.S. Left, with only a handful of individuals and actions excepted — is bogged down in timidity, ashamed of itself, choking on its own collar, stumbling over its broken promises, devoid of all daring, imagination, lucidity and initiative. It has never been more evident than today why Marx said "I am no Marxist." Once the idea of Revolution is reduced to the spectre of a halfheartedly awaited messiah, "theory" inevitably becomes merely the arbitrary preparation of retrospective menus for the unattended banquets of an entirely abstract and illusory future. In their mad dash in search of *ways out for themselves* (academic sinecures, low-level posts in this or that trade union, a page or two in the *New York Review of Books,* not to mention vague dreams of holding comfortable posts in the bureaucracy of a future "socialist" state) the Left sectarians have irretrievably compromised their revolutionary integrity. Quite simply, they are *not serious;* they are entirely lacking in *umor*;* Jacques Vaché has never existed for them. They dither over "theoretical" tremblings hardly capable of cracking an egg-shell, much less the crust of everyday life. Meanwhile, several million workers have come to agree with the surrealists on the fundamental point: the necessity for the abolition of work.

*see "What is Surrealism?" *Selected Writings of André Breton.* Pathfinder Press, 1974 (forthcoming)

But if the Left is largely the captive of a retrograde mythology (*economism* in one form or another) the class struggle assuredly is no myth. In spite of the grotesque confusion of the various "parties," the surrealists are indissolubly united to the *party of the proletariat* in the sense intended by Marx. It cannot be emphasized too strongly that there is no solution to any social problem outside the absolute power of workers' councils. But as surrealists we are concerned above all with problems of the *human condition* which, because they arose before the advent of capitalism, cannot be expected to disappear automatically with its overthrow. If the surrealists have assumed, within the party of the proletariat, the position of *moral lookout*, it is because the surrealist perspective looks beyond the proletarian seizure of power.

For evident historical reasons surrealism here and now assumes, on the organizational level, the form of a militant minority. Between the old poetry (which maintained its position, however uneasily, within the shoddy framework of "Culture") and the generalized poetry, entirely outside the poem, as announced by Lautréamont, current surrealist poetic practice serves as an indispensable revolutionary transition. The poetic conquests of surrealism, no less than its conquests in the plastic arts, are merely the first skirmishes in a protracted war.

It would be absurd to deny that for most of our contemporaries a surrealist poem or painting retains an element of the incomprehensible. But it would be more than absurd, if not merely dishonest, to mistake or misrepresent the character of the obstacle between surrealist works and the majority of society. What prevents most individuals from immediate appreciation of a surrealist poem or painting is not a product of any attempt by the writer or painter to exalt his or her own personality above and beyond all other beings in the name of a supposed "individual liberation." Rather such a barrier, or more precisely such a challenge, is the natural consequence of the authenticity of the surrealist message in a world in which human beings are forced, every day of their lives, to accept and pass on false promises, to call each other and themselves by false names, to admit in their most sincere moments to a terrible deceit. The foundation of all surrealist efforts, whether in poetry, the plastic arts, political action, or scientific research, has always been the destruction of all forms of exploitation by forms of inspiration, asserting the primacy of human motives and needs: love, freedom, the marvelous.

As defined by the title of Lenin's first periodical — *Spark (Iskra)* — the task of the revolutionary communist in capitalist as well as in the monstrously bureaucratized "socialist" countries is to grasp and expand the transitory moments of lucidity that pass back and forth among the workers on the factory floor, in mines, on the decks of ships. The task of the surrealist is no less in the other, ceaselessly alternating spheres of everyday existence — in the hallways of a million apartment buildings, in public parks, above all in the streets: to amplify the occasional gleam between men and women together, between men and women themselves (summarized by the perpetual expectation that at any moment a decisive revelation will emerge from the crowd and be recognized without hesitation) into an illimitable beacon of freedom.

The permanent surrealist revolution is the permanent revolution of everyday life, the permanent festival of men and women celebrating the *becoming of freedom.*

With the realization of poetry and philosophy in the streets, on rooftops, in railroad yards, on the seacoast and everywhere else; with the abolition of the contradictions between dream and action, collective and individual, subjective and objective, city and countryside, etc., surrealism will at last cease to be minoritary. As poetry advances from the last vestiges of its alienated forms into the living dream of everyday passional attraction, the surrealist game will be played by all.

Treason Is Sweeter Than Honey

We refuse to content ourselves with being merely the best-hated men and women of our time.

The language of the birds has not been forgotten.

Anyone who accuses us of changing the subject deserves a punch in the nose.

We could say, in the spirit of Pythagoras, that it is never too early to learn to dream the undreamed.

The imagination is revolutionary or it is nothing.

The Revolution will be surrealist or will not be at all.

THOM BURNS, LUCY CATLETT, JEAN-JACQUES DAUBEN,
ROBERT DAY, PAUL GARON, ROBERT GREEN,
LOUISE HUDSON, JOSEPH JABLONSKI,
TIMOTHY R. JOHNSON, JOCELYN KOSLOFSKY,
WAYNE KRAL, PHILIP LAMANTIA, PETER MANTI,
DIANE MEUCCI, PATRICK MULLINS, RONALD LEE PAPP,
JANET PARKER, NANCY PETERS, FRANKLIN ROSEMONT,
PENELOPE ROSEMONT, STEPHEN SCHWARTZ,
RICHARD WAARA, LAURENCE WEISBERG

F. R.

Sonata

*Many years had passed
since the stranger fled
in a violent fright
He traversed the marrow of my bones
cutting a pathway
of emerald wreathes*

*Now the window perched
a falcon of silken alertness
beside a pool of evening
Outside there were unstable
fluctuating portraits
of exchanged glances
seas of turbulent crimes
dances of naked wind*

*As he turned to look
they ceased
A touch of bewilderment
discovered the darkness like a knife
Like a child I slept
thick with incident
The words beneath the palm tree
flew faster and faster
through an empty space in the street
The far horizon held a figure
of spreading wings
The stones began their minuet
The wild owl of midnight
chanted his evening song*

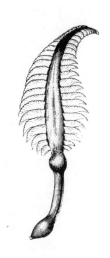

*The narrow paths of black
the clock of polished shells
the bed of voices
the shadows of unfamiliar doorways
and the soft network of pistols
beside the aurora borealis*

*Little whispers of hidden madness
arose to light the candles
for the drama of the eclipse
under a bright green crimson sky
of elephants
The wild owl of midnight
chanted his evening song*

PENELOPE ROSEMONT

The Golden Times

to Nancy

The boat tilts on your image on the waves between a fire of foam and the flower of moon-rays, these *the flags of your dreaming lips. I'm watching Venus on the ogred sky and a continent in cocoons.*

Soon all the butterflies of desire shall manifest o prescience of life becoming poetic and poetry, the incense of the dream . . . A street and a forest interchange their clothing, that *tree of telephones,* this *television of nuts and berries — the air, edible music.*

King Analogue
Queen Image
Prince Liberty
. . . Garden of imperious images . . . life is a poem someday to be lived: the feast of our hearts on fire, the nerves supplying spice, blood coursing a glow of insects, our eyes the dahlias of torrential ignition.

The whisper of the inter-voice to wrap you in the mantle of marvelous power, with the secret protection of the forest that falls asleep in fire whose ores become trans-mined only for human love — all your steps shall lead to the inner sanctum none but you may behold, your shadow putting on a body of metaphoric light.

The stone I have tossed into the air of chance shall come to you one great day and exfoliate the original scarab, the carbuncle of delights, the pomegranate inviolate, the sonorous handkerchief of the *Comte de Saint-Germain,* all the re-invented perfumes of ancient Egypt, the map of the earth in the Age of Libra when the air shall distribute our foods, the sempiternal spectrum of sundown at *Segovia,* the stork carrying the golden egg from the Templar's Tower, Chief Seattle's lost medicine pouch, our simultaneous presence in all the capitals of Europe while traveling Asia and listening to the million-throated choir of tropical birds, your lost candlewax empire, a madrone forest to live inside of which we can wrap up in a set of "secret bags" and open on our wanderlusts, the turbulent cry beneath the oceans, the extinct-birdcalls in a magical vessel *Christian Rosenkreutz* dropped on his way out of *Damcar,* beads of coral dissolving the last motors, the redolent eyes of firstborn seers, the key to the bank of sanity, the ship of honey at the height of storms through which we sail to new islands rising from the sunken continents and the bridge between sleep and waking we shall traverse in constant possession of "the great secret" become transparent as a teardrop — then, *with no other work but the genius of present life.*

Atlantic Ocean, passing the Azores Islands,
January 1968-San Francisco, December 1973.

Green Lion

At the street of caves where the fourheaded gnomes
Arrive in pairs followed by arrows
Gliding on our footsteps
The flowers basking behind the chandeliers
Have thrown buckets of dragon paint
To overflow into the suburbs
Keyless windows open to the touch of meteorites
Which are nonetheless hallucinatory shadows
Wherever I live at the raging scabbard's signpost
We march through the swamp of the moments
With the gilt tongue of grail venom
With the venom of adamant ferment
We shall find the talons of the three-colored process
As our eyes close to the checkerboard
And the night rushes through her own envelopes
Interspersed with salacious lakes
At the coming-to-be of militant swans
The odoriferous stream of ocular telephones
Connecting the vial bearing a watery armor
To the geomantic tablets exalting revolution
No one but the crimson bed-calmer deciphers

The Element You Love

*I can see you from the headgears navigating the beach lined with cement,
motioning the fallen arch of a comet that pelts a falcon's river, unheard
of jostling submerging the lamp posts.*

A waylaid victor at his flying pyramid, ochre is the window of the salutory
eye . . . *and a blast of doorways eludes a lion here and there nonchalantly
signaling* sudden ladies *about to vanish through the rain's escutcheon
where the civilized lusts plumed with anti-cephalic inanities bid their
guests go up in flames.*

*No less than a burnished chicken machineguns the greasy light of preachers
sinking into the docks the woman sets free by water, combing a vitreous
dress out of which fall foxes-in-hand and a macaw whose beak softens
to become her cachet of liquid poetry.*

PHILIP LAMANTIA .

Wayne Kral

The New Argonautica

Few would contradict me if I said that the day-to-day catatonic miasma, abstracted from its polar coordinates of good and evil, signifies as little as the continental drift of the seven conventional wonders. Nothing would be gained, moreover, by asking why. One might as well ask why hats are held in higher esteem than heads, or why the lobster dreams of the sea. Speaking of the sea, everyone too hastily disregards its carefully groomed sleep, the sleep of gulls soothed in the fireplace and filled with despair, always on the verge of ascension, as if the riddles of existence, cut like diamonds, were to collide suddenly, one by one, across the lonely bay of lucky guesses —those serene but light-hearted "stabs in the dark." But think of what could be done with sparks such as these. And then think of what it means to laugh out loud alone on the shore!

For my part I want nothing if not the full measure beyond all mirrors, the true fork of *this is it* in the crow's nest of memory nourished by the elliptical migrations of extinct animals returning triumphant for our infinite heyday. Make no mistake—*These dragons wax no dashboards*. The game is aloof in the once and for all.

It is well known that the night packs its own secret weapon in the vest-pockets of an irrepressible longing, and this longing (woven slyly into the constellations of thought like a huge overcoat of solid ice) calls to mind the frostbitten ears of those who, on their honeymoons, hear only the clanging waves of the Aleutians or the inscrutable resistance of a bear's bedraggled shadow in the runaway silences captured in a single hurled stone. This longing, too, reminds me, whenever I run headlong into the unexpected, that I should like to button up the moaning leeway, with its moonlight and mosquitoes, suspiciously given to the vanished or vanishing hands on deck. For when the sails are set and everything is ready, I invariably prefer above all the Jolly Roger, its light green ghost of Aristotle soaked in brine.

Thus the skeleton key of chance prowls with certainty in the deep lock of the mysterious flesh of necessity. And the treasure always turns up at the sign of the x, harbinger of all revelation, insignia of every breath of true life. Yes, the treasure of treasures always turns up at the implacable and magisterial x, marinated in the magic source of all adventure: love, love and always love.

And yet in the harried and haunted system of fossilized afterthoughts, that *frenzied glacier* known as western civilization, everything human is out of whack. Everyone knows, for example, that children—poets and dreamers all—are "matured" into obedient robots, or at least into uninspired golfers, bank tellers, bureaucrats. This maturation comprises far more than the myelination of the cortico-spinal tract and the cumbersome, heart-rending process of so-called reality testing. It consists of nothing less than a self-perpetuating vicious cycle of backfiring accommodations and treacherous compromises which add up to a penthouse (combustible, it is true) for everything sniveling and an early grave for whatever manages to survive of human dignity. Let us not tarry over the notorious alibis of "Culture." Children know what the Marvelous is without asking for definitions. But how short-lived is this knowledge! Born with silver spoons of the wildest expectations in their mouths, it is not long before the steel blades of a ridiculous asceticism are plunged indifferently into their ribs. Thus every-day life is compelled to surrender, bit by bit, every trace of paradise and fairy tale, eventually becoming a barren stage on which barren apologists for alienation rehearse their barren pantomimes. The roads of everyone's good intentions are paved with this babbling hell of evasions, each more squalid than the last.

Of course there are accidents, intrusions, disturbances. How could one expect that the poetic spirit, proud and unremittingly resourceful (one will find that the poetic spirit and the human spirit are fundamentally indis-tinguishable) to endure insults and outrages without plotting its many-sided revenge? From the standpoint of the revolution of everyday life critical thought could hardly be more usefully employed than on the systematiza-tion and interpretation of these bold and (perhaps only apparently) dis-continuous eruptions of the Marvelous. I say "usefully employed" although obviously such eruptions call for the elaboration of completely non-utili-tarian—or rather *sur*utilitarian—modes of apprehension and frames of refer-ence. It was Benjamin Paul Blood who warned us: "The Hound of Heaven is on its own trail, and the vestige still lures the scent of a foregone con-clusion." The conclusion may be foregone but the implications are far-reach-ing. The considerable influence exerted on the mind by the arrangement of objects in a room (a phenomenon well known to psychiatrists) leads us to deduce that the influence exerted by far more complex and extensive ar-rangements—a city, for example—must be incomparably greater, not only for the individual but for the collective sensibility. The task before us is nothing less than the determination and analysis of the entire repressive network in all its multifarious dimensions and through all its camouflaged mutations. Only by thus exposing the mechanism in its entirety can we ascertain its least protected areas, its weakest links; and only thus will we be enabled to assist decisively in breaking the whole chain.

But this problem interests us not only, and not even chiefly, from the merely critical angle. When Rimbaud remarked that "true life" was "absent" he impelled poetic explorers to attend to every manifestation, however fleet-ing, of its *presence*. Rimbaud himself, as is known, proved unwilling or unable to carry out his own program. After him we have a few hints from Jarry, O. Henry, Apollinaire, Mayakovsky, Saint-Pol-Roux and a few others; special credit must be given to Freud, whose *Interpretation of Dreams* and *Psychopathology of Everyday Life* greatly facilitated such exploration. In a completely distinct realm of inquiry Charles Fort, especially in his *Lo!* and *Wild Talents*, drew attention to a wide range of "unaccountable" human data which he approached with considerable theoretical rigor enhanced by consummate humor (when the Canadian Ambrose Small disappeared some years after Ambrose Bierce disappeared in revolutionary Mexico, Fort posed the question: Was somebody collecting Ambroses?).

Only in 1928, however, with the publication of *Nadja* by André Breton, was proper focus brought to bear on certain convulsive and irreducible en-counters in which the real and the ideal series of events compose a single sustained moment of "true life" in an inspired and inspiring dialectical move-ment grounded in "the real functioning of thought," pivoting on the very "stuff that dreams are made of," and implying, every inch of the way, the complete reconstruction of human relations and the total transformation of the world.

The point is not, of course, to cover reality with dreams but rather to unveil the continuity of oneiric activity concealed by reality behind its tech-nologically perfected blushes of shame. Reality, after all, in the commonest usages of the word, is merely an ugly extortionist racket, submission to which is exemplified by fatalistic shrugs of the shoulders and intolerable sayings such as "That's the way it goes." Like many other frauds, reality is done with mirrors, each reflecting a vast emptiness into which the hurried passerby projects his or her anguished search for meaning. One can find these dead-end mirrors nowadays on almost any corner. A few days ago I noticed that the Cubs' baseball park is embellished with numerous signs reading "*Spectators not permitted to enter or throw objects onto playing field.*" There we have, as a comic book might put it, the whole kettle of fish in a nutshell. A mere handful of people wear all the "special" clothes, do all the playing, enjoy all the privileges, take all the money and bask in all the glory. The others, the *spectators*—and it is worth considering for a moment exactly what is meant by spectators—have only the dubious honor and pleasure (?) of paying for every bit of their own rigidly enforced passivity and alienation. This universal narcissistic parody of the blind leading the blind harbors a multitude of seasick dervishes, all at the end of their ropes. The only thing to do is to leave the accepted playing fields to their vicarious specialists and to proceed elsewhere full speed ahead, *anywhere out of the running*. This very deliberate divergence from the beaten paths is prerequisite to the discovery of an endless array of enticing lyrical improbabilities provocative of reveries at last worthy of the name—reveries which overlooked and even scorned in a society governed by the fetishism of commodities, will yet have their dawn, placing in our hands the key to lost continents, hidden valleys, secret caverns, ancient cities, new planets. And we ourselves, if we wish, shall be comets soaring through midnights in which the very stars will be at our beck and call!

I confess that I live entirely for those moments of insatiable eeriness in which the unforeseen bursts in brandishing its automatic menagerie and announcing that the tide has turned, that from now on, without irony, the pleasure will be all ours. Because such moments seem to me to comprise the only "solutions" that are really capable of solving anything, I think it is permissible to speak of an ascending spiral leading from revery to revolution, from the dream of action to the actualization of the dream (revolution being, in a sense, the collective equivalent of an individual dream in pursuit of its fulfillment). The road of permanent revolution is also the road of permanent revery.

Following this road it is of prime importance to heed, ever more closely, the seemingly inexplicable solicitations that rise phoenix-like from the ashes of boredom, distraction, hypnagogic states or anxiety, coalescing into a luminous train of disquieting associations regarding which, it must be admitted at the present state of our knowledge, it is futile to attempt to draw conclusions except as one draws a revolver—that is, as a *challenge*. Phenomena such as this pass incessantly and it is more than ever necessary to seek their laws. This effort, in turn, requires first of all breaking the proscriptive laws of positivism and sweeping away the musty inhibiting hoax of common sense, so that one may enter the fray of a volatile actuality with a single demand: the *desirable*, known by its enemies as the impossible. This arrogant demand for the realization of the impossible has the elementary virtue of automatically provoking the apparition, or at least the awareness, of new possibilities. It is a matter of inventing new needs and new emotions; it remains to be seen whether they are "impossible" or not. Lenin pointed out that "in revolutionary times the limits of the possible increase a thousandfold." And in his brilliant conspectus of Hegel's *Logic* the author of *The Threatening Catastrophe and How to Fight It* wrote in the margins, without so much as a glint of the enigmatic, the single word: *"Leaps!"* Useless to demur behind the most superficial and indefensible of intellectual defenses, to decry as sophistry that which has no other ambition than to throw a small footbridge over the chasm of syllogistic half-truths where human understanding lies in a state of irremediable putrefaction. "It is from conforming to finite categories in thought and action," as Hegel wrote, "that all deception originates."

I consider myself fortunate to have as friends only those who, if they should stumble on a magnificent revelation, still possess enough of a very rare sense of life (a sense that usually disappears with the passing of childhood) to be able to look it straight in the eye. And this is doubtless why, on various expeditions across the city, there has been no lack of ephemeral chimeras whisking by with a baffling word or an unfathomable glance. I am fond of the feeling, as we set foot out the door, that none of us has the faintest idea of where we are going—yet our footing is sure, our confidence supreme.

It hardly need be noted that it is precisely the exceptional details of everyday behavior, all essentially under the sway of *pure psychic automatism* (sexual promptings, orgasms, dreams, parapraxes, jokes, criminal urges, nocturnal emissions, etc.) that most effectively pull the rug from under the mouldering ideologists of rationalist humanism. It is true that the elucidation of such exceptional details has not prevented these ideologists from continuing to profess "faith" in altogether untenable notions of "responsibility" —behind which, to be sure, there lurks a legion of cops, priests, and other agents of capitalist law and order.

But this is all the more reason why it has become indispensable now to increasingly fix our attention with more or less maniacal rigor and a truly obsessed indifference to the consequences, on all the singular configurations, lustrous oversights, unlikely juxtapositions, explosive anachronisms and other *symptomatic accidents* whose intrinsic disavowal of complicity in the "unredeemed dreariness of thought which no goading of the imagination could torture into aught of the sublime" (to quote Poe's *Fall of the House of Usher*) makes them actually *cry out*, as it were, in a tone of unmistakable prophecy. A silver fox caught in a trap beseeches the universe for the prolongation of the night in order to multiply its opportunities for escape; when one is trapped escape is always foremost in one's thoughts, and this is no less true when a whole world is caught in the trap of ordinary logic. Even though one lies bleeding and half-dead it is still possible, not to mention admirable, to desire above all *and to find* a new and terrible innocence. Who do we think we are—always in pursuit of the most uncontainable materialist miracles, always hoping beyond hope and despairing beyond despair, always letting go of the truncated agonies of June only to catch the inexpressible devastations of July, but still holding out for a deliriously utopian August; always hurling the most easily fomented and just as easily sacrificed psychic disorders and social disasters into the whirlpool of euphoric diversions, as if one were seated in the bitter light of an attic window merely contemplating souvenirs no more nor less amazing, perhaps, than a flea circus in which all the fleas were dead. "What next?" we ask, so imperturbably that Diogenes himself cannot resist dropping by, tapping us on the shoulder, and requesting a match.

I am the first to admit that all this doesn't carry us far enough; but I have no intention of marking time. There is reason to insist on the fundamental discrepancy in any and all attempts at premeditated self-evaluation

Poetic Evidence: *Anarchist Militia aiming at statue of Jesus during the Spanish Revolution (1931-1939)*

which fail to take into account the mounting irrational evidence. Pure Heraclitian fire will guide our footsteps a long way. One cannot step twice into the same street, because it is never the same street: from one moment to the next it is four, five, six, a thousand different streets. And yet, on the affective plane, everything depends on a few salutary temptations, scattered here and there like dice, but which we do not hesitate to qualify as *permanent*: a few unassailable signposts of magical eternity, strategic intersections of internal and external necessity that let us know, concretely, that we are on the right track, that something momentous is about to happen, and that it depends on us in some still obscure and unsettling fashion. These defiant signals offered on the run convey the certainty that they are meant for us alone. They are signals of "something else," premonitory glimmers of *that which will be* perceived darkly and hazardously through the cracks and fissures in the repressive structure of everyday life.

It is remarkable how such glimmers, which are unforeseeable and uncontrollable, and which normally betray their existence and return to oblivion in less time than it takes to flip a coin, nonetheless instantly and solidly implant themselves in the fertile soil of the mind's eye, establishing brave outposts on which everything touching on the destiny of the imagination must sooner or later rely. It is also remarkable how these glimmers ceaselessly arrange and rearrange themselves into kaleidoscopic patterns swollen with mythological cunning, permitting us to seize from the flotsam and jetsam of the most idle hurricanes of silence and the most resolute minutiae of ordinary conversation a hundred thousand visible and invisible possibilities for symbolic development, all interlaced in a vast panorama of experimental poetic hallucination which erects, let us say, a *castle* constructed of Ignatz's bricks, with Blake's liberty bonnet pinned above the door, a gatling gun on the mantle, a few heads beating against the walls for good measure, the usual hands reaching into the goldfish bowl, oversize portraits of Peetie Wheatstraw and Giordano Bruno, a hippopotamus from the river Nile, a copy of *Bugs Bunny and the Magic Sneeze*, a gigantic dodo to serve as an *example*, etc. Here, in a perfect negation of the ignoble and preposterous "House of God," the mind can truly wander without fear of getting lost. But there is always a slap in the face, and far worse, for anyone who pretends to reduce this adventure to a mere virtuoso exercise or an indulgently individualistic "way out." Those who try to cheat the Marvelous, those who try to play tricks on freedom, those who regard the philosophers' stone as a universal checkbook, learn soon enough that they have only shut themselves off. For it is especially remarkable how these tremulous glimmers, demanding to be read like a book (the words of which, however, remain undeciphered) have become the astonished and astonishing bearers of an overriding *cause*. Assuming before our eyes the shapes of heretofore unimagined and highly intelligent beasts of prey, they are already organizing perilous voyages to the far corners of the unknown.

These voyages, come what may, must be followed through all the way to the end.

For some time I have attempted to record the incidents which make up such voyages; it is from this record that the following notations are excerpted. I have included here all the notes from a three week period, to illustrate the intricate interrelationships and superimpositions in the unfolding of these events.

21 February 1973. In the afternoon Penelope and I happened to be in the Chicago "Loop," attending to various chores, after which we intended to have dinner at a German restaurant, the Berghoff, 17 West Adams Street. (We had never dined there together before.) Arriving at the Berghoff, however, we found it closed; we then repaired to Miller's Pub, just down the street (another place at which we had never previously dined). There, following the peculiar terminology of the menu, I ordered a "Diamond Jim Brady" steak and Penelope a "Lillian Russell" steak.

The following morning, as a result of circumstances beyond my control, I went to Stein's Book & Novelty Store, 526 South State Street. I had been there only once, years before. This time I learned that this store is also the site of the Stein Publishing Company, publishers of a number of curious dream-books and magician's manuals, as well as a strange work titled Pow-Wows, the Long Lost Friend, *a copy of which Joseph Jablonski had sent to me from Pennsylvania over a year before. At Stein's Penelope purchased three very old German postcards of the Chicago Water Tower, which has always been among our favorite buildings in the city. I inquired of the proprietor about some old volumes in a room in back. She regarded some of these to be quite rare and, as proof, handed me a kind of scrapbook full of old theater playbills and newsclippings pertaining to the theater. As I took this book in my hands it fell open to a full page picture of Lillian Russell.*

That evening, resuming a task I had begun several days earlier, I leafed through about five books verifying some references made in my introduction to the writings of André Breton, which I was completing at the time. Among these was Henry Miller's Cosmological Eye *in which, on page 164, I noticed the name of Diamond Jim Brady.*

During this period Penelope was reading the book Stonehenge Decoded *by Gerald S. Hawkins. I recalled that when I brought this book home three years before I brought two others with it, on widely disparate subjects, but as Penelope pointed out at the time (for I had not noticed it) the covers of both bore unmistakable images of Stonehenge. I have always been fascinated by Blake's Stonehenge relief etching (in his* Jerusalem) *and I returned to it at this time.*

27 February. Penelope and I took a plane to Florida, a journey she had decided to take for some time but which for my part was decided only on the spur of the moment. Such a journey seemed to me so unanticipated, so improbable, as to be somehow perfect. I had never been to Florida before. There—in Key Largo, where we watched the starfish, searched for corals and shells, and were continually surrounded by pelicans, egrets, herons, osprey, gulls, grackles, black-eyed vireos and hundreds of other species of birds; and later, in the Everglades, along the Anhinga Trail, where all these marvels reached a crescendo far exceeding my grandest hopes—I experienced a peculiarly sustained sense of elation. I had the feeling that we had entered a privileged place at just the right moment.

Certain incidents of the Florida journey loomed large in my consciousness at the time and have fully retained their particular light. I was intrigued by the discovery of information regarding a little-known pirate, Henri Caesar, known as Black Caesar, an ex-slave who had fought in the Revolution led by Toussaint-L'Ouverture, later turned to piracy and disappeared in 1820. I visited the Key Largo library in search of works on Florida pirates, but found little; at a supermarket, however, I purchased a locally produced booklet, Pirates and Buried Treasure of the Florida Coast, *which includes a short sketch of Black Caesar.*

Among the handful of books I had taken with me to Florida was Benjamin Franklin's Autobiography, *which I had never read. I was quite surprised to read therein that Benjamin Franklin had visited Stonehenge, a revelation he offered "in passing" but which sufficed to provoke a whole series of disquieting meditations.*

On the last day of our Florida visit we went to the Circus Hall of Fame in Sarasota. Intending to return to Chicago that afternoon, we had little time to look at all the exhibits. But we were especially attracted by one of the exhibits devoted to Buffalo Bill's Wild West Show. Buffalo Bill himself —murderer of the Indians, decimator of the buffalo herds, repulsive commercial schemer—hardly interests us, of course, although his legend (as developed in countless dime-novels and subsequently in movies) certainly commands critical attention. Indeed, an investigation of the "popular mythology" that relies so heavily on such second-rate but "famous" personages could reveal much of the deepest mechanisms operant in the "American dream." But what caused us to linger before this exhibit was not so much Buffalo Bill but rather a large and charming portrait of Annie Oakley, the celebrated marksman known as "Little Sure Shot."

On 7 March we returned to Chicago. Almost immediately Penelope noted in the newspaper a long article on Key Largo and the coral reef which we had visited. A few days later she called my attention to a newspaper advertisement for a movie opening in Chicago titled Black Caesar, *about a Harlem gangster.*

11 March. In the evening I was reading T-Bone Slim's I.W.W. pamphlet Starving Amidst Too Much. *Penelope, meanwhile, and without knowing what I was reading, was looking through the Chicago* Tribune's *Book World supplement in which, on page 3, she found a review of a biography of Buffalo Bill. She read aloud a few lines from this review. including this sentence: "Annie Oakley could never explain to [Sitting Bull] why in the midst of plenty children starved."*

15 March. During a walk with Penelope I noticed the same photograph of Marilyn Monroe twice within approximately ten minutes, both times in specifically "foreign" contexts: at a Japanese store on Diversey and at the Europa Bookstore on Clark Street.

16 March. At approximately 1:00 a.m. I was musing over the peculiar manner in which certain friends expressed their anger. While considering this problem three shots rang out, their volume indicating their proximity. From the front window I noticed several police cars and signs of commotion. The morning paper explained that two German tourists who had been visiting a local German restaurant, the Munchner-Hof, had been shot: one died immediately; I learned later that the other died in the hospital.

Thus, beginning down the street from one German restaurant and reaching a violent climax down the street from another, proceeding infallibly through a veritable maze of unlikely contingencies and obeying the laws of symmetry that give to the whole range of incidents the character of a self-contained series, we are left with evidence which, no matter what, will never be swept under the carpet. It is worth remarking here, as a technical point, the necessary role of *dislocation* (the unexpected trip to the "Loop" and later to Florida) in provoking the awareness of the encounters described above. This lends support to J. W. Dunne's hypothesis, in his *Experiment With Time*, regarding the prophetic dream, that one can recognize the intrusions of the future only if one frequently alters the background against which these intrusions occur. It seems to be a question of emphasizing contrasts that are too often blurred in the muddy chiaroscuro of workaday life. One whose existence consists of the habitual repetition of the same dreary exercises in futility cannot, with such a deadened sensibility, be attuned to these dissonant intrusions which therefore pass him by in silence. It is possible, in fact, to speak of the deliberate cultivation of these intrusions, of developing one's susceptibility to them, of tempting them out of the twilight. This is not a mere recapitulation of Rimbaud's well-known "systematic derangement of the senses." It is no longer a matter of pure and simple introspective agitation but of an action on the external world as well. As Joseph Jablonski has said, it is "the ability at a moment's notice to regard anything whatsoever from a new perspective, to radicalize meaning by the application of juxtaposition," an effort requiring above all that we place ourselves unreservedly at the disposal of the possibilities of the dream of freedom.

This strategical dislocation doubtless in turn presupposes a more determining, all-embracing sensibility, which I cannot regard as otherwise than fundamentally *erotic*. The foregoing examples from my own experience seem to me of such a nature as to confirm once more the rule that the most decisive encounters of life cluster by unfailing preference under the sign of love. There alone, where the mind's wildest flora and fauna revoke the very principle of domestication, is the air truly breatheable; there alone does life become luminously livable at last. Only love can overwhelm the stifling hesitations built into the loathsome tyranny of the monotonous and the habitual; only love permits each and every intractable windfall to flourish far beyond the scope of mere "refusal" and to establish an emotional terrain where the imagination can mobilize its forces with ever greater freedom; only love can immunize us to the innumerable infectious distractions passed off as "Culture," that absolute commodity which gloatingly reigns over the empire of boredom.

To the too superfically defined objects and images of everyday use in which the misery of the human condition is most agonizingly reflected but also perpetuated in an endless charade presided over by the hydra of hopelessness, love opposes a myriad of as yet insistently indefinable interpenetrating spheres of negative light and transparent eclipses from which there unceasingly emerge new objects and images instilled with the increasingly objective vertigo of the "surprise-event." At this cataclysmic vortex of inspired intersubjectivity, where a man's and a woman's reciprocal negation of each other's separateness enables both to overtake the farthest reaches of their individual internal galaxies, the white-hot generative collisions of love — love that is always excessive and outside all laws but its own — offer us unequivocal hints of the concrete means by which the irrational is transformed into a vehicle of revolutionary action. Within the eruptive solitude and erosive silence of a single glance or a sudden embrace, love restores the androgynous vision and the oracular voice. At the same time it imparts the distinctively *lyrical* motion, the suggestive *magnetic* fluidity underlying those moments that are uniquely "momentous," those that are worth all the others.

Everything leads us to believe that these still isolated and relatively unobtrusive molecular transformations are leading up to something epochal and irreversible: an explosion of consciousness from which the outmoded "real" and "rational" world will never recover. There is every reason to expect that it is precisely along the lines of such research that we will eventually unravel the tantalizing mysteries of inspiration, intuition, the prophetic dream, *déjà vu*, telepathy, various "mysticisms," genius itself. The sinuous paths by which the various "matters of the day" impinge on and filter through the prime matter of the night are the same paths by which the prime matter of the night imposes its alternating current on subsequent matters of the day. We are concerned here with "charges" of unverifiable magnitude and duration, but which can no longer be ignored. At once compass, mojo, lantern, sword, we have here an instrument of knowledge that must be secured.

It is striking to observe how the clock of chance *outruns*, so to speak, *its own hands* in the cancellation of all moments but "the one and only." Benjamin Paul Blood, in a letter to William James, wrote: "I always get a hint of the mystery *when the clock stops by itself*." The timeless navigations of objective chance may certainly be regarded an explicit confirmation, or rather extension, of Blood's aggressive thesis in his *Anaesthetic Revelation* (1874) regarding the experience of "coming to" — that "the naked life is realized only outside of sanity altogether." Fortunately we are no longer confined, as Blood thought he was, to nitrous oxide as the only road of access to this "naked life." I am convinced, moreover, that it is for this very domain that the dialectic has reserved its most stunning, most elegant, most resonant bursts of humor, which cannot fail to work entirely in our favor: for who else even suspects the existence of, much less holds in their hands, that unique golden thread that permits the legitimate heirs of Eiranaeus Philalethes to pass at will through every labyrinth, to emerge whenever they wish from *the open entrance to the closed palace of the king* and find themselves standing before the iridescent hearth of Thelonious Sphere Monk?

I hope the introduction at this point of this last name will not be considered gratuitous. Aside from the fact that it would be impossible for me to exaggerate the overpowering effect Monk's work had on me from the moment I discovered it around the age of 15, so that ever since it has served me as talisman and catalyst, an always renewable exhilaration, always capable of mobilizing whatever opaline forces compose the "occult stream" of my own destiny; aside, that is, from such "personal" reasons, it seems to me an incontestable fact that Monk's 'Round Midnight, Epistrophy, Misterioso, Blue Monk, Crepuscule for Nellie, his collaborations with John Coltrane — his whole work, for that matter — are among the most compelling invocations to, and poetic touchstones of, that unconquerable dream, always the dream of freedom, that awaits the definitive steps of its realization in our time. In Thelonious Monk we have the admirably sustained, inescapable prelude to the nocturnal annihilation of every hypocritical empiricism. His work is an endless dream palace, a new fountain of youth, Atlantis restored and revised.

Of course in essence it is not a question of a solitary mage but of a whole magic tradition. Jazz, through which there runs the imperishable Artesian well of the blues, unquestionably is one of the most fertile and imaginatively radioactive "secret societies" of true initiation in our time. Its focussing on the ever greater freedom of improvisation; its shedding of the last traces of hybrid sentimentality, formal (European) rigidity, eclectic inhibitions; its courageous plunges and flights into automatism and chance; its intrepid humor and celebration of love closely parallel the major poetic advances of this century. Jazz may be regarded, in fact, an independent manifestation and reinforcement of that specific, all-pervasive *climate of readiness for the actualization of the Marvelous* that defines the revolutionary poetic spirit today. In jazz, especially since bebop, the white heat of "expecting the unexpected" (in the expression of Heraclitus) plays havoc with every standstill, every death-wish. The hand that feeds the dreamy interlinear motion that drives us beyond the grip of the past is also the hand that reaches, the hand that waves, the hand that holds, the hand that lets go, the hand that already caresses the infinite, the hand that sooner or later will turn the pages of time *inside out*.

Wayne Kral: *The Threat of Clouds to a Deaf Woman*

Jazz is crucial here and now not only for its manifold autonomous revelations—though these alone would suffice to oxygenate the spiritual atmosphere to a wondrous degree — but also because it comprises a succession of anticipatory and confirmatory echoes of those aleatory meanderings across the shifting gravitational field of everyday life that I have attempted to outline above. I have tried to show that in the midst of these meanderings a certain *quest* takes shape and assumes direction. Phantoms gather in the garden, do they not? The fragility of dawn incarnated in a screech-owl's predatory take-off prepares the victory of unrestrained enchantments. One good enchantment surely deserves another. The monoliths of Easter Island have not spoken their last word! I am not at all trying to impose Basil Valentine's *Twelve Keys of Philosophy* onto the keyboard of the jazz piano. But it seems perfectly clear that the "clavecin of sensibility" invoked by Diderot in 1769, recalled by Lenin in 1908 and elaborated by René Crevel into a detailed critique of bourgeois-Christian values in 1932, is clamoring at last for its full development, its full freedom. The poetic cause today would be defeated at the very onset if it failed to recognize in jazz a fraternal movement, a powerful ally, above all a complementary adventure. One must admit at the very least that jazz has covered inestimable ground *entirely on its own* and that its most ardent adepts show every sign of their willingness to go all the way. It would be simply unforgivable, in any case, to go on as if Ornette Coleman's *Free Jazz* did not exist. The implications of this work, which is nothing less than the declaration of independence of jazz, are *staggering* from the point of view of the triumph of the human spirit — and no other point of view is worth considering. Nothing is so sublime as the radiant crystallization of the "unhoped for," whenever and wherever it occurs. It is only at the elusive junction of a "passing glance" and a long low shudder from the Great Invisibles that the unlivable retreats behind the restless march of untamable events. Jazz, in the hands of its greatest dreamers, intervenes precisely at that junction: I am thinking especially of those abruptly demonic arabesques with which Thelonious Monk, beyond all categorical imperatives, galvanizes the hibernating fury of "a man or a stone or a tree" (Lautréamont); I am thinking of the inexhaustible pocket tidal wave with which Ornette Coleman multiplies the margins of the miraculous in resplendent fits of grace warmed by the sphinxlike shadows of ancient kazoos, Robert Johnson's dialogue with Satan, and the bebop boomerang always aimed at worlds to come and always bringing back a little taste of tomorrow.

Let us proclaim, in letters of phosphorous if need be, that the quest to remove the obstacles to the free development of the imagination (which alone gives to the "surprise-events" described above their exalting significations)— let us proclaim in letters of fire that this quest is advanced inexorably not only by a long and continuing revolutionary current of poetry and painting — from Lautréamont to Malcolm de Chazal, from Benjamin Péret to Guy Cabanel, from Samuel Greenberg to Philip Lamantia, from Bosch to Toyen, from Van Gogh to Arshile Gorky, from Tanguy to Mimi Parent — but also by the long and continuing revolutionary current of jazz, associated particularly with the names Charlie Parker, Bud Powell, Thelonious Monk, Sonny Rollins, Charles Mingus, John Coltrane, Eric Dolphy, Cecil Taylor, Sun Ra, Pharoah Sanders, Archie Shepp, Albert Ayler, Anthony Braxton, Joseph Jarman. The torches with which we proceed into the abyss of the unknown may vary, but they are lighted from a single flame.

All discovery in one way or another is self-discovery; all inspired expeditions beyond the boundaries of established knowledge are worth making. The insipid notions of success and failure are merely dust in the eyes of the timid, counterfeit icons for false witnesses. Entirely aside from the tired alibis of teleology, the myth of "destiny" resolves its equations like the hairs that never cease breaking the backs of camels. When the streets begin to dream; when things begin to click; when the bastilles of habit and remorse are stormed and leveled; when the wind of lyricism gives wings to every word; when appearances recede behind the lacework of unfettered insolence; when creatures large and small, of forest and jungle and desert and sea, transform the latitude and longitude of what *can be;* when everyday life, that is, begins to rise at last to the level of our legitimate expectations, then — and only then — shall we have a life in every sense worth living. Already it is beyond dispute to those who know, from within, the free zone of objective chance, that these pulsebeats of the Marvelous alone define the rhythm of true life. All that remains to be done — a large task, to be sure, but one that makes all competing tasks seem ridiculous — is systematically to remove, in alchemical terms, the "superfluous matter" that impedes the universal proliferation of this infinite grandeur.

One day, sooner than you think, the hegemony of these meteoric moments will abolish time as we know it and lead us into the golden age of the spirit, in which, like the ancient Greeks, we shall drink from the measureless cup of love and dance to the *music of the spheres.*

Franklin ROSEMONT

THE JEALOUS EXCURSION

Claw moustaches bark into labyrinths
creating angry candelabras

as the lampost severs abused gorillas
that drool upon the laughing creamed
cheese

you are the propeller and I am the
Pronghorn

Iced perfume smoldering, bonded seashells
reflecting tightropes of clay

as the cornfields feed deserted cubs
that drip secret codes

you are the propeller and I am the
Pronghorn

Jocelyn KOSLOFSKY

Greeted by horned effluvium
The cancerous zero will bloom a lagoon of human torches
when she has turned back the storm from which I came
I am handed the hermetic keys of blood
which will not open the Earth
but only its shadow

The actual neuron escarpment of excited sheep
A vague harmony like a fruit drops
The milky-way goes down my body
as my body goes up through the milky-way
In this way only is the world wedded to me
and all will weep with me

Night where mirrors held me up to their faces
to witness the jewel of the blaze of her body
reflected in the sun my crown
as her circle broke and Yanged into personality
a gull's robe
The sister the moon her green lips hungry
She is the trap I have set in the world
The trap is baited with human flesh
Obstinate sign

Away under a snowing oak
her eye does not stir in the movement of hours
for the hawk is hung upsidedown like bread
as the claw of the dew caught her echo
and she was brought to the mouth of my death

The question of will slips from the air
and mates with the agate of the month
The mirage has no will
yet its teeth punctures the theory of windows
Evolution takes its toll
even among the great invisibles
The fog is there
It is sitting in its faun-chair
It is harder than her liquid cameo of sunlight
Her eye a brother to her will dies
in the wolf's jaw of music
The wind returns its power
to the ocean's heart of human water
as the mountain devours my bloody feet
in the roaring fog

Says sleep shimmering
the full flux of light that dream is
its core is motionless
its center is empty
the word is wood
the center is empty
where the honey sings
and its song pulsates

LAURENCE WEISBERG

Hypnotic obelisks impel the dolphins of jews' harps
The abacus of desire limewashes the cleaver of antipodes
Satyromaniac goggles spew blue helices
expunged from the ciliated reefs of vertigo
THE MASK I WEAR YESTERDAY
Oh the inverted "v" over the lips
in that grotto where the incisors of lightning sleep
Ah the black face mask of fur
Hands whiter than a convocation of nuns' tits
Nocturnal ceremonies such as your hair hanging loose over the
*   riffraff of crow feathers*
Night of suicidal equilibrium
Your eyelashes as a door opening and closing
The tumescence of your nipples is a memory erasing device
I can remember only
Mucous snails
parachuting above
the mating ground of the sabretoothed sphinx
Your lips cower in a satin tumbril which is drawn away
*   by praying mantises*
The tuft of fur on your cheek coos at my penis with its wings
*   flying by*
Your buttocks flanked by marmosets unscrew their triangular
*   anaglyph and walk away*
THE MASK I WORE TOMORROW
How could naked transvestites have lunch
Laser teeth for the lords of the smoking mirror
while behind the lair of black lace
a lighthouse slips off its manacles

RICHARD WAARA

Tincture of Night

If I said that books *by* Freud should be read at night, but books *about* Freud should be read during the day, no one would misunderstand. Likewise, one could say that Baudelaire should be read during the night, but his letters should be read during the day (if they should be read at all, which is doubtful). But if we do not choose Freud or Baudelaire as our examples, things become more complex; and if we choose the blues, we are confronted with the fact that the blues is indeed a music of the night, regardless of when it is played. The blues, then becomes a point of departure for our inquiry, for not only is it of the night, but it reveals something of the nature of the night.

> *In the wee midnight hours, long 'fore the break of day. (repeat)*
> *When the blues creep up on you and carry your mind away.*
>
> *While I lay in my bed and cannot go to sleep. (2x)*
> *While my heart's in trouble and my mind is thinking deep.*
>
> *My mind was running back to days of long ago. (2x)*
> *And the one I love, I do not see her anymore.*
>
> *(Leroy Carr — Midnight Hour Blues)*

It takes no citing of a blues song as evidence, however, to suggest that the night is associated with fear and loneliness — and often the fear is of things that partake of the supernatural. It is at night, too, that we fall prey to those peculiar afflictions that result in insomnia and nightmares. Yet there is also the hope of the coming dawn.

> *The big star falling, mama, 'tain't long 'fore day. (2x)*
> *Maybe this sunshine will drive these blues away.*
>
> *(Blind Willie McTell — "Mama T'ain't Long Fo' Day")*

Or:

> *Hurry down sunshine, see what tomorrow brings. (2x)*
> *It may bring drops of sorrow, and it may bring drops of rain.*
>
> *(Leroy Carr — "Hurry Down Sunshine")*

The despair that grips us at night and the promise of dawn are both so taken for granted that a glass of bourbon at night is considered normal while a glass of bourbon in the morning on awakening is considered a sign of a "serious disturbance." The night of despair and horror is typical and it is not infrequently dissipated by the coming dawn, the effect of this dissipation being often miraculously revitalizing and euphoric. But there is no doubt that the *dawn of horror* is worthy of the utmost despair. The despair that begins to close in on us as night progresses is nothing compared to that feeling of horror and desperate isolation that solidifies rather than dissolves at daybreak. Against this we have few weapons; the proverbial "promise of dawn" having been broken, there is very little one can do. The very abstract and vague nature of the coming day is often source of hope enough but for those who cannot draw even this hope, the terror of night and the terror of day become only the two halves of a total despair.

While I have said that night is associated with the supernatural, fear, and loneliness, we must also remember that for most of us it is associated with sleep and dreams, and that it is only with the introduction of these two states that we begin to understand the essential nature of night. When we begin to explore its less superficial aspects, it becomes obvious that *unconscious* phenomena play a significant and even major role. At night we may have witnessed the sexual activities of our parents; at night we most regularly engage in dreaming; at night, too, our needs and desires find expression (in the dream and subject to distortion); and at night we regularly face our fear and horror of these same impulses (or, more likely, our fear of punishment for these impulses). At night, moreover, we most ardently confirm the possibilities of our lives, projecting our wishes first into dreams, and later into myths and poetry.

Yet I think the most significant fact is that nearly all our emotional states can be traced back to moments of greatest intensity *at night*—through the dream and through the vicissitudes of our own infantile sexuality and aggression, but primarily through the dream. I do not think it rare for decisively traumatic incidents to befall the infant during the day, but I am convinced that except in unusual cases, even daylight events do not secure their decisiveness without the characteristic effects and elaboration of the night and the dream.

One needn't apologize for reintroducing the blues at this point, even for personal reasons. Several years ago I described a night visitor known as "the hag," a woman long dead who prowls about my home. I described how women that I loved were likely to be transformed into horrible grave-eaten monsters, all the work of the hag. But the description of this transformation astounded me anew when I heard "You Brought It On Yourself" (!), by Smokey Hogg, recorded thirteen years ago:

> I went to Texas with a suitcase, I came back to California with a bag. (2x)
> I thought I had a wife in Texas, I didn't have nothing but a hag.

Some have said that the old tricks are the best ones — yet no one is deceived; certainly not Smokey Hogg, not the women I have loved, not even I, except for a moment. For there was a quick stab of paralysis, a stopping of breath, a total fear for just a few seconds late at night, when I was alone, and when I heard the hag calling my name, using the voice of my lover. I think of Smokey Hogg again:

> All in my sleep I can hear my doorbell ring. (2x)
> When I turned my light on, Lord, there wasn't a doggone thing.
>
> ("Dark Clouds")

Fear? As I said, only for a moment. Yet the night lasts twelve hours, and I can no more take it away from her than she can from me. The fact that she is my enemy does not make the night my enemy. The exasperations of the night must be exploited until they fade into revelation. Indeed, even though it be her domain, I am at home there, often without despair, just as I feel most comfortable during the winter and am puzzled at those who expend so much energy seeking warmer climates. Unfortunately, however, she sleeps during the day, and I must sleep at night — and I cannot. My earliest memories are not only of fear of the night but of fear of sleep. I can remember with horror when I was four years old being forced to sleep during the day. Even then I could not sleep, day or night, it made no difference; and we see now that quite definitely part of the nature of the night is the act and idea of sleep. But only two memories emerge: I remember lying on a cot seeing the legs of the woman sitting next to the cot, as if that would make me sleep. And I remember lining up to urinate, girls and boys, and the teacher saying, "That's right, the girls sit down, the boys stand up. No giggling."

Frog, *Haida*

In any case, the hag doesn't giggle and neither do I. And sometimes what emerges cannot really be called a memory:

M.'s attitude toward darkness is mitigated by the fact that her face glows with the sheen of a harbor bat in quart size bottles of cream. Triptych lines reveal M. as the first to recognize me as a true *Rana*, the first to bare real teeth and not fangs in the reminiscence of a youthful centipede. A slope of blueberries and peppers descends into concrete tombs that have long ago been abandoned by their breath. Is recognition theoretically important? For I've forgotten to have intentions, and my windmills stir only patches of potato peels in the lilac monstrosities of octagonal porcupines. (Day has no chance with the pleas of the despairing who only cry for no night.) Give me a slipper with no dial tone. Keep the dime. Inflate a chair for portable bayonets, the resurgences of typical incandescent rib cages and amphibious barrages of mold. A time to hop and a time to think. Whatever gave you the idea that the night held out its hands to tumors, benign or malignant? To emperors, in power or dethroned? To priests, defrocked or otherwise? No, the night is mine for whatever blasts the scaly harpsichords from the balustrades of traditional sponges. A pint of soap to cool the burning of an insectivorous foot; the pain, he says, is inscrutable and confining.

Insomnia breeds its own plethora of difficulties; Kafka, in one of his letters to Felice Bauer, said that his nights were divided into two periods: a period of wakefulness and a period of sleeplessness. Not only is one incapable of writing except at night, but one is plagued at night, not only by the night itself, but by the number of associative ideas about the night that refuse to clarify themselves, i.e., the associations between blackness, night, anality, money, blacks, evil, etc. It could no doubt go on forever, for it involves one-half of our lives and probably the most significant half. I offer only two dreams, the first dream a night (sleeping) dream, and the second a day-dream or fantasy.

In the night dream, I am walking along 47th Street in Chicago *during the day*, and I turn the corner and see the entrance to a long, dark barn, much like a tobacco barn. It is open at both ends. I go in and see that it is full of junk dealers' tables with hundreds of items displayed. My eye immediately falls on a stack of old 78 rpm records, and as I approach them, I see that the top record is a blues record on the Vocalion label. I begin to go through the records, tremendously excited, and they are all blues records. At the peak of excitement, I awaken. I realize that I have been dreaming, and I'm terribly disappointed. It is morning.

In my day-dream, I'm driving along a deserted highway. Instead of coming across a dingy antique or junk store where old records are commonly found, I see a new, modern, brightly lit building, like a shopping center drug store. The store sells only 78's, all rare blues and jazz, all only $1 or $2. In my day-dream, *it is always night*.

PAUL GARON

Robert Day: drawing

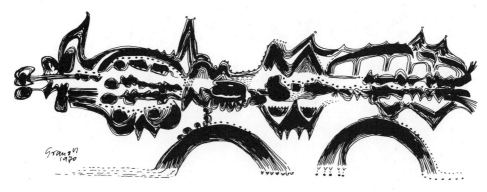

E. F. Granell: drawing

Precession

The sea is looking for its hat
forever hidden between the gulf of sighs
and the hermaphrodite machines
I build a garrison of webs where the desert
has grown antlers for my defense
Catapulted by the ashes of felons I arrive
at the door of Uranos whose shadow
continually powers a labyrinth
> *So wild the teeth of the rooftops*
> *so slippery the manacled dunes that*
I swim through moats where dragons play
hide and seek with the king of spades

We meet in this embargoed city
followed by a violent and inescapable smile
Comets hang bleeding from gallows as the men
stroll through the squared circle of their desires
The women careen into the headlights of chance
blinded by rabid vehicles which carry
the perpetual flags of anarchy
toward the last sleep

We meet in this city of a glass myth
we arrive at the somnolent corridor of sharks
a hot rush of wings upon our flesh
as your feathered face turns into an immense raft
We'll toss the seasons overboard
and sleep among mirrors and scorpions in flight.

NANCY PETERS

Salamandragora

(excerpts)

The fens of my thought encroach on the nostalgic star chamber
Where reading the newspaper is like an ancient map smudged or
    blank in the sites of terra incognita
Here on earth possessors of secrets are murdered without
    question
Saved sometimes by a network of accomplices clad in nuts and
    berries
It's the ignition of dreams which turns the lazy propeller
    billowing new myths in the open city here on earth
I've been seeing the yam vendor in her palace of hair
Who is so kind permitting me to kiss her on the eyes
Open or closed like the wonderment of the blue dahlia that only
    grows on me
Innumerable in diversion singular of choice
It nails high the condor in the hall of the mountain king
Displaying its pale cool opaquely naked entrails blinking
    furiously in the sun
Holiday greetings to Johnny Conqueroo in the emperor's new
    clothes
Pulsing stronger than whiskeyed coral the magnetism of axial
    horizons overcomes all hesitations
Silencing the caged minahs whose coat is alternately where else
    else where
Here on earth
No I never saw the hope you speak of but maybe
It's because it's all in my arm beyond the teetertotter of the
    this or that of hope and despair
Quite distinct from the registrar of deeds a pike to haul down
    flags with
Bowls hollowed in the night by the sea that shares your bed
A floating mine for intellectual tugboats
Yesterday named me king of today
But here on this good earth it's you
Who places tomorrow on my fingertips

    Sunstroke of the rose in a long drink on the water
    Lobster call as exotic as a hammer striking bronze
    As faithful as the instrument of the prophet
    This so imperfect world another lobster
    Which shall not prevent us from delighting in it
    Which cannot prevent us from changing it penguin chief
    Whose task it is to transparentize the skin of
        conjecture

A solar catastrophe from Kitai to Merlin's Wood
Turning the tables on the poppies of vigilance

Reason coils as the serpent strikes
But the red thread of the prophetic dream unwinds from the
    labyrinth
For where it goes is an act of creation
Courage and the powerful spell of a certain glint of heart
Hands across the water thrust from the earth
But where they can only clasp they come from
The heart in its cookpot of burning breasts of olive oil
Seasoned with pungent sesames of thought

    And so the weather changes its shoes below the ports
        of lapis lazuli
    Singeing pearls with an eye dropper one by one
    Pelicans watch learnedly sweep the coasts of Brazil
        with bread and fresh blood
    Feigning ignorance from the Cape of Good Hope
    To all other ironic geographies lying beyond the Horn
        of Plenty
    Easing a ring into the nose of day

    Chinese box with an hidden spring
    The gleaming skin of Fan Tan players
    In the upper reaches of mint sprigs opening and
        closing to the skirling of the pipes
    With a woman whose finger always points to the ceiling
    Slowly eating spongy wafers
    I crush completely in my palm

We must paint all the walls in witch hazel and let the dogs hunt
    in packs those they will
From the last to the first a gorgeous bouquet from me to you
Festooned with a wrought iron aphorism
Which like the prize in every Cracker Jack
Arises peering from a caramel latch

    And as luck would have it
    Never does one foot kick in the door without
    Four and twenty blackbirds baked in a pie
    Causing tin wars and bauxite rebellions
    To be continued
    Ice cream you scream we all scream for I scream
    But nostalgia that old shoe is on the wrong foot

PETER MANTI

Thom Burns: illustration for RESONANCES

RESONANCES

(an excerpt)

It had been raining.

The graceful bleakness of the street complemented my room's severity. Though spacious enough, I had limited it to almost bland furnishings, except the floor where within a carpet from the Mongolian frontier, its lustre undimmed after five centuries, a grave blue was suspended like a foraging storm that swings between the farthest points of a barren horizon. I returned to work. I chose a little cigar from an open box on the table, lighting it as I sat and resumed typing.

By four I was tired enough to pull my glasses off, rub my eyes, and return to bed for a nap. I undressed, smoothed the counterpane, and lay down. I picked up Darwin's VOYAGE OF THE BEAGLE from the nightstand. I glanced up at the nearby chest of drawers; though it wore only brass handles, I had often wakened believing its grain concealed unsuspected features. I put the book aside and drew sleep to me.

A clash of swords disturbed me.

I lay still until I recognized the telephone, then groped to the worktable and clumsily lifted the receiver.

A tense, unfamiliar woman's voice asked "Auburn?"

I assumed it was a name. "Wrong number," I replied, hanging up. I turned back to bed. But before I could lie down again the telephone repeated itself more shrilly, and the same voice demanded "Auburn, don't hang up. You must come. This is Julie."

I was about to ignore the plea and replace the receiver wordlessly. The name stopped me. I knew nobody named Julie, but it reminded me of something I tried to identify as she spoke. When she said the word "drift" I recalled it: a comet I had seen when very young. I had expected the bright marauder would streak madly overhead, but it only hung, shaking its head indecisively, from the throat of the sky. Julie. I wanted to meet her.

"All right," I responded. "Where should I go?" She murmured an address and hung up.

I dressed and hurried out of the hotel, doubtful. I had no idea how to recognize her. And no way to pass myself off as any Auburn.

But the scent of morning rain soothed me. The brooding afternoon was eager to embrace and fondle the mannequin-like buildings. I walked to a stone bench at the corner.

I waited for the bus. A sense of detachment, then of another, deeper apprehension, beleaguered me, growing trance-like. I stood and began pacing. Glancing back, I was startled by the aspect of the hotel. Its dozen windows peered rodent-like into the street and insinuated decay, even disaster, against the shops that flanked it. The gold leaf on the glass doors read *Hotel ANCHORITE*.

The bus stopped and I stepped past its mechanical doors, shaking off my disquiet. Remembering the woman's address was near the waterfront, I muttered "Transfer" as I pushed a coin into the chattering farebox. The driver offered me a very delicate object about the size of an infant's head resembling a wasp's nest and a half-open book.

I knew what it was: a redrift. But I could not recall its function. I glanced inquiringly at the driver. He averted his face.

I carried the redrift to a seat. The object consisted of erratically shaped but sturdy leaves of musty paper joined at a common edge. Each leaf was irregularly pierced by taut threads. Certain strings and holes were marked with arrows and concentric circles. I knew it was supposed to expand, but it resisted my efforts to pull it open, and the attempt made my head ache.

I glanced through the bus window, and as we passed the Civic Center, with its monument to Florian Geyer and the Black Troop, the woman's address effaced itself from my memory. I clutched the redrift with one hand and angrily signaled the driver with the other. The bus slowed and I alighted. Night had fallen.

My gaze around the Civic Center was swallowed by the demolished Museum of Art. I was better acquainted with the long abandoned building and its looted collection than most of the city's inhabitants. Now I entered it almost involuntarily, drawn along the sagging, defaced galleries to an immense painting whose size alone, I supposed, had discouraged theft.

The painting was profoundly arousing.

On the canvas an adolescent woman was poised, nude, as within a dubious refuge. Her hair plunged as if seeking the waters under the earth. Her pale face was avid with rumor and tremor. The landscape around her stood among fire and flood, invaded by glaciers and general strikes.

Behind her the artist had affixed a living bush of black roses. Her hands were occupied with some just-vanished object.

Every other time I had viewed the painting the black roses had shielded a tiny male figure whose look of exalted solitude reminded me of the identity quests pursued for many days and nights by Siberian hunters. Now the human was replaced by an immense ebony wolf. Its eyes glowed so deeply beyond me that, turning, I was not surprised to find Michael Flood staring at the canvas.

I knew Flood from the University. I never liked him. The way he showed off his money did not attract me; I was convinced his crisp dress, his carefully trimmed beard, and even the precision and amplitude of his studies concealed some degeneracy. Perhaps what I really resented was the way some students treated me and Flood as two of a kind. There was no reason for me to speak to him, but I did. Smugly, I asked "Do you like this painting?" He did not reply. That irritated me. I stepped forward and slapped his face. He stared as the bruise darkened his flesh. I grasped his arm, shouting "Flood! Don't you recognize me? It's Schwartz! Stephen Schwartz! From the University!" I was about to slap him again when, his eyes still fixed on the painted female figure, he laughed slurringly and pointed aim-

Thom Burns: illustration for RESONANCES

lessly. "Julie," he whispered. "My sister." I tensed. He continued, his voice clearer, as if bearing a message. "My sister, my sister. She's thirteen, always returning, always first." He reached for the frame. As his hands sought the painting, he collapsed.

I bent and gripped his left wrist, then his right. There was no pulse. I stood, and was prodded from behind.

My back was so close to the painting that the gesture could only have come from within the frame. I did not look behind me.

Subtle paws, as of a wolf, settled at my shoulders, and, within me, directed me back to Flood's corpse. My right hand raised itself awkwardly and searched his pockets, finding a key ring and a business card engraved MICHAEL FLOOD, Altair Road, Mill Valley, California.

The address was vaguely familiar. The invisible grasp maintained itself cautiously as I picked up the redrift and left the museum. I recognized Flood's Mercedes at the curb. I unlocked the door, tossed the redrift on the back seat, and climbed behind the steering wheel. I started the car.

The being at my spine merged with the groping headlights, guiding me like a draught of opium.

I followed the highway across the Golden Gate Bridge to Mill Valley, a town a few miles north, besieged by redwood trees, under a mountain that rainlight had aroused erotically.

On each side of the road the weighted sky smothered the landscape. I stopped the car at a junction and located Altair Road on the map in the glove compartment. It was an avenue hewn among the redwoods, and I sensed while reducing speed the forest's impatience to avenge so wanton a wound. I had always loved the redwood trees, like a dynamo whose working I could not comprehend.

At the end of Altair Road I recognized my hotel. The wolfling light that had preceded me dragged itself away to the woods.

I parked the car. I took the redrift and strode to the building. The door, flaunting the single word ALASTOR in gold leaf, opened as I neared it, framing a young, distantly-glowing woman in a white silk kaftan.

Her erect posture, her waist-long, falcon-like hair, the eager disdain of her smile suggested the fabric of the kaftan concealed, in place of breasts, two denizens of an abyss.

"Auburn," she declared. "I knew you'd come. Do you have the redrift?"

STEPHEN SCHWARTZ

Franklin Rosemont:
Bride of the Iconoclast

The Chariot of the Hourglass

You are the threshold of succulent orchards
that bear the secret of the restless dreamer
The orange trees caress me and share their miraculous sap
salvaged from some aging well

I trip over gold doubloons and ancient fortunes
        a priceless encounter
The wind speaks of past lovers with chastising tongues
and spits its bloody venom on slumbering telephones

Time whispers its promise in the corridors of today
and hastens to corrupt the voices of dreams

The letter fell from your bloody lip
        and I turned to face the window
            where before me stood a man in black
                with a dagger through his heart

From the scarlet fluid emerged
        white swans bearing gold boxes that held priceless promises

DIANE MEUCCI

OLD CUSTOMS OF THE EARTH

You eat the purple newspaper of the north
segments
identified
at the turning pole
a filthy flame cut from ice

The weaver's face has a musical profile
You are the bandit holding the telephone in your gullet
and
there is poison of winter
the lines all down
the sea abolishing the air

injuring cigarettes

Objectivity waddles and cracks in the ice-bucket
perfect mystique of cantilevers
I am sitting on the couch in my rope suit
a bottled ape
the lawyers proved it

referring again
to the holes of sound

which sits where the grandfathers mustered their graves
like a vaccination
and the reporters made joy out of cheap rags
and the villages wore black pearls

THE STORY OF AN EXILE

In the village church the head on the altar speaks to the convocation of the Whistlers.

"The swamp eat . . ."

"Pay the sum . . ."

"After growing, cut the multiple . . ."

"A wild goose . . ."

"Frames . . ." And so forth.

The village is always quiet, except for the sunday speaking done by the head. If it rhymes the people hold their ears and grimace horribly. The rhyme is like a sin the whole village must atone for, by silence. The extreme caution of the head has infected everything about village life by now, the slow deliberate phrases spoken so uneasily finding reflection in the ominous demeanor of the Whistlers.

When I came to the village they greeted me with characteristic solemnity. A slow procession bearing baskets of red moss for me to eat. I had a picture of the murdered man pinned to my coat. Nevertheless, my brisk manner of walking frightened the timid day fish who scurried back under piles of dung. After the welcoming preliminaries I sought out a place of lodging, settling in the rear of a shop kept by a grave.

The grave, smiling, unspeaking . . .

This was a sinful town. Why am I here? The law allows us to avoid execution by going into the country.

One finds differences in the villages, some dull, some exciting. At times the villages burn very brightly and the rumor goes around that there is a moron eating crabs.

One evening as the grave slept and the red moss loafed about, I stole into the little village church to confront the head. As I shouted rhymes the whole village began to awake and scream. The head swelled and swelled and swelled and finally exploded like a balloon.

Suddenly I was standing in a valley, on a road bordered by fields of tall grain. Each of my little fingers had become a gerkin, so that I knew I would never again be hungry, unless I wanted crabs.

The swamp eat . . .

Pay the sum . . .

After growing, cut the multiple . . .

A wild goose . . .

Frames . . .

JOSEPH JABLONSKI

Ronald Lee Papp: *Deaf Recollection*

POEM

Rainbows appear on the horizon
to melt the crystal women of darkness
who stand on the hill
a pot of sugar hanging from their lips

The machine guns sound closer tonight
your fingers glowing as they
tuck themselves behind the
stars
Can you see the owls calling us to the end?
Can you solve their equations
with the bloody revolt of your mind?

Look for the yellow butterflies
they know you

Lucy CATLETT

Penelope Rosemont: *Hermes' Bird*

Louise Hudson: drawing

SUPPER - TIME

A table was set for a fine supper, and I was expecting my guest to arrive shortly. I was shocked when she appeared carrying a painting of the Nativity and an extra nose. "I'm going to need one of these before the night is over, I think," she said. I stared in amazement, not sure which to cast first into the fire, and distracted as I was by the smell (coming from either her or the painting), I decided to do nothing for the moment. As we sat down at the table, soup was ladled into large bowls and either consumed with a spoon (she) or drunk directly from the bowl (me). "If you are trying to draw attention to yourself with your disgusting table manners, you will not succeed," she said. Then she approached my chair, which was just preparing itself for flight, and broke one of its wings; she tied down the other wing, making it unusable for all practical purposes. "Did you bring the postcards I asked for?" I said, thinking it a rhetorical question, for I saw her carrying nothing when she came in except the nose and the painting. "Oh," she said, "I brought these instead." She produced a rather large stack of books from under her dress (the smell again): Proust, Joyce, a bible, a hymnal, and some torn manuscripts which were unidentifiable and uninteresting. The whole lot went immediately into the fire, but the next morning I discovered that neither the Proust nor the manuscripts had burned. There were also some crusts of toast in the ashes which I do not remember throwing there. Meanwhile the nose began a very boring monologue on the Nativity scene, all done in the manner of a high-school art teacher, concentrating on color, form, perspective, etc. Then it continued, "we see in the blood of christ a device for catching carp."

"Not too good for this nose," I thought.

"The blood of christ is not a redeemable coupon."

"Ho hum."

"The blood of christ has a meaning beyond that which is given it in the church."

Yawning, vomiting.

By this time, my guest had not only removed all of her clothes but had taken all the left-over food from our plates as well as from the serving dishes, and put it into a giant bowl. She had pounded and mixed it to a mush and was now serving it to this stupid, harping, simpering, conceited nose. I edged the Nativity painting into the fire, and it burned very quickly. Needless to say, I had similair plans for the nose, but a thunderous noise began, and a toad announced, barely loud enough for me to hear, "Your chair has been repaired—and not a minute too soon, either." Indeed, through the doorways and the windows poured police of all sizes and nations. I quickly strapped myself into the chair, and we took off immediately. I had time to see only a short, mustachioed policeman in a French uniform begin to fondle the breasts of my willing guest before I had to duck my head. Bullets were hitting the chair—ineffectively, I might add—as we crashed through the ceiling to freedom. I looked back and thought, "If a nose could be said to be all smiles . . ."

PAUL GARON

Jean-Jacques Jack Dauben: *Her Mouth the Distant Hoofbeats of the Mongols*

A Bird Which Slowly Sheds Its Leaves

The jungle dressed as a fisherman warms its hands over a flame of grasshoppers. The boat of this fisherman is a chandelier dodging bullets in a glass of milk. His catch, which are mirror-shaped and have for eyes the smoke emerging from factory stacks continue to whisper among themselves like the hairs on a woman's head. The dry ice coursing through this fisherman's veins reminds one of a bale of hay, of the day before yesterday when a lamprey hovered beautifully in the air, interrupting the embrace of a projector and the screen, much like a gymnasium biting into a sour apple.

Where in the wings of bees do the rippling marriages of sandstone and birdseed find their foliage as it calls from the backs of horses ensnared in the nets of rice?

In the flourishing carpet of snails leaking from a flame the darkness finds a match for itself as an airplane ducks glasses of water tied to sticks brandished by star-nosed moles whose gleeful digestion of the parallel rows of ear-rings hung on the traffic lights afterward is seen in a barn of tusks enflamed by the velvet whiskers of eyes just before it takes wing.

Baboon of Red-Eyed Candlelight

The jellyfish gallop like thunderstorms
as doors knock upon fists
their tentacles become entangled
in the underbrush seen from a great distance
which inhabits the prisms
proportionate to their altitude in the wounds
in the blister that wears a race track
on its head of singed flower petals
in the shadow of a squirrel
shaped like a beach ominously clutching
a cigarette lighter preparing to devour a parade
all day long the rays of light
disappear behind a pink ribbon
whose eyes are waterfalls of midriffs
that scald the pear trees dropped into the road
waving hello
to the canal of peppermint leaves that whinnies
like a rainbow tossing pebbles of water
into a puddle of standstone
to the railroad yards that disrobe so slowly
leaving a single ravenous pine needle
whose attic window opens
like the expanding fur of a kangaroo
for the swarms of hermit crabs

PATRICK MULLINS

244

Longitudinal Poem

Are there too many gazel roads
  as to touch
With the always growing fiber of my mill barrow
  of you
The always growing fiber of your match hair
When it falls like the darker diamonds
  of the internal sea victuals
  about your waist of dust that I am of magic
I can glance at least for an instant the preternatural energy
  that you harbor behind the orchard of the last will
  as I am there also as the testament

It is in the smile of tides as they torment angels
  that I can see you best
With the always present barometer
With the needles slightly warm and a changed locket
  at the shades of your perfect color
With the glow around the parameter of an educated man
  IT IS ALSO YOUR COLOR

I can not hear the sound of the afternoon's mirror

As if for a moment a fleet of ships
  drained the workers from their hammers and bellows
  from anvils to gears
  that steer us wrongly then retreat propelled by alphabets
So common there is a ghost before and after them
So much the better in the blasted desert
Massages of cigarettes smoked by eternal forks
These are what separate the mahogany penchant
  through which can be seen
  stones throwing matter at a menace
Closing in behind us as we walk

SECOND START

The way I see the crackling heights
In somber and strange weather
  is the light as straight as cherries
As milk from ten days of splashing
  the street lamp careens around the nape of your neck
  as you stand still
  while sliding your body through an antelope

Later you faded on this side
I found you forever brighter on the other side
Brighter on the road
so smooth sperm glistens on its hazardous turns
Gradually as sand escaping the desert
   the fortuitous sleeper held his means firmly under foot
   while it kept him there by violence

THOM BURNS

A Gown for My Divine, Dead Painters

Timothy R. Johnson.

"An Initiation of the Past" *

There was a time when there were no haberdashers' shops on the street.

There was a time when awakening was reaching into a cotton box of severed fingers to find only—more silence.

There was a time when my spiritual crystallization was taking place that I remember only too well. It was a time of viscous feet, its mouth full of futures, its eyes full of nets and spiny traps. But the beast had only paper claws and even if its hair was full of amber snakes, try as it might it could not drag "what had become" back into the abyss of the past.

Many claim that memories of their early years fail them. Ah, such good fortune, to be so innocent, unable to remember when rational history was invented, unable to notice in every eye the murderous intent. Yet none can remember a time when they were not! They deny even their dreams and refuse to notice the tiny feet one often sees flitting away into the darkness in corners and under armchairs.

What is the resolution of night? Can the problem be solved by the division of a fish into a suit of armour and a laundry ticket? The cloth panels of the sky snare the passing planes and put them into their baskets of clouds. Writing is still a primitive form of illusion that waits behind the grillwork of the unsympathetic forests of virtue. Writing exploits the wretched mountains of loneliness, the transparency of which contrasts tragically with the extravagent opacity of sea creatures. The unexpressed abundance of the past is called "external reality." But who understands the greatness and splendor of the hydra whose wishes lend significance to its adornments?

Those fierce and wrathful medicines, the mundane manifestations of life, the opening of the gates of despair—these let man know that he is without any "law" that shouts of spring. A life of darkness perpetually seeking its victims—what light does it give? An intense curiosity flowers from which the amusements have been emptied. But colors, wonders and spirit remain as locomotives which penetrate the mind discovering the fragile beauty of creatures who defend themselves with poison. The hummingbird is most beautiful in the darkness of an eternal mirror.

I had been living in this place only a short time. Each evening as the moon rose I noticed the old woman next door in her yard. The yard was covered with bright red and orange gloves that had fallen from the tree and just as many were left on the branches. She gathered these gloves into neat piles. I would carry them for her. She gave me a polished black box which contained only a miniature staircase, and hinted that some day I might learn its uses. She taught me to remove the bones from eyes and to keep live snails behind my ears to learn what would occur the next day. When I tried to look into the windows of her house I could see only the stars and distant planets. It was dizzying, like falling into the Milky Way.

Once I watched as she walked through the doorway and saw in her place an elegantly dressed and young woman. Her black hair which fell

* Benjamin Paul Blood (1832-1919), leading theorist of the anaesthetic revelation.

to her waist was crowned with a nest full of bluebirds. She called to a young man on the street and he boldly entered her abode. I remember only a very old man leaving who wore the ill-fitting clothes of a youth.

There was a wonderful electricity about these days that brightly gleamed like visions of peacocks. When the weather was fair and breezy, I stood next to the morning and built towers of darkness with the threads and ends of reckless dreams.

The wind finds eyes that extend from the fingertips of the summer's night over the four corners of the earth.

I found suddenly that roots held me fast with their glowing fibres.

I spend my days mending black sails.

I spend my nights beside the window waiting for a coal-black raven to carry me on his back to the treetops.

PENELOPE ROSEMONT

THE LAST DAYS

At the crossroads of surrealism, psychoanalytic theory and historical materialism we must inevitably encounter the constellated impulses of desire, repression, metamorphosis and revolution; radical and dynamic conceptions whose interrelationships enact what we could call the law of the *conservation of desire*. Under this aegis there occurs the process first of occultation and then of revelation, whereby Being avenges itself upon repression.

It is that which is born of nature with an organic direction, libido and natural aggression, that suffers repression. Repression always represents a negation on both the individual and historical planes of the natural movement of life. This movement cannot possibly be stopped, but only displaced to where it undergoes a long, labyrinthine odyssey of occult gratification and illumination until it rises at last into self-consciousness in surrealism. Far from being an escape from reality, surrealism is the expression of vital forces of being that aim to circumvent and smash that famous empty cage. It also represents the self-enjoyment of the indestructible nature of desire.

These realizations encourage me to paraphrase Breton and declare: the mind exists in the savage state. Language and all other symbolic behavior, including madness, share a common root in this state. We can thus speak of projecting the mind into a blot of words, or into automatic speech or writing, or into invented language, just as Da Vinci spoke of projecting the eye into a daub of paint on a wall (see *Beyond Painting* by Max Ernst). It should be obvious that by the savage state I do not mean "chaos," that most artificial of notions. What is clearly implied here is the existence of the repressed super-rational realm which achieves its expression in the only form of experience which liberates in us a total awakening, the Marvelous.

The capacity to bring the mind into focus upon the Marvelous requires a development as private and sensitive as a shamanistic initiation. Nevertheless the latent content of the mind is also the latent content of history. A legend has it that in the German Peasant Wars of 1525 the witch "Black Hoffman," a follower of the Swabian "United Contingent," strangled the town crier in the town of Bockingen after he proclaimed the annulling of the Twelve Articles. What strengthened her hand to so prophetically annul the voice of the annullers? Only madness, only history, only desire.

This wild figure from the past seems reborn again in gigantic terms in Buñuel's image of the angel with the scourge, the Exterminating Angel, blotting out the sun with shadowy wings of black fire. The scourge in the angel's hand does not destroy. Rather it serves to drive everything and every creature into the crucible of the present where the force of innate human drives and genius slams the clattering scaffolding of our civilization against the still erect structure of repression. The door is closing, the margin is disappearing and the heats and pressures are building up that will force this world to transform itself utterly.

"Desire is the greatest force," sang Apollinaire in *Collines*. He invented the word "surrealism" but never lived to see its efflorescence.

Toward the end of *Collines*,

> *"Arms of gold support this life*
> *The golden secret must be pierced"*

JOSEPH JABLONSKI

Fortress St. Elmo,
Malta

The Crime of Poetry

Fabre d'Olivet, prodigious philologist of the early 19th century, contradicted the classical-academic etymology of the words "poetry" and "poet" as, respectively, "making" and "maker", thereby superseding the false consciousness exuding from connotations of this dictionary and literary "definition" persisting to this day even among the allegedly "avant-garde." Fabre d'Olivet's erudition discovered that the Greek word for poetry derived from the Phoenician which translated signifies: *"the superior principle of language."* Developing correspondences with this central etymological key in the lengthy preface *(The Essence and Form of Poetry)* to his book, *The Golden Verses of Pythagoras*, Fabre d'Olivet signaled his profound agreement with the poetics of Sir Francis Bacon who, from the following viewpoint, can be justly claimed as a precursor of surrealism: "Poetry does truly refer to the Imagination, which may at pleasure join that which nature has severed and sever that which nature has joined and so make unlawful matches and divorces of things . . . it does raise and erect the mind by submitting the show of things to the desires of the mind, whereas reason does buckle and bow the mind to the nature of things." Rejecting "craftsmanship", the surrealist viewpoint, respecting sovereignty of mind, the primacy of human desires and oneiric exaltation, considers and finds true poetry to be an instrument of knowledge, of discovery, of unveiling, and of human freedom. Authentic poetry is certainly the highest principle of language, but one which has generally been lost and which surrealism aims to restore, illuminating André Breton's saying: "Language has been given to man so that he may make surrealist use of it," together with Benjamin Péret's genial affirmation, "poetry is the source and crown of all thought." Surrealism's fifty years of poetic evidence demonstrate the initial steps taken towards this supreme *disalienation* of humanity with its language, an emancipatory leap in opposition to the civilized debasement and fragmentation of language by reason, that is, language conditioned to serve as aesthetic object, submission-to-reality, national chauvinism, entertainment, neo-formal energy-fields, stylization, mirror-trickery, everyday speech, pseudo-revolutionary mystification, personal confession, conscious self-expression and other idiocies—all of which, I insist, can be summed up in the self-condemned monstrosity that was Ezra Pound, his worthless emulators and what generally passes for poetry and good writing in this country.

Furthermore, the object of surrealism is *moral*. The demands it may elicit from you do not fall short of a furious revolutionary perspective concerning language, poetry, love, science, erotism, politics, dependent on an imaginative exaltation of disquieting materials and potential renewal of latent powers requiring a purification of means well within your grasp, *as easy as the day swallowing the night*.

PHILIP LAMANTIA

Harmonian Research

If you are deliriously (and seriously) attracted to the principled expressions of surrealism revealed in the pages of *The Surrealist Movement in the United States* and desire to take preliminary steps towards liaison (assuming knowledge of, and your vital affinity to, the basic principles of the movement and *attending occultation,* found, to mention only the most available texts, in Breton's *Manifestos* and *Surrealism and Painting)* you are invited, *at the risk of your present life,* to correspond with us by furnishing a comprehensive statement of your understanding of surrealism, indicating the forms of your co-relatable motivation, experiences and potential contribution. Replies may be expected only if terms of the invitation are coherently fulfilled through which the desired reciprocity can germinate a significant *complicity*.

Address:
MAGNETIC FIELDS, P.O. Box 26205, San Francisco, CA 94126.

NOTICE

Publishing projects *at the service of surrealism* are in formation, necessitating sympathetic and competent translations into English from French, Spanish, German, Portuguese, Czech and Slovakian, etc.

Contact: Philip Lamantia
MAGNETIC FIELDS, P.O. Box 26205, San Francisco, CA 94126.

SURREALIST PUBLICATIONS

Black Swan Press

Fata Morgana by André Breton
A long poem written in 1940, illustrated by the Cuban surrealist painter Wifredo Lam. "This poem," said Breton, "fixes my position, more unyielding than ever, of resistance to the masochistic undertakings which tend in France to restrain poetic liberty or immolate it on the same altar as the others." 32 pages. 85c

Athanor by Penelope Rosemont
Seventeen surrealist poems illustrated with alchemical engravings. "A as in *Athanor*, cormorant-poems by Penelope Rosemont" (Joyce Mànsour). Second printing. 16 pages. 50c

The Morning of a Machine Gun
by Franklin Rosemont
Twenty surrealist poems profusely illustrated with drawings by the author. Also includes the essay *Situation of Surrealism in the U.S.* (1966) originally published in the French surrealist journal *L'Archibras*, and the texts of various leaflets issued by the surrealists in Chicago. Cover by Eric Matheson. 64 pages. $1.75

In Memory of Georg Lukacs
Contributions to the demystification of the late Stalinist mystic. 20 pages. 50c

Remove Your Hat by Benjamin Péret
Twenty poems by one of the greatest poets and theorists of the surrealist movement. "What is Benjamin Péret? A menagerie in revolt, a jungle, liberty" (Marcel Noll and Raymond Queneau). 32 pages. 75c

Surrealist Insurrection
Wall-poster periodically issued by the Surrealist Group in Chicago. 25c

The Devil's Son-In-Law by Paul Garon
Lyrical biography of the great blues-singer Peetie Wheatstraw. Illustrated. 111 pages. $2

ARSENAL/Surrealist Subversion
Journal of the surrealist movement in the United States. Subscriptions (four issues) $6. Single copy $2.

SURREALIST RESEARCH & DEVELOPMENT MONOGRAPH SERIES

1. *The Apple of the Automatic Zebra's Eye*
Seventeen surrealist poems and "A Note on Automatism" by Franklin Rosemont, with positive and negative drawings by Schlechter Duvall. 28 pages. 75c

2. *Hidden Locks*
A collection of surrealist texts by Stephen Schwartz, with a frontispiece by Max-Walter Svanberg. 12 pages. 50c

3. *The Poetical Alphabet*
An inquiry into language by the American presurrealist philosopher Benjamin Paul Blood (reprinted from *Pluriverse*, 1920), with an introduction by Stephen Schwartz. 24 pages. 50c

4. *Rana Mozelle*
Fifteen surrealist texts, authentically amphibious and automatic, preceded by a succinct treatise on the "Fate of the Obsessive Image," by Paul Garon, author of *The Devil's Son-In-Law*. 20 pages. 50c

5. *Down Below*
Leonora Carrington's classic account of her adventures in Spain on the other side of the mirror, after being pronounced incurably insane (reprinted from *VVV* No. 4, 1944). With detailed map. 48 pages. $1

6. *Music Is Dangerous*
Translation of a 1929 lecture by Paul Nougé (1895-1967), a leading figure of the surrealist movement in Belgium (reprinted from *View* magazine, 1946). 32 pages. 75c

7. *Fair Game*
Nineteen surrealist poems by Peter Manti. Illustrated. 20 pages. 75c

8. *Specters of the Desert*
A cycle of drawings by Toyen, with a poem by Jindrich Heisler (translated by Stephen Schwartz). 24 pages. 75c

9. *In a Moth's Wing*
Surrealist poems by Joseph Jablonski, with drawings by Franklin Rosemont. 28 pages. 75c

---

Address all correspondence to:
Franklin Rosemont, 2257 North Janssen Avenue, Chicago, Illinois 60614.

Please add 25c postage on all orders

CITY LIGHTS BOOKS

Antonin Artaud, ANTHOLOGY $3.00
Julian Beck, THE LIFE OF THE THEATRE $3.50
Robert Bly, THE TEETH-MOTHER NAKED AT LAST $1.00
Michael Bowen, JOURNEY TO NEPAL $2.50
Paul Bowles, A HUNDRED CAMELS IN THE COURTYARD $1.25
Charles Bukowski, ERECTIONS, EJACULATIONS, EXHIBITIONS AND
    GENERAL TALES OF ORDINARY MADNESS $4.50
Charles Bukowski, NOTES OF A DIRTY OLD MAN $3.00
William S. Burroughs & Allen Ginsberg, THE YAGE LETTERS $1.50
Neal Cassady, THE FIRST THIRD $3.00
CITY LIGHTS JOURNAL No. 3 $2.50
Gregory Corso, GASOLINE $1.00
Albert Cossery, MEN GOD FORGOT $1.50
René Daumal, MOUNT ANALOGUE $2.00
Alexandra David-Neel, SECRET ORAL TEACHINGS IN TIBETAN
    BUDDHIST SECTS $2.00
Diane diPrima, REVOLUTIONARY LETTERS $2.50
George Dowden, BIBLIOGRAPHY OF ALLEN GINSBERG $17.50 (cloth)
Paul Erlich, ECO-CATASTROPHE 50¢
Ernest Fenollosa, THE CHINESE WRITTEN CHARACTER AS A MEDIUM
    FOR POETRY $1.50
Lawrence Ferlinghetti, CITY LIGHTS ANTHOLOGY $5.00
Lawrence Ferlinghetti, PICTURES OF THE GONE WORLD $1.00
Jean Genet, MAY DAY SPEECH $1.00
Allen Ginsberg, THE FALL OF AMERICA $3.00
Allen Ginsberg, HOWL AND OTHER POEMS $1.50
Allen Ginsberg, INDIAN JOURNALS $3.00
Allen Ginsberg, IRON HORSE $3.00
Allen Ginsberg, KADDISH AND OTHER POEMS $1.50
Allen Ginsberg, PLANET NEWS $2.50
Allen Ginsberg, REALITY SANDWICHES $1.50
Ernest Hemingway, COLLECTED POEMS 50¢
Journal for the Protection of All Beings No. 2, ON THE BARRICADES $1.50
Journal for the Protection of All Beings No. 1, GREEN FLAG $1.50
James Joyce, POMES PENYEACH 50¢
Bob Kaufman, GOLDEN SARDINE $1.50
Jack Kerouac, BOOK OF DREAMS $2.50
Jack Kerouac, SCATTERED POEMS $2.00
Philip Lamantia, SELECTED POEMS $1.50
Timothy Leary, EAGLE BRIEF 50¢
Malcolm Lowry, SELECTED POEMS $1.50
Norman Mailer, THE WHITE NEGRO $1.00
Michael McClure, MEAT SCIENCE ESSAYS $2.00
Henri Michaux, MISERABLE MIRACLE $2.00
Daniel Moore, BURNT HEART $2.50
Mohammed Mrabet, M'HASHISH $1.50
Harold Norse, HOTEL NIRVANA $2.00
Frank O'Hara, LUNCH POEMS $1.25
Charles Olson, CALL ME ISHMAEL $2.00

Thomas Parkinson, PROTECT THE EARTH $1.50
Kenneth Patchen, LOVE POEMS $1.00
Kenneth Patchen, POEMS OF HUMOR AND PROTEST $1.00
Pablo Picasso, HUNK OF SKIN $1.00
Tom Pickard, GUTTERSNIPE $2.50
Charles Plymell, LAST OF THE MOCCASINS $3.00
Janine Pommy-Vega, POEMS TO FERNANDO $1.25
Jacques Prévert, PAROLES $1.00
Kenneth Rexroth, THIRTY SPANISH POEMS OF LOVE & EXILE $1.00
Charles & Janet Richards, CLASSIC CHINESE & JAPANESE COOKING
    $1.50
Ed Sanders, POEM FROM JAIL 75¢
Paul Jordan Smith, A KEY TO THE ULYSSES OF JAMES JOYCE $1.50
Carl Solomon, MISHAPS, PERHAPS $1.50
Carl Solomon, MORE MISHAPS $1.50
Italo Svevo, JAMES JOYCE $1.25
Roland Topor, PANIC $1.00
Charles Upton, PANIC GRASS $1.00
Andre Voznesensky, DOGALYPSE $1.50
Arthur Waley, THE NINE SONGS $2.50
Alan W. Watts, BEAT ZEN, SQUARE ZEN, AND ZEN $1.00
Walt Whitman, AN AMERICAN PRIMER $1.50
William Carlos Williams, KORA IN HELL: IMPROVISATIONS $1.50
Colin Wilson, POETRY & MYSTICISM $2.00
Pete Winslow, A DAISY IN THE MEMORY OF A SHARK $2.00
Yevtushenko, Voznesensky & Kirsanov, RED CATS $1.00